Melville, Beauty, and American Literary Studies

OXFORD STUDIES IN AMERICAN LITERARY HISTORY

Gordon Hutner, Series Editor

After Critique
Mitchum Huehls

Unscripted America
Sarah Rivett

Forms of Dictatorship
Jennifer Harford Vargas

Anxieties of Experience
Jeffrey Lawrence

White Writers, Race Matters
Gregory S. Jay

The Civil War Dead and American Modernity
Ian Finseth

The Puritan Cosmopolis
Nan Goodman

Realist Poetics in American Culture, 1866–1900
Elizabeth Renker

The Center of the World
June Howard

History, Abolition, and the Ever-Present Now in Antebellum American Writing
Jeffrey Insko

Not Quite Hope and Other Political Emotions in the Gilded Age
Nathan Wolff

Transoceanic America
Michelle Burnham

Genre and White Supremacy in the Postemancipation United States
Travis M. Foster

Modern Sentimentalism
Lisa Mendelman

Speculative Fictions
Elizabeth Hewitt

Transamerican Sentimentalism and Nineteenth-Century US Literary History
Maria A. Windell

Patriotism by Proxy
Colleen Glenney Boggs

Jewish American Writing and World Literature
Saul Noam Zaritt

The Archive of Fear
Christina Zwarg

Violentologies
B. V. Olguin

Transgression and Redemption in American Fiction
Thomas J. Ferraro

The Latino Continuum and the Nineteenth-Century Americas
Carmen E. Lamas

Time and Antiquity in American Empire
Mark Storey

Picturesque Literature and the Transformation of the American Landscape, 1835–1874
John Evelev

Literary Neurophysiology
Randall Knoper

Writing Pain in the Nineteenth-Century United States
Thomas Constantinesco

Slavery, Surveillance, and Genre in Antebellum United States Literature
Kelly Ross

Climate and the Picturesque in the American Tropics
Michael Boyden

Melville, Beauty, and American Literary Studies

An Aesthetics in All Things

CODY MARRS

Great Clarendon Street, Oxford, OX2 6DP,
United Kingdom

Oxford University Press is a department of the University of Oxford.
It furthers the University's objective of excellence in research, scholarship,
and education by publishing worldwide. Oxford is a registered trade mark of
Oxford University Press in the UK and in certain other countries

© Cody Marrs 2023

The moral rights of the author have been asserted

First Edition published in 2023

Impression: 1

All rights reserved. No part of this publication may be reproduced, stored in
a retrieval system, or transmitted, in any form or by any means, without the
prior permission in writing of Oxford University Press, or as expressly permitted
by law, by licence or under terms agreed with the appropriate reprographics
rights organization. Enquiries concerning reproduction outside the scope of the
above should be sent to the Rights Department, Oxford University Press, at the
address above

You must not circulate this work in any other form
and you must impose this same condition on any acquirer

Published in the United States of America by Oxford University Press
198 Madison Avenue, New York, NY 10016, United States of America

British Library Cataloguing in Publication Data

Data available

Library of Congress Control Number: 2022940174

ISBN 978–0–19–287172–5

DOI: 10.1093/oso/9780192871725.001.0001

Printed and bound in the UK by
Clays Ltd, Elcograf S.p.A.

Links to third party websites are provided by Oxford in good faith and
for information only. Oxford disclaims any responsibility for the materials
contained in any third party website referenced in this work.

Preface: Beauty in a Time of Pain

I wrote most of this book during a pandemic. As I contemplated Melville's roses, statues, whales, and other forms of "beauty strange with horror allied," a tragedy unfolded.[1] Something almost unimaginably small—a virus less than 1,000 times smaller than the width of a human hair—wreaked havoc across the globe, yielding disease, anxiety, and moral panic. Amidst this devastation I told a friend about this book, and he said out loud something I frequently wondered to myself: Is it appropriate to think about beauty at such an ugly time?

That question concerns not only the relationship between ethics and aesthetics but also the purpose of literary studies more generally. And there are several possible answers. One might respond—as I initially did when talking to my friend—by underscoring literature's ability to reflect on broader social, political, and historical circumstances. Recent scholarship on the environment, sexuality, and the literary histories of race and empire has underscored this point, disclosing the multiple ways in which American writing grows directly out of American culture and, oftentimes, reflects on the very circumstances of its production.[2] As Joel Pfister points out, most of the critical issues that currently organize American literary studies were "serious literary concerns" long before they became scholarly concerns. In fact, "American literature did cultural-theoretical work (for instance, aspects of materialist critique, poststructuralism, feminist theory, and transnational studies) . . . [years] before academics institutionalized the field of cultural theory in the twentieth and twenty-first centuries."[3] Melville is a case in point. His writing thoughtfully engages with a range of issues, from antiblack racism in "Benito Cereno" and *Moby-Dick* to revolution in "The Encantadas" and *Israel Potter*, communism in *Clarel*, corporal punishment in *White Jacket*, and colonialism in *Typee*. That is one of the reasons why Melville has become a perennial fixture of American literary studies: his writing unveils the thoughts and actions that spawned our historical present.[4] In other words, it is both fitting and necessary to consider Melville's treatment of beauty because it is part of the complex way in which he depicts the world, and Melville sees the world as full of conflict and injustice.

That is undoubtedly true. But that answer undersells the ethical and philosophical value of Melville's writing. In nearly everything Melville wrote, pain and beauty are woven together, providing one another with form and meaning. This is partly attributable to Melville's keen interest in the *chiaroscuro* method, or what Robert K. Wallace describes as Melville's Turnerian aesthetics, wherein everything is cast "in spheres of love and fright."[5] However, Melville's treatments of beauty also evolve out of his lifelong interest in the role of aesthetics in a cosmos full of suffering. The various qualities that Melville associates with beauty are not Idealist universals untethered from people's lived interests but situated effects that are conditioned and informed by experiences of pain.

The value that Melville places on beauty not despite but because of suffering is evident in *Battle-Pieces*, his 1866 volume of Civil War poetry. One of the most perceptive poems, "Running the Batteries," is ostensibly an account of the Union Navy's 1863 assault on Vicksburg, but the poem is as much about light and beauty as it is about warfare. In the "moonless" night, a "lampless boat" glides through the water, just breaking through the mist then melting into the shade (Figure 1). A second ship then passes by unseen, followed by another, and another. Dispatched in the cover of night, these ships ferried down the Mississippi's "shadowy shore" until they finally fired their guns, illuminating their hulls and providing hazy, half-lit targets. Far away on the high bluffs a "golden" flame leaps up, then arcs down, turning into a "silvery" meteor. It strikes one of the ships, which catches fire and becomes a kind of beacon, shedding its orange glow on the rest of the fleet. A furious exchange ensues, but the guns don't shoot, Melville says; they "flash," catapulting light, which rises and falls, "blazon[s]" and "flit[s]"

Figure 1. *Admiral Porter's Fleet Running the Rebel Blockade of the Mississippi at Vicksburg* (1863). Lithograph. Courtesy of the Library of Congress, Prints and Photographs Division.

toward "salamanders hard to hit, though vivid." When the Confederates light their torches, everything suddenly becomes visible:

> Whereby anew the boats are seen—
> A burning transport all alurch!
> Breathless we gaze; yet still we glean
> Glimpses of beauty as we eager lean.
>
> The effulgence takes an amber glow
> Which bathes the hill-side villas far;
> Affrighted ladies mark the show
> Painting the pale magnolia—
> The fair, false, Circe light of cruel War.[6]

What does war have to do with light? It almost seems as if there is no battle. There are neither soldiers nor cannons; instead, colored flames leap and descend, creating points of "converging fire." Given what we know about Melville, this luminous poem is rather fitting. The "false" light of war recalls the fires that flicker in *Moby-Dick*: the hellish flames of the try-works and the blazes that have consumed Ahab, a latter-day Prometheus "cut away from the stake."[7] The poem also shares an investment in luminism—in light's meaningful effulgence—with the painters of the Hudson Valley School. The dying beacon and burning transports are twisted versions of the light that breaks through in Sanford Gifford's Catskills and Albert Bierdstadt's Sierra Nevadas. "Running the Batteries" also stages a tragic play between darkness and illumination that links light with knowledge, in a manner redolent of Giovanni Piranesi's *carceri* sketches, with their "hushed cloisters" best dwelled upon "in the night."[8] In other words, this is yet another Melville text about the curse of knowledge, verbally and visually rendered.

If Melville treats the Siege of Vicksburg like a painter, that is not merely because the arts influenced his writing. It also because—however much we may wish to disavow it—this naval assault is stunningly beautiful. The silvery flames and streams of fire are pleasing and alluring. Even the smoke that billows up has a "mellowly brilliant" hue that provokes a sense of wonder. In that regard, the poem is typical of *Battle-Pieces*, which repeatedly associates violence with flashes of beauty. The dissolution of the armies in 1865 thus becomes indistinguishable from the *aurorae borealis*—another form of colored light—dissolving in the air, and the "voweled syllables" of the *Cumberland*, "Flowing, rolling on the tongue," survive "Unswallowed by the swallowing sea." In "The Prison Pen," Virgil appears, and in "The Slain Collegians," Apollo himself. And this doesn't even begin to touch on the volume's numerous ekphrases, such as the "dim inklings" of "The Coming Storm" or Melville's use of J.M.W. Turner in "The Temeraire."[9] Suffice it to say, *Battle-Pieces* is a book about war, beauty, and the relation between them.

That is one of the major insights of recent scholarship on *Battle-Pieces*: aesthetic concerns and commitments propel the poems from beginning to end. Hsuan Hsu points out that the volume adopts ekphrasis as both a poetic model and politico-philosophical claim by treating nature, warfare, and painting in analogous terms, while Timothy Sweet notes that Melville is drawn to "somatically satisfying" vernacular forms, such as the hymn and the ballad.[10] Other scholars have revealed the importance of Melville's visit to the National Academy of Design in 1865, the "exactingly calibrated" ambivalence of Melville's poetic grammar, and the relationship between Melville's view of democracy and his use of groundless metaphors such as "wind, water, and gravity."[11] This confluence between war and beauty presents a host of ethical problems, though. Melville almost seems to suggest, edging ever closer to the claim, that perhaps we "glean / Glimpses of beauty" because violence provides pleasure, like a painting or a song.

Melville therefore veers toward the "aestheticization of war" that Walter Benjamin identified as the ethos of fascism itself, the sensibility of a society that has become so alienated from its own humanity that it can "experience its own destruction as an aesthetic pleasure."[12] Benjamin directed his well-known adage ("'Let art flourish—and the world pass away,' says fascism") toward the Italian Futurists, who saw war and beauty as folded inexorably together. As Filippo Tommaso Marinetti declares (in his garbage-fire of a manifesto), "War is beautiful because it initiates the dreamt-of metalizing of the human body. War is beautiful because it enriches a flowering meadow with the fiery orchids of machine-guns... War is beautiful because it combines gunfire... into a symphony."[13]

Battle-Pieces evokes a very different view of war. Instead of aestheticizing violence like Marinetti, Melville cultivates experiences of beauty that fragment and disperse the very self upon which violence depends. In *Battle-Pieces*, as in so many of Melville's writings, beauty is the substance and spirit of intersubjectivity, a kind of *sensus communis* without individuated subjects. According to Iris Murdoch, beauty is an experience of "decentering," a felt recognition that the self is not, in fact, the center of anything, least of all our own experience.[14] That type of experience is repeatedly elicited in *Battle-Pieces*. Throughout "Running the Batteries," boundaries erode: forts have spleens, guns speak, beacons die, and people too partake in the warp and woof of life's exchangeability—

> Breathless we gaze; yet still we glean
> Glimpses of beauty as we eager lean.[15]

This is nothing short of a collective action. There is no "I," only a loose and ambiguous "we" that literally acts in unison, leaning toward the light *en masse* and exhaling in response. There is no discrete soldier here, and the speaker is certainly not Melville. It is a non-individuated consciousness that forms—or, at least, is felt—when "glimpses of beauty" break through the chaos. That is why the poem comes right before two poems about Stonewall Jackson (one Northern, one Southern), a diptych that similarly proceeds from a plural, disaggregated perspective: for Melville, "Running the Batteries" is part of an extended meditation on the meanings of multiplicity. In that respect, the fragmentation of Melville's mind, which prefaces the volume ("The aspects which the strife as a memory assumes are ... variable, and at times widely at variance") characterizes Melville's broader treatment of the war, as the poems migrate not simply from perspective to perspective but from fragmented sensation to fragmented sensation, evoking an ever-expanding range of non-individuated experiences.

Battle-Pieces thereby comments not only on the phenomenology of war but also on the ethics of organized violence. Throughout the volume, Melville repeatedly carves out a sense of peace, either supported or enabled by beauty, that cuts against war's brutality. In poem after poem, *Battle-Pieces* suggests that beauty has the power to pacify us—indeed, when war is viewed through art or nature, it becomes more terrible, and more reprehensible. There is a remarkable moment, for example, at the end of "Donelson," that bears directly on this question about the relationship between beauty and pain. After the Union Army declares victory, some of the villagers rejoice, but others, Melville writes, remain haunted by the "pale sheets" of death (i.e., the lists of the deceased read out loud).

> Ah God! may Time with happy haste
> Bring wail and triumph to a waste,
> And war be done;
> The battle flag-staff fall athwart
> The curs'd ravine, and wither; naught
> Be left of trench or gun;
> The bastion, let it ebb away,
> Washed with the river bed; and Day
> In vain seek Donelson.[16]

In short, let us forget this battle and rid our hearts of any will to violence. To be sure, it is notoriously difficult to know where Melville himself stands at any given moment, but the view offered here is in keeping with the objections to violence that run through so many of his other writings. A disregard for life itself, whether human or non-human, is what makes Ahab Ahab and it is what makes Bildad and Peleg, those pacifist investors in bloodshed, hypocrites. The impossible call lodged in "Donelson," let "war be done!," resounds throughout *Battle-Pieces*: this is the flipside of the volume's sense of cyclical historical decline, an accompanying sense of ethical *correction*, a moral light made possible by beauty's "dark knowledge."[17]

Many of the speakers in *Battle-Pieces* are aghast at what they witness. The British observer in "Battle of Stone River" reflects on the tendency for violence to induce memories that cannot reckon with loss or justify destruction, and the urban dweller in "Ball's Bluff" laments the waste of youth ("Ah war, thy theft!") repeated in every conflict. Nonetheless, as Melville moves across the struggle, shards of life remain in spite of the war's astounding violence. In "The Rebel Color-Bearers," "the color-bearers facing death, / White in the whirling sulphurous wreath," become works of art, "planted statues" enshrouded in "living robes." When the Union soldiers see these statuesque men, they intuitively stop firing. Taking Colonel Stuart's admonition as an example ("'No, no,' he said, 'they're too brave fellows to be killed'"), Melville pauses, wondering: If spite can be suspended and violence halted even at Shiloh (of all places), might it cease elsewhere? What if every soul has the same worth as these color-bearers? And what if beauty is what makes us alive to that fact by awakening us to life's equitable distribution? "Spare Spleen her ire," Melville implores.[18]

The desire to view the war aesthetically in a way that challenges, or at least elides, it politically also plays an important role in "Running the Batteries." When the fires become aesthetic objects, it is a result of stillness, of movement's cessation. "Breathless we gaze; yet still we glean / Glimpses of beauty as we eager lean." On the one hand, this is utterly perverse: the soldiers, like Melville's poem, are drawn to destruction like a moth to flame. This could be glossed as an aestheticized version of Freud's death-drive or, as Benjamin might say, a fascistic consumption of our own annihilation.[19] On the other hand, Melville's syntax—as always—complicates matters. "Yet still," he says: a spondee that both announces and clarifies. The "amber glow" cast upon the shore of the Mississippi yields a momentary sense of peace—it literally takes the breath away—and *that* produces a kind of revelation: a discovery, by aesthetic means, that war is cruelty.

That realization is made possible by the poem's genre. It is a ballad, a narrativized retelling that acquires insight as it nears its conclusion. Like *Battle-Pieces* more generally, "Running the Batteries" models the very experience it describes, at once enacting and enunciating beauty's antipathy toward war: the felt discovery—whether through weapons or words—of what is fair and what is cruel, of what is beauteous and worth preserving. Poem and volume alike are remarkably self-reflexive in that respect, using encounters with beauty to make sense of the pleasures that the text affords, until we, like soldiers leaning toward the fire, peel away, breathlessly delighted at our escape and newly aware of the precariousness, as well as the preciousness, of life itself.

In this book, I follow Melville's example and consider how beauty clarifies and counter-balances suffering. In Melville's writing, beauty resembles what the Pyrrhonists dubbed *ataraxia*, a pleasurable yet temporary release from pain. According to Sextus Empiricus, *ataraxia* was not a transcendent state but a world-bound condition that underscores the mutability of existence and the relativity of all things ("All things are changed as their relations become changed, or as we look upon them in different points of view"[20]). In viewing beauty and suffering as inexorably linked, Melville anticipated recent scholarship in literary studies that emphasizes the connection between aesthetics, history, and politics. Kandice Chuh, for example, has argued for the intellectual and ethical value of alternative humanisms modeled on non-individuation, humanisms that emphasize "visceral multisensory experiences" and view human beings as "defined not by discrete and self-possessed individuality but instead by constitutive relationality." Scholars have also emphasized the importance of beauty to the study of black art, the history of sexuality, and the literature of revolution, all of which indicate that beauty, far from being antithetical to experiences of pain, might be indispensable for understanding those experiences.[21]

In this regard, Melville will continue to be an important interlocutor. His work reconceptualizes beauty in ways that are of utmost relevance to emerging discussions about citizenship, ecology, personhood, race, sexuality, and ethics. Across his writings, beauty is a medium of experiential change, a mode of being that reframes perspectives and reveals connections between forms. As students and scholars explore the ugliness as well as the beauty of American literary history, Melville's writings thus launch us forth, providing—with every story and every poem—"delightful inducements to embark."[22]

Acknowledgments

Although I am listed as the author, this book is the outgrowth of many conversations I've had with friends, family, and colleagues.

First and foremost, I wish to thank Gordon Hutner. He saw what this book could become from the beginning, then helped me create it. Without Gordon's patient and intelligent guidance, this book would not exist.

Oxford University Press has been wonderful to work with. Hannah Doyle is a superb editor and consummate professional. I am also grateful to Jacqueline Norton, Joy Mellor, and Tara Werger for their peerless work, and to Edward Sugden, who provided an insightful and nuanced reader's report. The other readers, whomever they may be, offered invaluable advice that has strengthened this book considerably. Tripp Sandifer did an excellent job as a fact-checker, and I am thankful for all that he did.

Many people talked to me about this book and encouraged me to see things differently. To Theo Davis, Paul Downes, Elizabeth Duquette, Jennifer Greiman, Christopher Hager, Christopher Hanlon, Paul Hurh, Michael Jonik, Casie LeGette, John Wharton Lowe, Richard Menke, Eric Morales-Franceschini, Samuel Otter, Adam Parkes, Jason Payton, Eliza Richards, Kelly Ross, and Brian Yothers: thank you so much. I am indebted to Robert S. Levine, who generously invited me to come to the University of Maryland and share some of my book-in-progress; and to Ronan Ludot-Vlasak, Edouard Marsoin, and Cécile Roudeau, who brought me to the University of Paris and the University of Lille, where we got to talk about Melville, aesthetics, and matter. I am also grateful for the colleagues I spoke with at C19 and the Melville conference in London, where I workshopped early versions of this material. Those conversations were very important to me.

Last but certainly not least, I wish to thank my wife, Kristin, and my children, Harper and Caleb, for their immeasurable love and support, which sustains me in all that I do. Everything I learned about beauty I learned from my family. To my parents, Monte and Betty Marrs, and to my in-laws, Kim and Don Ristow: thank you for all of your warmth, generosity, humor, and kindness. This book would not be possible without you.

Contents

List of Illustrations	xvii
Introduction	1
1. Ancient Beauty in *Timoleon*	25
2. Floral Beauty in *Weeds and Wildings*	52
3. Appalling Beauty in *Moby-Dick*	77
Postscript: A Note on Method	107
Notes	115
Index	147

List of Illustrations

1. *Admiral Porter's Fleet Running the Rebel Blockade of the Mississippi at Vicksburg* (1863). Lithograph. — vi
2. The Dioscuri (Castor and Pollux), Rome. Photograph. — 2
3. "Sperm Whale Goes Down for a Dive" (2014). Photograph. — 8
4. Sebastiano del Piombo, *The Raising of Lazarus* (1517–19). Oil on canvas. — 11
5. Marcel DuChamp, *Fountain* (1917). Photograph. — 20
6. Praxiteles, *Hermes and the Infant Dionysus*. Photograph. — 26
7. Leo Von Klenze, *The Acropolis at Athens* (1846). Oil on Canvas. — 35
8. Hans Holbein the Younger, *Lais of Corinth* (1526). Oil on Canvas. — 35
9. "Fragment from the Ergastinai ("Weavers") Frieze, from the Parthenon in Athens." Photograph (2005). — 36
10. Claude Lorrain, *Morning in the Harbor* (1637). Oil on canvas. — 40
11. *Bust of Epicurus and Metrodorus* (second century CE). — 43
12. John "Warwick" Smith, *Entrance to the Grotto of Posillipo, Naples. Watercolor over graphite* (1778–9). — 45
13. Jiugang Wang, *Milan Cathedral from Piazza del Duomo* (2010). Photograph. — 47
14. *Gothic Window on the Basilica di S. Marco*. Photograph (2004). — 50
15. Jacob Vosmaer, *A Vase With Flowers* (1613). Oil on wood. — 55
16. *Delphinium*. From John Lindley, ed., *Ornamental Garden and Shrubbery*, Vol. 1 (1838). — 67
17. Photograph of Melville's copy of *Mosses from an Old Manse*. — 74
18. George Cooke, *Interior of St. Peter's in Rome* (1847). Oil painting. — 85

Introduction

Beautiful Melville

Poet of terror. Writer of the sublime. Chronicler of "all truth with malice in it." This is how Herman Melville is typically remembered: as a writer who plumbed the depths of nature's dark side and dared to put it down in books.

Yet to read Melville is to repeatedly encounter beauty. Whales, gliding through the water, glisten like "living opal." Swallows skim "lightly...over the field in clouded days."[1] In Melville's writing, even the smallest of acts—finding a palm tree in the desert, or seeing a handsome sailor—can spark a vivid, felt awareness of life's intricate web. For Melville, to be alive is to experience beauty, sometimes when you least expect it.

If that is the case, then beauty is quite different from what it is often reputed to be. It is the dynamic outgrowth of life itself, a vital charge that is variously experienced and broadly distributed. As Melville puts it, "The mind, instead of being bewildered in itself, is drawn out by the symmetry and beauty of the forms it beholds."[2] Beauty pulls us out of ourselves, whether by surprise or by quiet recognition, and discloses the eclectic ways in which the self is entangled and the mind is anything but self-contained. For Melville, beauty is an experience of non-sovereignty, a feeling of weakened or blurred autonomy that reconnects us to the world.

As Geoffrey Sanborn contends, Melville views existence as momentum, and that belief in universal motility leads him to "lateralize just about everything that is capable of being hierarchically arranged."[3] Beauty emerges out of nature's ceaseless change; it has no center or apex. As Melville writes in his poem "Venice" (1891),

> With Pantheist energy of will
> The little craftsman of the Coral Sea
> Strenuous in the blue abyss,
> Up-builds his marvelous gallery
> And long arcade,
> Erections freaked with many a fringe
> Of marble garlandry,
> Evincing what a worm can do.

> Laborious in a shallower wave,
> Advanced in kindred art,
> A prouder agent proved Pan's might
> When Venice rose in reefs of palaces.[4]

Though "no great and enduring volume can ever be written on the flea," Melville did write a great poem about worms.[5] The poem marvels at the humblest of artisans: the coral worms that burrow in oceanic reefs, sculpting "marvelous" honeycomb-like galleries amidst the "blue abyss." The poem's sense of meaning and movement derive from its conceit, namely that worms are our "kindred" creatures, artists in another medium. The creation of Venice does not merely parallel the creation of oceanic reefs; those acts of beauty-making involve the same "energy of will" and collective artistic labor.[6] Whether on land or shore, beauty both requires and produces communal being. That is why the poem traffics so prolifically in metaphors of combination and dispersal: beauty grows prodigiously out of nature and the connected experiences it sets into motion.

That view of beauty bubbles up in the lectures about Roman statuary that Melville delivered in the late 1850s, shortly after traveling through the Mediterranean world. Rome's statues enraptured him in countless ways, provoking everything from astonishment to distress to muted awe. The Vatican's statue of Demosthenes filled him with disappointment (the "thunderer of Athens," he said, resembled an ancient ambulance chaser), while the equestrian statues of Castor and Pollux reminded him of nature's egalitarian beauty (Figure 2).

Figure 2. The Dioscuri (Castor and Pollux), Rome.

The relation depicted by these statues has nothing to do with possession or domination. Although Castor and Pollux are reining the horses, the four figures appear to partake in a symmetrical exchange of wills, a coeval action legible on each sculpted body and mien. "The horse," Melville notes,

> was idealized by the ancient artists as majestic next to man, and they loved to sculpture them as they did heroes and gods. To the Greeks nature had no brute. Everything was a being with a soul... In truth, nothing even in the statues of gods could be more noble than the appearance of these horses.[7]

The beauty of these statues derives not merely from their fine forms and exquisite lines, but from the way they underscore the bruteless nature of the cosmos.[8]

If Melville is right, then beauty knows no fundamental distinctions, whether between high and low, inside and outside, or human and non-human. It is the aesthetic equivalent of Shelley's vision of love, that "powerful attraction towards all we conceive, or fear, or hope beyond ourselves... and seek to awaken in all things." Or, as Melville puts it, a "circumambient spell" that dissolves boundaries and differences: "I... speak of the impressions produced upon my mind as one who looks upon a work of art as he would upon a violet or a cloud, and admires or condemns as he finds an answering sentiment awakening in his soul."[9] Melville's twofold point here—that a work of art is essentially no different from a flower or a cloud, and that sentiments emanate through various phenomena—is far-ranging. This is the opposite of the Cartesian ego, or any other paradigm that views the human mind as sovereign and distinct. If feelings are awakened by such objects, that is because aesthetic experience, and perhaps even consciousness, flows between forms of life. Beauty is as boundless and egoless as nature itself.[10]

This book is about this "answering sentiment" and what it makes possible. In the following chapters, I retrace Melville's engagements with beauty as both a concept and a shared experience. Melville's writings, I argue, convey a distinct set of ideas about beauty that are rich and meaningful on their own terms and highly significant for American literary studies. In short, Melville reveals that beauty is associative, it inheres in natural forms, and it tends to dissolve and re-form individual identities. In all of these ways, beauty makes us reconsider who we are and how we are tied to the rest of the world.

In placing beauty at the core of Melville's writing, I draw upon two compelling strands of recent scholarship: criticism that has reframed Melville as a philosopher and as a stylist. On the one hand, scholars have thoughtfully assessed the numerous ways in which Melville approaches literature and philosophy as allied mediums. Recent work in this vein has disclosed Melville's connections to philosophers who preceded him, like Thomas Hobbes and Baruch Spinoza, as well as those he may be said to have anticipated, like Friedrich Nietzsche, Ludwig

Wittgenstein, and Gilles Deleuze. Contemporary scholars have also examined the roots of his epistemological skepticism, his interests in Enlightenment method and the limits of personhood, his fascination with analogical thinking, and his anticipation of later movements such as ecology and posthumanism.[11] At the same time, scholars have turned their attention to the aesthetic ideas, sources, and effects that distinguish Melville's writing. Compelling work along these lines has revealed significant links between Melville and visual artists such as Claude Lorrain, Elihu Vedder, and Thomas Cole, and expounded some of the defining features of Melville's style, such as his canny manipulations of form, genre, and tone.[12] From Sianne Ngai's analysis of "the vocabulary of affective 'transfer'" in *The Confidence Man* to Theo Davis's examination of "ornamental metaphor" in *Moby-Dick*, scholars have demonstrated that meaning in Melville is inevitably tied to the textures and rhythms of his language.[13]

Collectively, this criticism has yielded a twenty-first-century diptych of Melville. The first portrait shows us a Melville who does not merely engage in philosophizing, or whose writing simply involves metaphysical speculation, but who thought obsessively about the process of thinking. Melville, scholars have discovered, was less of a "philosophical writer" than a philosopher who saw the act of writing as an opportunity to test out beliefs and refine ideas. The second portrait shows us a Melville who conceives of literary texts as works of art: highly resonant mediums defined by their formal architecture and aesthetic charges. One purpose of this book is to merge these two portraits. Melville almost always couches his philosophical claims in aesthetic terms, and vice versa. I take this to be a corollary of Branka Arsić and K.L. Evans's insight that Melville's writing involves a kind of "world-making" that combines literature, ethics, philosophy, and the arts, as well as "palpable and concrete remakings of material environments."[14]

The following pages also build on recent scholarship on the aesthetics of nineteenth-century American literature.[15] Studies such as Erica Fretwell's *Sensory Experiments* (2020), Theo Davis's *Ornamental Aesthetics* (2016), Édouard Marsoin's *Melville et l'usage des plaisirs* (2019), Samuel Otter and Geoffrey Sanborn's *Melville and Aesthetics* (2011), and Christopher Looby and Cindy Weinstein's *American Literature's Aesthetic Dimensions* (2011) have not only mounted a "resistance," as Looby and Weinstein put it, "to the resistance to aesthetics"; they have helped us look, with fresh eyes, at canonical works we thought we already knew quite well and revealed the centrality of aesthetics to a wide range of literary genres, cultural practices, and political phenomena. Scholars have examined important exchanges between American literature and the visual arts, and they have disclosed myriad ways in which writing traffics in sensation.[16] As Fretwell argues, many works of nineteenth-century American literature can be read as "sensory experiments...[that] explored and exploited bodily sensations, pressed in on by historical events."[17] This book extends and deepens this work by examining the role of beauty in Melville's writing and exploring how Melville can help us apprehend beauty's intersubjective dimensions.

Melville, I contend, is persistently interested in beauty as both an idea and an experience, and over the course of his life he develops distinct modes for representing beauty. Two major objections to this argument might reasonably be made. First, one might posit that Melville is less invested in beauty than he is in the sublime. Regardless of his occasional invocations of beauty, accounts of the sublime proliferate in his writing. This is why Ahab's speeches, in all of their twisted eloquence, are so affecting, and it is why nature, whether in the form of a white whale or of a Polynesian landscape, always tends to stun or overwhelm: Melville's writing—indeed, his entire worldview—is anchored in experiences of power and immensity, experiences that are most aptly understood as manifestations of the sublime. When he does explicitly move beyond the sublime, Melville often does so through the language of the picturesque, which in the eighteenth and nineteenth century was taken to be the sublation of the sublime and the beautiful—a subject Melville addresses in writings such as "At the Hostelry." That leads us to the second objection: for all of Melville's talk of beauty, his writings are full of what we might call the unbeautiful. Ugly thoughts, ugly actions, and ugly landscapes abound in stories such as *Typee*, *Billy Budd*, "Benito Cereno," and "The Encantadas." It is Melville, after all, who writes about the hell unleashed by the Civil War ("What like a bullet can undeceive?"), the "wantonness of malignity" in the *Bellipotent*'s master-at-arms, the "serrated teeth" of the Maldive shark ("Pale ravener of horrible meat"), and the possibility that "the palsied universe lies before us a leper" ("Nature absolutely paints like the harlot, whose allurements cover nothing but the charnel-house within"), which are difficult if not impossible to square with the notion that Melville is a writer deeply interested in beauty as such.[18]

The first counter-argument certainly has the weight of most Melville scholarship behind it. Melville's status as a writer of the sublime has been one of the most consistent through-lines for Melville studies. Regardless of which schools of interpretation rise or fall, Melville is almost always identified with sublimity. The sublime has become a lodestar, at once guiding Melville's readers and providing a shared destination for interpretation's many paths. Scholars have connected Melville to Longinus, J.M.W. Turner, Frederick Douglass, and other prominent artists of the sublime. The sense of the sublime in Melville's works has been described alternatively as "ecological," "technological," "American," "Miltonic," and "Kantian."[19] And many interpretations approach sublimity as a kind of skeleton key that unlocks all the other doors, revealing the secrets of Melville's philosophy, style, politics, and biography. Nonetheless, I propose that the nature and terms of Melville's interest in the sublime have been misconstrued in ways that have obscured his powerful, enduring, and nearly omnipresent interest in beauty.[20]

My departure from this line of interpretation is perhaps best understood by repositioning Melville vis-à-vis Edmund Burke. Burke's aesthetic philosophy, it has been argued, greatly influenced Melville's thinking in general and *Moby-Dick* in particular.[21] This is true. Melville's undoubtedly read Burke's treatise, *A Philosophical Enquiry into the Origin of Our Ideas of the Sublime and the Beautiful* (1757), and many of Melville's writings, from *Mardi* to *Billy Budd*, bear the traces of this intellectual encounter. But Melville did not read like Captain Vere for verification of "his own more reserved thoughts," nor did he see books merely as educative instruments. Instead, he treated books as living, breathing interlocutors. For Melville, books were dialogic mediums that opened him to the world, and the world to him. In reading's "harborless immensities," he tested out ideas, gauged impressions, and speculated alongside a motley crew of fellow writers, artists, and philosophers.[22] Far from a unidirectional source of information which might yield something as simple as "influence," reading for Melville resembled a long conversation with a friend: a life-giving exchange of ideas and feelings, the outcome of which could never be anticipated.

His marginalia indicate that such an exchange could be experienced with authors regardless of where or when they lived. Books provided intellectual and emotional transport, and he responded to them in the same way that he responded to Roman statuary, admiring or condemning as he found "an answering sentiment awakening in his soul."[23] Those sentiments varied widely, not only from book to book but also from page to page. His responses to Emerson, for example, swerve from adulation ("All this is nobly written, and proceeds from noble thinking") to outrage ("My Dear Sir!"), to contemptuous dismissal ("God help the poor fellow who squares his life according to this"), and vehement correction: "No, no, no," Melville wrote next to Emerson's claim that "dissipation" deadens the poetic faculty; "Titian—did he deteriorate?—Byron?—did he[?]—Mr. E is horribly narrow here."[24]

Melville's writing stages a similarly spirited dialog with Burke.[25] Both thinkers pose, and try to answer, a shared philosophical question: To what degree are feelings rooted in sensations? For Burke, different feelings are the result of different types of sensations, both real and imagined—being immersed in total darkness, for instance, provokes fear, while smoothness generally produces a sense of delight. Melville, too, views matter as intimately bound up with the mind. Whereas Burke posits axiomatic correlations between particular experiences and particular mental states, Melville finds that reactions vary and feelings are never singular or discrete. Melville probably bristled at several parts of the *Enquiry*— such as Burke's dismissal of passion as animalistic and, therefore, disconnected from aesthetics[26]—but they especially differ in the way they view beauty. According to Burke, beauty is the obverse of the sublime: they are not merely dissimilar; they are seamless reversals of one another. The sublime is defined by vastness; beauty, by smallness. The sublime is rugged, beauty is smooth. The sublime is obscure, beauty is clear. The sublime is "dark and gloomy," beauty is "light and delicate." As Burke remarks, the sublime and the beautiful are "ideas of a very different nature, one being founded on pain, the other on pleasure... [and their] causes keep up an eternal distinction between them."[27]

Burke's aesthetics are bound up with his politics. Burke uses highly gendered language to divide the sublime from the beautiful and elevate the former over the latter because he sees aesthetic experience as part of an immense cosmic hierarchy, a great chain of being handed down directly by God. The *Enquiry* provides in aesthetic philosophy what his *Reflections on the Revolution in France* (1790) provides in political philosophy: a defense of traditional distinctions and a vigorous critique of any attempt to muddy them. This link between Burke's aesthetics and politics was surely not lost on Melville, who sustained a lifelong fascination with the French Revolution. It is even possible that, as Ray Browne has argued, Melville modeled Captain Vere—that unyielding, aristocratic stalwart who believes in the inviolability of established forms—on Burke himself.[28]

While Burke saw the world in terms of balanced divisions, Melville was an inveterate mixer who valued "ruthless democracy on all sides."[29] As a writer, Melville repeatedly crossed boundaries, not only between literary subgenres but also between modes of intellectual endeavor, intermingling literature with science, sculpture, painting, and metaphysics. In Melville's writing, the sublime and the beautiful blend and blur until they become nearly indistinguishable. *Moby-Dick*, for example, underscores the absurdity of Burke's segregated aesthetics by rhapsodizing about the beauty of the sperm whale's tail (Figure 3). Those bannered flukes, Ishmael says, may be terrifyingly massive and full of "amazing strength"— in short, utterly paradigmatic of Burke's sublime—yet that power makes the whale *more* beautiful, not less:

> In no living thing are the lines of beauty more exquisitely defined than in the crescentic borders of these flukes... The whole bulk of the leviathan is knit over with a warp and woof of muscular fibres and filaments, which passing on either side the loins and running down into the flukes, insensibly blend with them, and largely contribute to their might; so that in the tail the confluent measureless force of the whole whale seems concentrated to a point. Nor does this... cripple the graceful flexion of its motions... On the contrary, these motions derive their most appalling beauty from it. Real strength never impairs beauty or harmony, but it often bestows it; and in everything imposingly beautiful, strength has much to do with the magic.[30]

What is beautiful about a sperm whale's tail? In part, it is the astounding symmetry. The "broad, firm, flat palms" mirror one another with utter fidelity, paralleling in shape, size, and function. In part, it is the graceful curve, the undulating line that rises and falls around the tail, a crescentic beauty reminiscent

Figure 3. "Sperm Whale Goes Down for a Dive." Courtesy of Marine Mammals and Seabirds of the Pacific and GRID-Arendal. Photograph (2014).

of palm trees, rolling hills, or waves of water. In part, it is the tail's sloping gradient: from the "compact round body of its root," the tail slowly tapers, "gradually shoaling away to less than an inch in thickness."[31] Nonetheless, these beautiful features are only bestowed by the animate power that endows them with motion and sensation. Melville thus provides a subtle but significant correction to Burke, suggesting that power and beauty are inseparable.

Later in the chapter, Melville advances another idea that eludes Burke's aesthetic philosophy: that whales like to *play* with their tails, and such playfulness is wonderful to observe. That play takes a few different forms:

> [Occasionally, when] stealing unawares upon the whale in the fancied security of the middle of solitary seas, you find him unbent from the vast corpulence of his dignity, and kitten-like, he plays on the ocean as if it were a hearth. But still you see his power in his play. The broad palms of his tail are flirted high into the air; then smiting the surface, the thunderous concussion resounds for miles. You would almost think a great gun had been discharged; and if you noticed the light wreath of vapor from the spiracle at his other extremity, you would think that that was the smoke from the touch-hole.
>
> [At other times,] when he is about to plunge into the deeps, his entire flukes with at least thirty feet of his body are tossed erect in the air, and so remain vibrating a moment, till they downwards shoot out of view. Excepting the

sublime *breach*... this peaking of the whale's flukes is perhaps the grandest sight to be seen in all animated nature. Out of the bottomless profundities the gigantic tail seems spasmodically snatching at the highest heaven... Standing at the masthead of my ship during a sunrise that crimsoned sky and sea, I once saw a large herd of whales in the east, all heading towards the sun, and for a moment vibrating in concert with peaked flukes. As it seemed to me at the time, such a grand embodiment of adoration of the gods was never beheld.[32]

We find here another answer to the question, "What is beautiful about a sperm whale's tail?" Its physical characteristics alone—its massive size, graceful tapering, and so forth—do not make it beautiful. Nor is the tail beautiful simply because it embodies the whale's astounding power. Rather, the tail combines these material and immaterial elements in ways that enable the whale to experience unfettered joy, to unloose its being and partake in life's cosmic drama. If, as Friedrich Schiller argues, beauty derives from a "play instinct," an impulse that combines ideas with actions and frees us from the iron rule of necessity, then the leviathan's tail is the fullest articulation of that principle.[33] David Graeber postulates that play—and more specifically, "action carried out for the sheer pleasure of acting, the exertion of powers for the sheer pleasure of exerting them"—is not exclusive to human beings; in fact, it is exceedingly common across the animal kingdom.[34] Whether it is toying "kitten-like" in the ocean's shallows or gloriously peaking flukes in the deep, the whale combines grace and power, joy and astonishment, form and formlessness—experiences that, according to Burke, are utterly alien to one another. Turning Burke on his head, Melville depicts the whale as sublimely beautiful, or beautifully sublime, by reconstituting those categories in ways that emphasize the collective nature of life on earth.

Melville is a dialectical thinker through and through, and nearly all of his reflections on death, violence, and injustice are shadowed by their opposites. I take this to be a fundamental feature of what Paul Hurh calls Melville's "dialectical method."[35] Melville's writing routinely merges supposedly oppositional categories, identities, and positions. In *Moby-Dick*, a sailor is both free and subservient, the ocean is a space of death as well as of possibility, and Ahab is at once a singular Captain ("Ahab stands alone among the millions of the peopled earth") and a representative personality ("one in a whole nation's census—a mighty pageant creature"). In "Bartleby," the phrase "I would prefer not to" functions as both speech and non-speech, a negative locution that is marked as much by liminality as Bartleby's screened-off workstation.[36] The list goes on. For Melville, beauty is not a historically contingent concept or elitist topic of concern but a force generated out of multiple phenomena, the apprehension of which clues us in to the nature of reality. It is the combined effect of many different feelings, perspectives, and sensations, including but not limited to the sublime.

Beauty is therefore quite different from the picturesque. Melville's attention to non-sublime experiences has sometimes been attributed to his interest in the picturesque tradition, which prioritized the balancing of colors and textures, particularly in landscape painting.[37] Philosophers of the picturesque, such as William Gilpin and Uvedale Price, certainly influenced Melville's ideas about art and nature, and some of Melville's later poems meditate at length about the specific properties of the picturesque. However, Melville never considered the picturesque to be the defining form or expression of beauty. He persistently inquired into beauty in all of its redoubtable power and multiplicity, and Melville's engagements with the picturesque grew out of that sustained inquiry. The picturesque, according to many of its eighteenth-century theorists, requires a "toning down" of extremes, whereas Melville *amplifies* the ideas and feelings that come into his purview, turning the volume up. The picturesque also focused primarily on landscapes, whereas Melville tends to find beauty throughout the entirety of nature, locating it not only in mountains and groves but in everything from splashes of color (and colorlessness) to ideas, actions, ships, stones, weeds, water, trees, moss, and the physiognomy of the human face.[38]

This leads us to the second counter-argument, about ugliness. Melville apprehends beauty through different ways of writing and thinking, and sometimes that involves inquiring into beauty's opposite. The ugly in Melville is almost always associated with brutality, from the tyrant Radney ("ugly" and "malicious") to the heartless "gunner's gang of every man-of-war" (who are "invariably ill-tempered, ugly... and quarrelsome") and the grotesque ironclads ("The *Monitor* was ugly"). For Melville ugliness has little to do with imperfection or deformity—indeed, some of the most beautiful people, actions, and objects in Melville's work are decidedly less-than-perfect, such as Billy Budd who stutters. Ugliness is instead associated with antipathy toward the mutuality that defines the natural world.[39] Amasa Delano, the racist captain in "Benito Cereno," has "ugly" thoughts, and the hideous "steam-tug" that pulls the *Temeraire* embodies the "deadlier lore" of modern warfare—aesthetic judgments that are freighted with moral significance. As Melville proclaims in *Mardi*, "the only ugliness" is "of the heart."[40]

Melville encountered similar ideas about beauty in some of the books that he read. In *Modern Painters* (1843–60), which Melville owned, John Ruskin identifies beauty with self-erasure: "Every great writer... [guides] the mind far from himself, to the beauty which is not of his creation, and of the knowledge which is past his finding out." In Madame de Staël's *Of Germany* (1813), Melville discovered a more hopeful vision of the sublime, in which it has two corresponding effects: even as the sublime "crush[es]" us (as Burke likewise argues), it also "raises [us] up," conveying a "spark of sacred fire."[41] William Hazlitt's *Criticisms on Art* (1843) expounds the centrality of beauty to human existence ("The contemplation of truth and beauty is the proper object for which we were created, which calls forth the most intense desires of the soul") and reflects on the diverse aesthetic qualities that enliven works of art. For Hazlitt, the very best paintings tend to combine numerous techniques. When reflecting on Sebastiano del Piombo's *The Raising of Lazarus* (1517–19; Figure 4), for instance, Hazlitt is struck by its exquisite mixture:

Figure 4. Sebastiano del Piombo, *The Raising of Lazarus* (1517–19). Oil painting. Courtesy of the National Gallery, London.

We might dwell on the masterly strength of the drawing, the gracefulness of the principal female figures, the high-wrought execution, the deep, rich, mosaic colouring, the messiness and bustle of the background.... The artist has not relied merely on the extent of his canvas, or the importance of his subject, for producing a striking result—the effect is made out by an aggregate of excellent parts.[42]

Several of Melville's interlocutors saw beauty as something akin to a law of nature. As James Jarves writes in *The Art Idea* (1864)—a copy of which Melville received as a gift—beauty is a primary "instinct" that "enters into all things." Art is simply a "material form" in which this instinct is expressed.[43] Melville's approach to beauty also dovetailed, in certain respects, with William Ellery Channing's. Melville owned and read copies of Channing's works and, as Dawn Coleman has documented, Channing's Unitarian theology stirred Melville's ever-evolving interest in the divine.[44] Channing holds that beauty is an "all-pervading presence" that is "infinite in the universe," manifesting in everything from the growth of trees to "the numberless flowers of the spring," and the splendid hues of rocks and shells.[45]

That affirmation of beauty resounds in many of Melville's works. From the alluring music that vibrates from the strings of Isabelle's guitar to the "strange... [and] exceedingly beautiful" grottoes of Rock Rodondo and the opening reflections of "The Piazza" ("beauty is like piety"), beauty recurs across Melville's writing because it is integral to his understanding of the world and his attempts to render it through language.[46] It is an inextricable part of everything that makes Melville Melville: his fervent, lifelong interest in the complexities of perspective; his searching meditations on the nature of belief; as well as his reflections on identity, power, and the relations between forms.

Resituating Melville

This study seeks to revise our understanding of Melville by recentering his treatment of beauty. As we will see, Melville's interest in beauty was profoundly philosophical, not only its historical sources but also in its implications. That echoes what scholars have discovered about Melville's philosophical engagements. Melville wrestled with ideas that he encountered across multiple media, not only in books of philosophy (e.g. Baruch Spinoza, Plato, Immanuel Kant, John Locke, Friedrich Schiller, Arthur Schopenhauer) but also in paintings, prints, poems, novels, histories, memoirs, and encyclopedias. Melville frequently wove philosophical sources into his fiction, exploring metaphysical ideas and perspectives through "the fusing power of [his] imagination."[47] In their volume *Melville Among the Philosophers* (2017), Thomas Nurmi and Corey McCall highlight the importance of mutability and contingency for Melville—qualities that aptly describe his writing as well as his view of the world-at-large. The question of how to respond philosophically to a universe of constant change, they point out, "framed Melville's writing in various ways for [most] of his career, giving shape to some of his most famous passages and the philosophical problems that underlie them."[48] For Melville, philosophy and aesthetics are inextricably linked.

"The Tail" is a case in point. On the one hand, the chapter is clearly about the acquisition of knowledge. Trying to ascertain the biological purpose of the sperm whale's tail, Ishmael proceeds through several enumerated claims, arguing that the tail is defined by "five great motions": "First, when used as a fin for progression; Second, when used as a mace in battle; Third, in sweeping; Fourth, in lobtailing; Fifth, in peaking flukes."[49] As such, the chapter partakes in the epistemological inquiry that sustains so much of *Moby-Dick*, anchoring Ishmael's relentless exploration of the relation between parts and wholes and the bond between the material and the immaterial. In "The Tail," Ishmael attempts, yet again, to access truth through empiricism and synecdoche, using the tail's material movements as a basis for understanding the whale's immaterial essence. On the other hand, "The Tail" is clearly about aesthetics. The entire chapter revolves around considerations of "lines of beauty" (a term that comes from eighteenth-century aesthetic philosophy[50]), the perfect curve of which reminds Ishmael of elephants sublimely hailing "the morning with their trunks uplifted in the profoundest silence." The muscular fibers that entwine the tail (another source of beauty) resemble classic architecture: the "dense webbed bed of welded sinews" composed of "three distinct strata" echo the stout walls of ancient Rome. The chapter even begins with Ishmael likening himself to a poet, crowing that he seeks not to philosophize upon the tail but to "*celebrate*" it. That sense of praise is redoubled at the end of the chapter when Ishmael recalls a glorious morning when he saw something he'll never forget: a large herd of sperm whales, heading eastward at daybreak, lifting their tails to mark the rise of the blazing sun. "As it seemed to me at the time, such a grand embodiment of the gods was never beheld."[51] Even in recollection, Ishmael is overcome with awe.

In Melville's view, these two ways of apprehending the world—philosophy and aesthetics—are codependent. "The Tail" famously concludes on a note of failure: "dissect him how I may, I only go but skin deep; I know him not, and never will." But the chapter is not a failure in the manner that Ishmael imagines it to be. It advances our understanding of the whale's physiology and behavior, and it imparts a keen sense of beauty's co-extensiveness with "all animated nature."[52] To assess the sperm whale's tail, Ishmael enlists a range of analogies—elephants, Dante's *Inferno*, the first law of thermodynamics, Michelangelo's Sistine chapel, Roman walls and statues, antelopes, Ptolemy Philopator—that collapse distinctions between science and art. What if the "lines of beauty," so evident in the whale's flukes, organize the cosmos and our perception of it? That question, which animates the entire chapter, encourages us to think about philosophy and aesthetics as a paired totality, as interconnected as a sperm whale's flukes.

If the aesthetic and philosophical dimensions of Melville's writing are impossible to disentangle, that is partly due to Melville's understanding of literary form. For Melville, form has very little to do with fixed or established structures. As Samuel Otter argues, Melville treats form as something that, rather than enclosing meaning, opens it up and makes it multiply.[53] In Melville's writing, form becomes a web of relations, a verbal and visual network that explicitly draws attention to how information is conveyed.[54] I want to extend Otter's analysis in a slightly different direction, asking how Melville's aesthetic treatment of information is also an act of philosophy, and how Melville's investment in meaning's proliferation might help us better understand beauty itself.

This book is also in conversation with the wave of recent scholarship on Melville and personhood. In recent years, several critics have recovered a key feature of Melville's writing: how it conflates the human with the non-human. Melville, Thomas Nurmi observes, is a writer "attuned to the intricate entanglement of human and nonhuman realms, not in pantheistic or transcendental terms but in terms we now recognize as hallmarks of ecology."[55] Melville's characters do not resemble people or characters as much as they form "irresolvable aesthetic problem[s]," or as Michael Jonik puts it, "intertwined 'personae'...unmoored from personhood, [and] cast into the 'whelming sea' of the impersonal." Sharon Cameron draws attention to Melville's penchant for treating "persons as if they were not governed by a set of constraints that differentiate them from other phenomena, as if...a person were not different from a stone or a manifestation of light," while Paul Hurh shows us how Melville "degrade[s] and disperse[s]" the self in ways that subvert the romantic subject.[56] We have also learned that Melville does not approach personhood solely in terms of negation. He also reveals just how entangled humans are with a variety of natural forces, from gravity to numbers and sounds.[57]

This breakdown and dispersal of the self has an immanently aesthetic dimension. Impersonality rarely reveals itself through logic alone; it has to be felt on a sensuous and intuitive level. This is where beauty comes into play, by arousing the senses and revealing the copious ways in which we are constituted by other modes of life. At once catalyst and medium, beauty dispels the fictions of selfhood that so often parry and degrade our understanding of reality. Approaching beauty in this manner involves following the trajectory of Melville's own thinking, which uncannily anticipates many of the political, philosophical, and environmental concerns that prevail in the twenty-first century. Encounters with beauty open up these concerns by taking us outside of ourselves and imparting a sense of connection.

Melville deftly described that sense of connection in an 1851 letter to Nathaniel Hawthorne. After recounting his intellectual growth as if he were a flowering plant

("I am now come to the inmost leaf of the bulb, and... shortly the flower must fall to the mould"), he recalls one of Goethe's adages, "Live in the all." What might it mean to truly do that, to live and think and move "in the all"? For Melville, it means discarding the notion that you have a "separate identity" and finding ways to "get out of yourself, spread and expand yourself, and bring to yourself the tinglings of life that are felt in the flowers and the woods, that are felt in the planets Saturn and Venus, and the Fixed Stars." Melville then offers something like a confession. He says he knows that this is a bit of "flummery," but he cannot help believing there is an important underlying "truth in it":

> You must often have felt it, lying on the grass on a warm summer's day. Your legs seem to send out shoots into the earth. Your hair feels like leaves upon your head. This is the *all* feeling... [W]hat plays mischief with the truth is that men will insist upon the universal application of a temporary feeling.[58]

However much Melville hedges against Goethe's adage, he insists on its aptness. The letter articulates a series of intimate connections he feels with Hawthorne, with Goethe, with humanity, and with nature. Melville's intimate letters to Hawthorne, as Jordan Alexander Stein observes, are "rich in metaphor and guileless in their meanings, giving their reader glimpses of feelings that often look astonishingly unguarded," and here Melville confesses to a deep-seated intuition about collective being.[59] The entire passage is about mutuality; it describes a life-force that passes through individual selves and onward and outward into the cosmos. Melville's famous skepticism rears its head but it is accompanied by the recognition of a basic truth, a fleeting realization of the interdependency of life on earth. This is where philosophy emerges, in the moments before and after that "all feeling": philosophy enables one to move from feeling to thought and back again, providing that heady sensation of having roots for feet and leaves for hair with a sense of order. Yet the reverse is true as well: philosophy equally depends on that "all feeling" and the sense of boundless connection it makes possible. Otherwise, it withers on the vine.

Melville, Beauty, and American Literary Studies acknowledges this entanglement and adopts it as an analytical method. To elucidate Melville's treatment of beauty, the following pages focus on Melville's philosophico-aesthetic modes. By "mode," I mean a style of thinking, a pattern of expression that is at once verbal and ideational. Over the course of his career, Melville developed several such modes which enabled him to try out perspectives, describe worlds both real and imagined, and measure the artistic, ethical, and intellectual worth of various ideas. Melville's modes thus resemble the ancient idea of *modus* ("measure, way, or method" in Latin).[60] For the Greeks and Romans, mode referred to a distinct melody or pitch structure within a given work, or more accurately "the internal relationships of notes within a scale, especially of predominance of one of them over the others as a tonic."[61]

In this book, I analyze three modes that organize some of Melville's major writings. Chapter 1, "Ancient Beauty in *Timoleon*," ponders how and why Melville persistently returns to the ancient world. For Melville, the ancients had something crucial which has since been lost or forgotten: a sense of beauty's radical ubiquity. *Timoleon* turns back to antiquity to apprehend the beauty of natural forms, which ancient artists took as both raw material and a source of inspiration. As they migrate through ancient places and stories, Melville's poems identify three defining features of beauty: it inheres in nature's shapes and materials, it is mixed rather than pure, and it is a common part of earthly life. I track the ways in which these features of beauty appear in various sounds, lines, and phases of matter throughout Melville's poems.

Chapter 2, "Floral Beauty in *Weeds and Wildings*," explores Melville's uses of flowers and the communal experiences they bring about. *Weeds and Wildings* distributes aesthetic experience in ways that underscore the unnaturalness of sovereignty and property alike. Despite the apparent smallness of their subject, Melville's floral poems contain a rather big idea: if possession is in fact "the whole of the law," beauty is its absolute other, its reversal and negation. This is what Melville means when he writes, in the preface, "we are communists here": beauty is a widely shared experience, a force that binds the world together.[62] And that idea, which is woven into his late works, reframes our understanding of Melville's relation to a wide range of writers, artists, and philosophers, from Claude Lorrain to Arthur Schopenhauer.

Chapter 3, "Appalling Beauty in *Moby-Dick*," considers types of beauty that stun or bewilder. Such beauty recurs throughout Melville's work, but it plays a particularly important role in *Moby-Dick*, leading Melville to distinguish between two points of view: Ahab's theory of individuated personhood, according to which everyone has an identifiable self (including a whale who is capable of shocking violence), and a more open perspective that views personhood as broadly distributed and marked by interdependence. Whenever something beautiful comes into view, it subtly but powerfully dissolves the self—or what we previously considered the self—and pulls us toward one of these perspectives. Chapter 3 assesses this dialectical treatment of personhood, attending in particular to the way the novel connects the beautiful to the sacred and depicts whales as akin to works of art.[63]

I focus on this particular set of writings for a few related reasons. Melville's career spanned nearly half-a-century, and during that time he experimented with a multitude of genres, from odes and lyrics to essays, sea-fiction, and floral poetry. To understand Melville's modes, it is essential to study the early and the late writings together, and to treat his poetry and prose as related forms. Although it is customary to divide Melville's career into antebellum and postbellum halves, there is a great deal of continuity across Melville's work, and that continuity is particularly evident in his abiding interest in beauty's characteristics and consequences.[64] Furthermore, I consider these writings—*Timoleon*, *Weeds and Wildings*, and *Moby-Dick*—to be among Melville's very best. As we will see, they are finely crafted, ingeniously conceived, and acutely aware of beauty's role in everyday life.

Reclaiming Beauty

By focusing on aesthetics, this book taps into a minoritarian strain in American literary studies. Minoritarian thought, as Deleuze and Guattari define it, involves variation from "from the majoritarian standard" and an attention to "the powers of becoming."[65] For a rather long time, the major trends in American literary studies have focused on considerations of history, politics, and culture. When the term "American literature" first emerged in the 1810s in 1820s, it was a defensive concept, a historicized rejection of the popular British assertion that "American literature" did not exist.[66] When the first anthologies of American literature were assembled and disseminated in the ensuing decades, they presented their contents (which, from the beginning, included colonial documents, travel writings, and historical studies) as examples of strong but not necessarily beautiful writing, works that are culturally if not artistically significant.

In the nineteenth century, this defense made a lot of sense. If the case for American literature depended on texts such as Michael Wigglesworth's *The Day of Doom* (1662) and Benjamin Franklin's *Autobiography* (1791), when British anthologies could boast writers like William Shakespeare, John Milton, Mary Shelley, John Keats, Samuel Taylor Coleridge, Jane Austen, and William Blake, then positing beauty as an evaluative standard was a losing hand.[67] In terms of the artistry of the writing, there was no comparison and everyone knew it. One of the first anthologizers of American literature, Evert Duyckinck, saw his work in strictly historiographic terms: "The history of the literature of the country [is not] ... an exhibition of art and invention, of literature in its immediate and philosophical sense." Rather, American literature is best conceived as a record "of facts and opinions which derives its main interest from its *historical* rather than its critical value. It is important to know what books have been produced, and by whom; whatever the books may have been."[68]

This disregard for beauty was reinforced by the rise of academic professionalization in the late nineteenth and early twentieth century. American universities, which took the German research model as their North Star, prioritized intellectual "rigor" and scientific (or, at least, science-like) analytical methods. As Elizabeth Renker demonstrates in *The Origins of American Literary Studies* (2007), the German model had an array of gendered consequences, elevating ostensibly "masculine" subjects like the hard sciences over "feminine" subjects like English, and denigrating American literary studies in particular (the "step-child of British literary studies," as Renker puts it).[69] It also molded the American canon, which valorized writers like James Fenimore Cooper who wrote about history and politics, and excluded writers like Harriet Prescott Spofford and Pauline Hopkins, who developed a "highly wrought" style that emphasized sumptuous form and verbal profusion.[70]

New Criticism sharpened and intensified this way of evaluating literature. Although they are frequently remembered as defenders of outmoded aesthetic ideals, the New Critics tended to be quite wary of aesthetic experience. From Cleanth Brooks to Yvor Winters and Allen Tate, the New Critics placed considerable emphasis on impersonal analysis and impassionate expertise. As John Crowe Ransom argued in "Criticism, Inc." (1937), literary criticism must be "scientific,...precise and systematic," and this requires excluding all "personal registrations, which are declarations of the effect of the art-work upon the critic as reader. The first law to be prescribed to criticism...is that it shall be objective."[71] William K. Wimsatt and Monroe Beardsley similarly claimed in "The Affective Fallacy" (1949) that "objective criticism" is possible only if one completely disregards the literary work's "psychological effects." The gravest mistake, according to the New Critics, is to pay attention to how a text makes you feel: to go down that path is to descend into mere "impressionism and relativism."[72]

There were exceptions, of course. R.P. Blackmur and Milton R. Stern's studies of Melville's craft, Walter Bezanson's work on *Clarel*, and similar scholarship explored the aesthetic dimensions of American literature and provided important insights into the development of particular careers, genres, and styles.[73] Nonetheless, a majority of Americanist scholarship in this era consisted primarily of what we would now call archival work. Throughout the twentieth century, scholars recovered and reprinted texts, discovered new sources, and inquired into the relationship between literature and history. Here is a fairly representative cross-section of the topics in Americanist scholarship from the early to mid-twentieth century:

"On the Development of American Literature from 1815 to 1833: With Special Reference to Periodicals"

"The Origins of Brown's *Clotel*"

"Poe's Knowledge of German"

"The Economic Interpretation of Literary History"

"Regionalism and Nationalism in American Literature"

"Literary Aspects of American Anti-Imperialism, 1898–1902"

"Walt Whitman's Politics"

"Hawthorne and Politics"

"Lanier and Science"
"The Negro's Contribution to American Art and Literature"
"Nationalism and International Copyright"
"The Frontier in American Literature"[74]

This past is not exactly a foreign country. Nearly all of this scholarship examines the material histories of American literature and tries to develop objective understandings of its political, cultural, and intellectual contexts. American scholars' desire to rise to the standard of Germanic academic rigor also yielded an early push for quantitative analysis. Decades before the advent of computers, Americanists were already undertaking what Franco Moretti would later dub "distant reading," producing studies such as "A Statistical Survey of American Fiction, 1774–1850" (1939) and "Social Themes in Late Nineteenth-Century American Verse: A Quantitative Study" (1955).[75]

This was the intellectual and institutional backdrop for Melville's canonization and the growth of Melville studies. The priorities that guided American literary studies likewise guided many Melvilleans, who undertook scholarly projects that—apart from obvious differences in terms and concepts—look remarkably contemporary. Prior to 1970, Melville scholars

- Recovered previously neglected writings and expanded the archive. Scholars discovered, edited, and published previously unknown letters, lectures, and other pieces of writing (such as Melville's review of Cooper's *The Red Rover*).
- Examined Melville's views on race and slavery, focusing, for instance, on "Herman Melville and the American National Sin," "Slavery and Innocence in *Benito Cereno*," and "Evidence of the Slavery Dilemma in *White-Jacket*."
- Reconstructed the intellectual, biographical, and literary subtexts of Melville's work. Critics in this era deepened our understanding of Melville's relationship with editors and publishers; his connection to contemporaries such as Ralph Waldo Emerson and Richard Henry Dana, Jr.; and the lasting influence of Melville's experiences at sea.
- Positioned Melville as a writer profoundly interested in science and the natural world, researching his ideas about the earth and his uses of the scientific method.
- Examined the rich tapestry of Melville's spiritual engagements. Long before the rise of "postsecular criticism," scholars analyzed Melville's reading of the Bible, his uses of esoteric and ancient Christianity, and his encounters with various religions and philosophies.[76]

Not only does this older scholarship bear little resemblance to how it has sometimes been portrayed (i.e. as methodologically or politically naïve); it reveals an enduring scholarly concern with the historicity of American literature, and more specifically with Melville's relationship to his cultural and political contexts.

The decades in which the field of American literary studies was institutionalized were also the decades in which beauty was dethroned in the art world. Whereas the nineteenth century was marked by renewals and revisions of beauty (in Romantic, Realist, and Symbolist forms), art in the twentieth century moved in the opposite direction, rejecting the prior era's artistic ideal by deforming and de-emphasizing beauty. As Wendy Steiner has argued, the "break with history" inaugurated by the modernist avant-garde (then extended by the Late Modernists and Postmodernists) was rooted in "the Enlightenment notion of the sublime" and "a disgust toward women and the bourgeoisie that had been building throughout the nineteenth century among increasingly disaffected artists and writers."[77] This disaffection can be felt in works as far afield as Pablo Picasso's *Weeping Woman* (1937), Marcel DuChamp's *Fountain* (1917; Figure 5), and the abstract paintings of Mark Rothko, Jackson Pollock, and Kazimir Malevich.

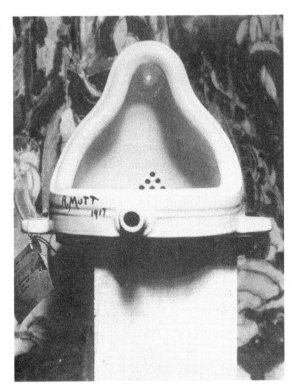

Figure 5. Marcel DuChamp, *Fountain* (1917). Courtesy of the San Francisco Museum of Modern Art.

Beauty was similarly devalued in a great deal of what came to be called "literary theory." In his influential study *Distinction: A Social Critique of the Judgment of Taste* (1979), Pierre Bourdieu posited that aesthetic terms such as beauty are politically contingent and historically variable concepts that cannot denominate anything like a shared, universal experience. Aesthetic judgments, according to Bourdieu, are the byproducts of "social coding" that inevitably reveal one's class position and social status. As Bourdieu writes, the Enlightenment notion of "the 'pure' gaze is a historical invention"; people "distinguish themselves by the distinctions they make, between the beautiful and the ugly, the distinguished and the vulgar," which provide ways of positioning oneself and others vis-à-vis society's power relations.[78]

Raymond Williams provided a related critique in *Marxism and Literature* (1977) and *Keywords: A Vocabulary of Culture and Society* (1976). Retracing the development of aesthetic philosophy, Williams identifies its most problematic assertion: that art is somehow separate from life and material activity. "It is clear from [its] history," Williams writes, that the very idea of the aesthetic, "with its specialized references to art, to visual appearance, and to a category of what is 'fine' or 'beautiful'... emphasized and isolated subjective sense-activity as the basis for art and beauty as distinct... from social or cultural interpretations." This false sense of isolation, he adds, is deeply "damaging."[79] Williams offers a solution, suggesting that students and scholars should focus on "texts" rather than "literature" since "*all* writing carries references, meanings, and values." Hence the problem with beauty as a concept or object of analysis:

> This recognition is lost if it is specialized to "beauty"... What we can practically though variably recognize in specific works has to be linked with the complex formations, situations, and occasions in which such intentions and such responses are made possible, are modified, and are encouraged or deflected. Thus we have to reject "the aesthetic" both as a separate abstract dimension and as a separate abstract function.[80]

Throughout the late twentieth century and early twenty-first century, as scholars worked to expand the canon and re-examine American literature, theorists such as Bourdieu and Williams provided fruitful models. Literary criticism came to be seen in interrogative terms—as a crime scene that one "investigates" or a battle in which one "intervenes"—and aesthetic considerations increasingly carried a taint of backwardness. Although beauty has been a cornerstone for philosophers, literary scholars have traditionally eschewed the term or viewed it in bracketed terms, understanding "beauty" as a false universal that cloaks its actual assumptions and effacements. For a rather long time now, "beauty" has been construed as an ideological effect—an outgrowth of distinct class structures, power relations, and social asymmetries that, whenever it is deployed, necessarily reinforces the status quo.

The most forceful version of this critique can be found in the New Americanist scholarship of late twentieth and early twenty-first century. The rejection of aesthetic judgment and accompanying categories such as beauty plays a prominent role in New Americanist studies such as Jane Tompkins's *Sensational Designs: The Cultural Work of American Fiction* (1986), John Carlos Rowe's *Literary Culture and US Imperialism* (2000), Janice Radway's *Reading the Romance* (1984), Sacvan Bercovitch and Myra Jehlen's *Ideology and Classic American Literature* (1986), and Walter Benn Michaels and Donald Pease's *The American Renaissance Reconsidered* (1985). For Radway the problem with aesthetics has to do with its subjectivism, or lack of "empiricism," whereas for Rowe aesthetics is always entangled in an "aesthetic ideology" that blinds one to political realities. More recently, David Lloyd has argued that nearly all of aesthetic thought—and in particular, its Enlightenment and post-Enlightenment forms—produces a "racial regime of representation" that fuels "the racism of [Western] culture."[81]

There are valid reasons for this skepticism toward aesthetics. It is not difficult to find prejudiced statements in eighteenth- and nineteenth-century aesthetic theory. Burke, for example, compared the feeling of the sublime to the "great horror" experienced "upon accidentally seeing a negro woman."[82] Yet in both direct and indirect ways, Melville's writing challenges racist theories of beauty and upends prevailing aesthetic standards. In his book *On the Natural Varieties of Mankind* (1775), Johannes Blumenbach posited that beauty was synonymous with whiteness, and that idea spread like wildfire in the nineteenth century. One can find versions of Blumenbach's theory expressed far and wide, from Charles White ("[whites are] the most beautiful of the human race") to Ralph Waldo Emerson ("The fair Saxon man, with open front, and honest meaning... is moulded for law ... [and] for colleges, churches, charities, and colonies").[83] Nothing could be further removed from Melville's commentary on the "ghastly" qualities of whiteness (a color of "transcendent horror"), or his treatment of characters such as Queequeg, Pip, and Babo.[84] Melville also subverted racist accounts of beauty in his poems about the ancient world. In Melville's day, writers sometimes viewed Greek and Roman art as evidence of white beauty and racial superiority. In *Timoleon*, Melville praises Greek and Roman art in radically different ways, finding beauty in the lines, forms, and very matter out of which it was made—aesthetic qualities that transgress boundaries not only between bodies but also between species. In Melville, beauty is open, communal, and almost endlessly inclusive.

Moreover, aesthetic theory is merely one version—a particularly abstract version—of aesthetics as such, and as Melville says, "There is an aesthetics in all things."[85] No matter how roundly beauty is dismissed or how vehemently the idea of the aesthetic is rejected, as a mode of experience beauty does not go away. On the contrary, beauty manifests in all sorts of daily actions and experiences. As Alexander Nehamas observes, "Beauty is the object of love and, for better or worse, love can be provoked by anything... [A]esthetic features inform our every waking hour and we are all—every one of us—aware of them."[86] To see things as beautiful or unbeautiful is not an elitist act but a fundamental part of being alive.

Scientists have discovered that this attraction to beauty extends far beyond *homo sapiens*.[87] From the gorgeous feathers of the Great Argus to the elaborate dances of the Red-Capped Manakin and the intricate patterns of tropical seashells, earthly life brims with beauty. From an evolutionary perspective, much of this beauty is extravagant and unnecessary, since it is irreducible to the pressures exerted by natural selection. As Richard Prum affirms in *The Evolution of Beauty* (2017), beauty has played an integral role in the history of evolution and created the "extraordinary aesthetic diversity" that is evident not only among but also within particular species.[88] And this fact has profound consequences for the humanities. It means that nearly all of the ways in which philosophers, writers, and critics have traditionally viewed beauty—from Kant's account of beauty's "subjective" contemplation to Bourdieu's critique of "the pure gaze"—have been woefully narrow and anthropocentric.[89] Prum compares the implications of this idea to the effects of the Copernican revolution: beauty, it turns out, does not revolve around us at all.

Melville, Beauty, and American Literary Studies takes beauty's ubiquity and heterogeneity as its starting point. I agree in this regard with Christopher Castiglia, who has called for a literary criticism based on hope and possibility rather than disenchantment. As Castiglia posits, hope is "very different from optimism": "Far from implying a cheery faith that all will turn out well," hope is a "perpetual openness to the as-yet-untried, is an end in itself. Hope is a disposition toward the imaginative value of dissatisfaction and the social value of illusion, whimsy, vision, reverie, daydreams, all sources of world making trivialized within disciplinary regimes of the 'real.'"[90] Beauty is one of hope's basic modalities, one of the primary ways in which hope is felt and expressed.

This was certainly the case for Melville. Whatever demons Melville may have battled (and they were legion), his writing is shot through with beautiful shapes, acts, bodies, movements, and ideas. From Vine's reflections on the Mar Saba palm (that glorious "stem of beauty") to the evanescent roses that enlace *Weeds and Wildings*, beauty courses through Melville's works, revealing itself to be a mode of experience that is as enduring as it is enlivening. As Melville writes in "At the Hostelry,"

> In best of worlds if all's not bright,
> Allow, the shadow's chased by light,
> Though rest for neither yet may be.
> And beauty's charm, where Nature reigns,
> Nor crimes nor codes may quite subdue...[91]

Beauty cannot stamp out injustice, Melville implies. But the reverse is equally true: neither "crimes nor codes" can destroy beauty because it is irrepressible.

Plato articulates a similar idea in *The Banquet*, the work upon which Melville modeled "At the Hostlery." Plato posits that beauty, rather than deriving from narrow self-regard, is social and open-ended. When someone or something beautiful comes into view, we are filled with wonderment and drawn to another spark of life. That particularized experience of beauty, Plato says, is never singular; it engenders *other* experiences of beauty, which widen and spread as we live and grow. "Beauty," Plato continues, "which exists in any [particular] form... is the brother to that which is in a different form." Each experience we have with beauty, each time we are washed by its waves, we wade into the "wide sea of beauty," which knows neither beginning nor end. Like energy, beauty can be neither "produced nor destroyed": it "exists forever," Plato argues, and is "manifold," always exerting a certain power to string experience together and produce change.[92] For Plato as for Melville, beauty erodes identities and folds us into the broader world.

My hope is that this book will contribute to our understanding of Melville's writing as well as the aesthetic dimensions of American literature more broadly. Might archives have aesthetic qualities as much as a violet or a cloud? What are reform movements but attempts to beautify the world and bring it into a more ideal order? How might aesthetic experience play a larger role in classrooms and curricula? What if the "texts" scholars recover for their historical or cultural representativeness are just as notable for the pleasures they afford and the imaginative experiences they foster? It would be a mistake to assume that Melville offers definitive answers to such questions. But his writings do open up a host of possibilities by encouraging us to reconsider what beauty is, where it comes from, and why it matters.

1
Ancient Beauty in *Timoleon*

In 1877, while excavating ancient ruins in southern Greece, archaeologists discovered something hidden in the rocky bosom of a building that had been constructed more than twenty-five centuries ago: a breathtaking and surprisingly well preserved statue of Hermes feeding grapes to the infant Dionysus (Figure 6).[1]

Melville was struck by this statue, which seemed to have been magically lifted from one era into another. In *Timoleon* (1891), his final volume of published poetry, Melville reflects on this felicitous discovery:

> What forms divine in adamant fair—
> Carven demigod and god,
> And hero-marbles rivaling these,
> Bide under Latium's sod,
> Or lost in sediment and drift
> Alluvial which the Grecian rivers sift.
> To dig for these, O better far
> Than raking arid sands
> For gold more barren meetly theirs
> Sterile, with brimming hands.[2]

Melville looks at the statue—as he looks at so many things—in several ways. This ancient work of art offers a lesson in historical difference, hinting that modernity might not be the grand march forward that many of its proponents imagine it to be. In fact, it might involve a tragic decline. We used to create divine art, Melville implies; now we just pan for gold. That decline is echoed not only in the poem's shift in imagery (from "rivers" to "arid sands") and movement (from lifting up to bending down) but also in the sense of loss that quietly echoes through the poem. Melville's description of Hermes as both "demigod and god"—an immortal whose form is utterly and touchingly human—also invites theological considerations. Sculpted by Praxiteles, the statue depicts Hermes, the semi-divine "messenger of the Gods," playing with the infant Dionysus (and protecting him from Hera)—a far more earthly conception of divinity than came to pass after the spread of Christianity and Islam.[3] Last but certainly not least, Melville is captivated by the statue's beauty. By linking the everyday and the divine, the human and the non-human, the airy and the earthly, this "hero-marble" sharpens our sense of connection. The marble out of which this statue was carved was slowly created

Figure 6. Praxiteles, *Hermes and the Infant Dionysus* (forth century BCE). Photograph (2019).

over the course of millions of years by the "sediment and drift / Alluvial" of "Grecian rivers": a beautiful process made even more beautiful by Praxiteles' hammer, chisel, and brush.

Melville's fascination with this rediscovered statue is part of his abiding fascination with the ancient world. Melville felt almost magnetically pulled toward classical Greece, Rome, and Egypt, and the effects of that fascination are registered in almost everything he wrote. Melville's verbal tapestries and imagined worlds are full of ancient ideas, characters, and references:

> "We think we are not human; we become as immortal bachelors and gods; but again, like the Greek gods themselves, prone we descend to earth; glad to be uxorious once more; glad to hide these god-like heads within the bosoms made of too-seducing clay."

> "While partaking of this simple repast, the inmates of Marheyo's house, after the style of the ancient Romans, reclined in sociable groups upon the divan of mats, and digestion was promoted by cheerful conversation."

> "But who shall hymn the roman heart?
> A stoic he, but even more:

The iron will and lion thew
Were strong to inflict as to endure."

"'And did you get that out of your silly Dream Book, you Greek?' howled Jackson through a cough. 'Don't talk of heaven to me—it's a lie—I know it—and they are all fools that believe in it. Do you think, you Greek, that there's any heaven for *you*?'"

"The sleek little pilot-fish, azure and slim...
Have nothing of harm to dread,
But liquidly glide on his ghastly flank
Or before his Gorgonian head."

"[Billy Budd] showed in face that humane look of reposeful good nature which the Greek sculptor in some instances gave to his heroic strong man, Hercules."

"Claggart was a man about five and thirty, somewhat spare and tall, yet no ill figure upon the whole... The face was a notable one, the features all except the chin cleanly cut as those on a Greek medallion."

"His pure tight skin was an excellent fit; and closely wrapped up in it, and embalmed with inner health and strength, like a revivified Egyptian, this Starbuck seemed prepared to endure for long ages to come,..."

"So that there are instances among them of men, who, named with Scripture names... and in childhood naturally imbibing the stately dramatic thee and thou of the Quaker idiom; still, from the audacious, daring, and boundless adventure of their subsequent lives, strangely blend with these unoutgrown peculiarities, a thousand bold dashes of character, not unworthy... a poetical Pagan Roman."

"And—more–is Nature's Roman, never to be scourged."[4]

As these invocations suggest, something is going on that far exceeds the bounds of mere "interest." For Melville, the ancient world is not simply a recurring setting or theme. Rather, this is one of Melville's major philosophico-aesthetic modes, one of the prisms through which he both apprehends and depicts the world. Melville's ancient mode is at once a style, a way of thinking, and an interpretive framework that influences a great deal of his writing.

Melville's modes frequently overlap. Always interested in contrast and juxtaposition, Melville enjoys putting multiple modes into motion and seeing the sparks fly. So there is ancient beauty in *Moby-Dick*, floral beauty in *Mardi*, and appalling beauty in *Timoleon*. But each work possesses a distinct philosophico-aesthetic architecture, and in *Timoleon* the mode that resonates most fully across the poems, impacting the volume in both implicit and explicit ways, attends to beauty that came before the modern world: the beauty of ancient art and religion;

of ancient places and actions; as well as the beauty of nature itself, which ancient artists took as both inspiration and raw material.

There are numerous reasons why Melville felt tethered to antiquity. He was born into a culture awash in neoclassicism, an early republic in which everything from buildings to political institutions and rhetorical ideals were based, to one degree or another, on Grecian and Roman models.[5] This American appetite for all things ancient yielded a prodigious number of books, many of which Melville bought or borrowed. With avid interest he read Plato's dialogs, Plutarch's *Morals*, Livy's *History of Rome*, Aristotle's *Treatise on Rhetoric*, Thucydides's *History of the Peloponnesian War*, Diogenes Laërtius's *The Lives and Opinions of Eminent Philosophers*, Edward Gibbon's *History of the Decline and Fall of Ancient Rome*; *The Odyssey* and *The Iliad*; the plays of Aeschylus, Sophocles, and Euripides; as well as diaries, journals, and travel guides that described ancient cultures and everything they left behind. Melville dove into Pyrrhonism, Cynicism, Epicureanism, Buddhism, and the other schools of ancient philosophy; he collected prints and paintings of ancient buildings and landscapes; and studied artists such as Claude Lorrain and Giovanni Piranesi, who channeled their artistic energy into depicting the legacies of Rome.[6]

Two of the authors he read with special care and attention, Arthur Schopenhauer and Matthew Arnold, wrote at length about the power and beauty of classical Greece. According to Schopenhauer, the Greeks

> developed a special, one might almost say, an instinctive sense of beauty, belonging to them alone of all the nations who have ever existed on the earth, peculiar, fine, and exact; so that their mythology took, in the mouth of their poets, and in the hands of their artists, an exceedingly beautiful and pleasing shape.

For Arnold, the Greeks' veneration of truth and beauty continues to provide a model to follow and an ideal to strive for: "The best art and poetry of the Greeks, in which religion and poetry are one, in which the idea of beauty...adds to itself a religious and devout energy,.. [represent] the happy moments of humanity." "To get rid of one's ignorance," Arnold added, "to see things as they are, and...to see them in their beauty, is the simple and attractive idea which Hellenism holds out before human nature."[7]

Melville traveled multiple times to this part of the world, first as a sailor then as a tourist, visiting Athens, Rome, Jerusalem, Milan, Constantinople, the Judean desert, and the Greek Islands. He drew on those travels in nearly all of his work, from his first novel *Typee* (roughly based on his experiences in French Polynesia) to his final novella *Billy Budd* (set on a British man-of-war during the French Revolution and about a sailor modeled on the ancient Greek beauty, Antinous).[8] In the journals he kept from his trips in the late 1840s and late 1850s,

Melville repeatedly comments on where he did and did not find beauty. The mountains and buildings of Judea, for example, proved to be humbler than the Bible had led him to believe ("Judea is [just] one accumulation of stones— Stony mountains & stony plains; stony torrents & stony roads; stony walls & stony fields,... The toes of everyone's shoes are all stubbed to pieces with the stones")[9], whereas Buyukdere, on the Turkish coast, was astounding:

> A challenge of contrasts, where by the successively alternate sweeps of the shores of both sides seem to retire from every new proffer of beauty, again in some grand prudery to advance with a bolder bid, and thereupon again & again retiring, neither willing to retreat from the contest of beauty.[10]

The ancient world represented to Melville not only a source of artistic and philosophical inspiration but also an example of all that modernity might lose or destroy: an intuitive sense of our connection to the earth, and an awareness that enjoying beauty—not making money or increasing efficiency—is an essential part of being alive.[11] The sense of decline intoned by "The Disinterment of the Hermes" is echoed by "The Ravaged Villa," another poem in *Timoleon*:

> In shards the sylvan vases lie,
> Their links of dance undone,
> And brambles wither by thy brim,
> Choked fountain of the sun!
> The spider in the laurel spins,
> The weed exiles the flower:
> And, flung to kiln, Apollo's bust
> Makes lime for Mammon's tower.[12]

Nor is this disenchantment limited to *Timoleon*. In a way, Melville's entire *oeuvre* is a meditation on the allures, dangers, and limits of modernity. That strain of Melville's thought can be found in *Typee*, which excoriates Christian missionaries and valorizes native culture, as well as everything else Melville created, from "Bartleby the Scrivener," which shows how the modern office strips humanity away and deadens the soul, to *Clarel*, which depicts modernity as a "skilled destroyer" incapable of providing spiritual succor or existential meaning.[13] As Lewis Mumford points out, Melville's writing "does not belong to this comfortable bourgeois world"; it is a "challenge and affront to all the habits of mind that typically prevailed in the nineteenth century, and still remain, almost unabated, among us: it comes out of a different world, and presupposes, for its acceptance, a more integrated life and consciousness than we have known or experienced."[14]

In Melville's view, that "more integrated life and consciousness" may be unrealized now but it was a part of everyday life for the ancients. *Timoleon* thus returns to antiquity to reflect on integrated consciousness and everything it makes possible, attending in particular to ancient perspectives on beauty. As we will see, the poems in *Timoleon* consider the relation between form and matter, the complexities of perspective, and the link between art and the environment, all of which were pressing concerns for ancient artists and philosophers. The account of beauty that furtively yet forcefully emerges in the volume emphasizes beauty's status as an elemental force that coheres in a variety of patterns and combinations. These beautiful poems thus sharpen our understanding of Melville's aesthetics, as well as how his aesthetics evolved in relation to his views on art and philosophy.

The following pages also extend recent scholarship on the biographical, artistic, and philosophical dimensions of *Timoleon*. Douglas Robillard and Elisa Tamarkin have elucidated Melville's intricate use of the visual arts in the poems, which frequently move back and forth between the eye and the ear as Melville stages intertextual and intermedial dialogs with artists such as Elihu Vedder, Charles Le Brun, and David Teniers the Younger. William B. Dillingham and Peter Riley have situated *Timoleon* in relation to Melville's changing circumstances in the late 1880s and early 1890s, namely his retirement from the Customs House and his late turn toward a particular "circle" of intellectual influences (e.g. Arthur Schopenhauer, James Thomson, Matthew Arnold, and Honoré de Balzac). Scholars have also examined Melville's distinctive use of ancient characters and poetic forms, which make *Timoleon*, as Edgar Dryden puts it, "historical without being antiquarian."[15] This chapter contributes to this burgeoning interest in *Timoleon* by elucidating the poems' philosophico-aesthetic treatment of beauty and the perspective they provide on the intermingling of the human and non-human world.

The Beauty of Natural Forms

In *Timoleon* beauty emerges in everything from lines to ripples of water, flashes of light, and moments of stillness. Even the poems that are ostensibly about the epic monuments of earlier civilizations are primarily about the natural shapes and materials out of which such monuments were composed. "Greek Masonry" and "Greek Architecture," for example, revolve around the relation between form and matter:

> Joints were none that mortar sealed:
> Together, scarce with line revealed,
> The blocks in symmetry congealed.
> ...
> Not magnitude, not lavishness,
> But Form—the Site;

> Not innovating willfulness,
> But reverence for the Archetype.[16]

The elegance and appeal of classic Greek buildings were not the byproduct of sheer human ingenuity. The beauty of the architecture derived from its relationship to the environment. Greek columns and crepidoma, made out of blocks of ashlar stone laid atop one another, resembled giant blocks of ice: masses of water suddenly frozen into place. "Congeal" has several connotations—to condense, for example—but congealing is also the process through which a liquid becomes a solid.[17] The beauty of Greek buildings has to do with their ice-like allure, which draws us into the cold grace of these structures composed out of some of the same elements that compose the human body. Perhaps that is part of the reverence: these buildings are us in altered form, transmuted through hammer and chisel.

In that respect these poems are emblematic of *Timoleon*, which finds beauty in fluidity, solidity, and evaporation. The poems tend to cohere around these states of matter, migrating from solid forms like the Milan Cathedral and Pisa's Leaning Tower to various liquids and atmospheres, as well as the forces that connect them, like geology and art ("a flame to melt—a wind to freeze"). "Magian Wine" is surprisingly watery, evoking the "liquid mirage" induced by drunkenness as well as the flowing sounds of the mages:

> And, seething through the rapturous wave,
> What low Elysian Athens rise:
> Sybilline inklings blending rave,
> Then lap the verge with sighs,
> Delirious here the oracles swim,
> Ambiguous in the beading hymn.[18]

Elsewhere, armies "gleam" like winding rivulets (in "The Night-March"), cataracts sing a pleasing "hymn" (in "Lamia's Song"), desire spouts like "Geysers" (in "After the Pleasure Party"), and icicles "glaze" the vines and "crape" the trees (in "Monody"). Even the vast blankness of the desert brings us back to water (which made the sand), appearing to the eye "Like blank ocean in blue calm"; and the Great Pyramid's blocks of stone are a beautiful series of "glaciers blank."[19]

Some of this, of course, is the result of Melville's oceanic style. Ever since his time as a sailor, he could never truly leave the water behind.[20] Melville's unyielding attachment to the sea, however, is only part of what's going on. As Ronan Ludot-Vlasak has demonstrated, Melville was keenly interested in antiquity throughout his life, and that interest crops up in writings such as *Typee*, *Mardi*, "Bartleby," and *Billy Budd*.[21] As Melville stated in a letter to Hawthorne, "I am like one of those seeds taken out of the Egyptian pyramids." In *Timoleon* that ancient perspective generates a set of poems concerned with interrelated states of mind and matter.

This is one of the things he learned from philosophers such as Lucretius and Democritus, who theorized elemental connections, the existence of atoms, and the beauty of earthly existence.[22] One can find no fuller refutation of "that snivel the world over, / That months are vacuums and the ground but wallow and filth" than the creation myth of Hesiod, according to which Aphrodite was born autochthonously from the water—an illustration of nature's evolution out of chaos as well as Plato's notion that the cosmos is "a living Creature." Metrodorus's teacher, Epicurus, likewise claimed that matter was not created but simply exists in and for itself, implying that everything in life comes from undirected but purposeful activity, finding form out of the void like the atoms that created the universe. No wonder Lucretius dedicated *De Rerum Natura* to Venus, the Goddess of Beauty, through whom "all that's born and breathes . . . [is] brought forth to see the sun."[23]

Melville combines that ancient point of view with modern science, whose "never-varying" method he evokes in "Lone Founts" and "New Zealot to the Sun."[24] As Thomas Nurmi contends, Melville seeks to "tell a different story of the human species through the prism of the non-human, a prism that refracts our constituent animal, vegetal, and mineral selves."[25] In *Magnificent Decay: Melville and Ecology* (2020), Nurmi reveals numerous ways in which Melville represents this interdependence between organisms and their environments, from *Mardi* to *John Marr and Other Sailors*. In *Timoleon*, Melville tells this "different story of the human species" by turning back to the ancient world. The resulting philosophy, which anchors *Timoleon*, suggests that beauty has little to do with the qualities with which it is routinely associated. It is not something that, as Kant says, happens in the human mind when pleasing objects elicit a "free play" between our imagination and our understanding. Nor does beauty reside, as Burke would have it, in discrete non-sublime qualities—smallness, delicacy, and so forth—that invite a feeling of love untinged by desire.[26] Rather, it is an inherent property of the earth, a connective force evident in everything from waves to clouds, whales, stones, and bursts of air.

Timoleon's attention to transitional states is part of what Elisa Tamarkin dubs the volume's "vaporous" quality. As Tamarkin has shown, *Timoleon* sustains a complex dialog with the art and aesthetics of Elihu Vedder, the late-nineteenth-century Symbolist who created illustrations for Omar Khayyám's *The Rubáiyát* as well as numerous paintings inspired by the ancient world. There is a stylistic and tonal convergence between Vedder's images and Melville's poems, which jointly explore the ephemerality of life and art. The poems in *Timoleon*, Tamarkin writes, are like

> hallucinations from a life that is lost or loses meaning by the day . . . They are hypnotic and dreamlike, but still hang thickly to the material world . . . Melville wanted his poems to have the special effects of Vedder's drawings, but to do this they had to acknowledge the vaporousness of art's whole enterprise.

That acknowledgment resounds in the "epiphanic vision" of "The Apparition," the fading idealism of "C—'s Lament," and other mirage-like moments.[27] To a large degree that is the volume's underlying point: everyone and everything is transient, like the mist in the epigraph to "Buddha": "For what is your life? It is even a vapor that appeareth for a little time and then vanisheth away."[28]

Yet even here, Melville is drawn to the beauty of matter and the materiality of beauty. Vapor is but the gaseous phase of a substance. As Pierre Bayle remarks in his entry on Lucretius, "The same atoms which compose water are in ice, in vapours, in clouds, in the hail, and the snow."[29] *Timoleon* is as much about solidity and fluidity as it about vaporousness. The poems evoke the beauty of these interrelated states of matter, which were the basis for so much ancient art and architecture. That might be what Melville means when he says,

> Gems and jewels let them heap—
> Wax sumptuous as the Sophi:
> For me, to grapple from Art's deep
> One dripping trophy![30]

Timoleon is an exercise in diving, a turning back to prior eras before the rise of modernity. What Melville finds is not something that is utterly gone, but, rather, something that is omnipresent: nature itself, which turns out to be more precious than "Gems and jewels." And nothing is more precious than water, which in *Timoleon* drips and evaporates, congeals and flows, in countless ways.

The poems' aesthetics touch on metaphysical considerations. To return to Tamarkin's point about the bond between Khayyám, Vedder, and Melville, all of whom create art premised on ephemerality: what is ephemerality but an expression of matter's inherent flux, a constant change of which our bodies and minds are inevitably a part? Greek fluted columns are "crescentic borders," and almost every feature of ancient architecture reflects this symbiosis between the human and non-human.[31] John Ruskin makes a similar point in *The Stones of Venice* (1851–3), stating that nearly every beautiful line—whether in a statue, column, or cornice—expresses a natural "action or force of some kind." The four-sided pyramid, for example, is the form of a natural crystal; "its use is quite limitless, and always beautiful." Other architectural figures recall shells (round arches, scalloped edges), foliage (the Greek acanthus, the Egyptian lotus, etc.), as well as other parts of nature, as Ruskin's categories denominate: "Branches and stems of Trees," "Reptiles and Insects," "Flowers," "Flames and Rays," "Quadrupeds and Men."[32]

As Samuel Otter and Geoffrey Sanborn observe, Melville is "unusually well-suited" to aesthetic considerations because of his "radically situational sense of form" and his "attentiveness to preconscious experience."[33] *Timoleon* reveals how Melville's interests in form and philosophy converge, especially in the entanglement between art and matter. No structure better illustrates that entanglement than the Parthenon. Initially constructed about twenty-five centuries ago, this great temple was designed to complement its environment—to align with the stars and rise out of the Athenian basin like a white stone poised atop a cliff.[34] Melville's poem titled "The Parthenon" lingers on this structure's astounding naturalness, a quality the poem mimics in its crystalline, four-sided structure, with each section viewing the temple from a different perspective. Melville begins at the furthest remove, "seen aloft from afar":

> Estranged in site,
> Aerial gleaming, warmly white,
> You look a suncloud motionless
> In noon of day divine;
> Your beauty charmed enhancement takes
> In Art's long after-shine.[35]

The Parthenon's beauty partly derives from its ongoing ruination. As Bryan Short puts it, "The Parthenon gains its effect not as a mute or forgotten divine origin or exemplum of the natural sublime but from the 'enhancing' power of its temporality."[36] The first stanza also lingers on the aesthetic effects of light. This is one of the aspects of Vedder's paintings that Melville most admired: the play with light and shadow as a means of adding emphasis, or "enhancement." "Seen aloft from afar," the Parthenon looks not like a crop of stones refashioned into a temple but a motionless cloud floating on a windless day, a great puff of air "gleaming, warmly white" as the sun's rays bounce off the surface (Figure 7).[37]

The poem then shifts perspective, looking at the Parthenon up close.

> Like Lais, fairest of her kind,
> In subtlety your form's defined—
> The cornice curved, each shaft inclined.
> While yet, to eyes that do but revel
> And take the sweeping view,
> Erect this seems, and that a level,
> To line and plummet true.
> Spinoza gazes; and in mind
> Dreams that one architect designed
> Lais—and you![38]

"Lais," to which Melville twice compares the Parthenon, probably refers to Hans Holbein's painting of Lais of Corinth (Figure 8), a contemporary of Pericles renowned for her beauty. If the Parthenon is "like Lais," that is because the painting and the temple share a peculiar aesthetic effect, making curves appear

Figure 7. Leo Von Klenze, *The Acropolis at Athens* (1846). Oil on Canvas. Courtesy of the Neue Pinakotheken.

Figure 8. Hans Holbein the Younger, *Lais of Corinth* (1526). Oil on Canvas. Courtesy of the Kunstmuseum Basel.

orderly and linear. And that formal technique, which ties each "cornice curved" to a "line and plummet true," is not without a philosophical point. The stanza's subtle suggestion is that all of this—every bit of stone in the Parthenon, every creature depicted in the frieze, even people like you, me, or Lais of Corinth—comes from the same authorless "architect," the same reservoir of atomic matter. That is why Spinoza appears here: he argued that the notion of separate and individuated substances is a fiction of the mind; in reality, everything is formed out a single substance. In his *Dictionary*, Bayle rails against Spinoza for this reason, chastising Spinoza's "foolish doctrine" that found "no distinction between God and the first matter," or as Spinoza put it, "that multitude and great variety of things that appear to us are one and the same thing,... as all our different numbers, ten, twenty, one hundred, one thousand, and [so on]... are but one and the same unity repeated several times."[39] The Parthenon takes this insight and turns it into art, converting a truth that could shadow "forth the heartless voids and immensities of the universe"[40] into a monument that makes you feel like you're looking at a cloud, so alluring that you feel pulled to it, as if by a magnet or a plummet.

The final two sections focus on a different set of rocks: the 500-foot-long set of marble structures that comprise the Parthenon's elaborate frieze (Figure 9).

> III THE FRIEZE
> What happy musings genial went
> With airiest touch the chisel lent
> To frisk and curvet light
> Of horses gay—their riders grave—
> Contrasting so in action brave

Figure 9. "Fragment from the Ergastinai ("Weavers") Frieze, from the Parthenon in Athens." Photograph (2005).

With virgins meekly bright,
Clear filing on in even tone
With pitcher each, one after one
Like water-fowl in flight.

IV THE LAST TILE
When the last marble tile was laid
The winds died down on all the seas;
Hushed were the birds, and swooned the glade;
Ictinus sat; Aspasia said
"Hist!—Art's meridian, Pericles!"[41]

Many features of the frieze solicit Melville's attention. The figures depicted in chiseled stone are incredibly detailed: one can see joints, muscles, expressions, and other evidence of living corporeality. As John Flaxman opined (in a quote reproduced in one of Melville's travel books),

> The horses appear to live and move, to roll their eyes, to gallop, prance, and curvet; the veins of their faces and legs seem distended with circulation; in them are distinguished the hardness and decision of bony forms, with the elasticity of tendon and the softness of flesh... [A]lthough the relief is not above an inch from the background, we can scarcely suffer reason to persuade us they are not alive.

Moreover, few other ancient works have such a complex history of division, dispersal, and recovery. In its original form the frieze consisted of more than a hundred blocks, created by a team of artists and artisans, narrating a single cogent story. Centuries later, the Parthenon was partly destroyed during a war; remade into a Christian church; remade into an Islamic mosque; remade into an ammunitions depot; ransacked by a narcissistic colonialist; recovered and preserved by archaeologists; then profusely described and depicted in countless letters, histories, paintings, sketches, travel guides, novels, and poems.[42] That coupling of unity and disunity is like aesthetic catnip for Melville.

Melville is struck by the beauty of the frieze, which is bound up with its sense of perspective. The frieze may tell the story of a single epic procession but it actually flows in two separate directions. It is like an ancient film etched in stone, and to watch it unfold one must view the frieze from several points of view.[43] That multiplicity is mirrored by Melville's poem, which shifts from perspective to perspective until finally landing on "The Last Tile." The seeming weightlessness of Melville's language, its airy quality, plays into the poem's philosophico-aesthetic design. Despite focusing on a massive temple made out of quarried rock, the poem almost floats on the page. Instead of a "marl-glen and slag-ravine," we find hushed birds, "frisk" light, and an artist's chisel applied with "airiest touch." That is another thing that is beautiful about the Parthenon as well as Melville's poem: it mixes the elements, lifting the earth into the sky and making it pause there. The frieze's men, women, and horses all seem to simultaneously move and be unmoved, partaking in a vast procession while staying perfectly still, mobile in stone yet utterly motionless in the air.

When the mind is unweighted or filled only with "happy musings," one can see the frieze's humans, horses, gods, and demigods for what they are: an equal set of beings, "contrasting" in their moods and actions yet tiled together in symmetric unity. The women filling the pitchers are "like water-fowl in flight" and the riders are inseparable from their horses, a vision of "Art and Nature lodged together," redoubled in the imagery of the final stanza. Indeed, the dying down of the seawinds is indistinguishable from the laying of the "last marble tile," and the architect Aspia's speech is paired with nature's acoustics ("swooned the glade"). That pairing is echoed in the concluding metaphor: in geometry, a meridian is a point between two arcs; a place of convergence.[44] The beauty evoked by "The Parthenon" is the ego-dissolving, non-essentializing beauty of natural relationships rendered through human art.[45]

Such poems are less invested in delimiting beauty than in apprehending its effects. That aspect of the volume ties *Timoleon* to a range of similar efforts by nineteenth-century scientists, artists, and philosophers to determine the material grounds of aesthetic experience. As Benjamin Morgan has documented, this inquiry was carried out by poets, biologists, interior designers, and fellow travelers who were deeply influenced by nineteenth-century science and modern materialism:

> If Enlightenment and romantic aesthetic philosophy had often seen aesthetic experience as providing access to a transcendental or spiritual realm, many writers ... [in this era] instead described aesthetic experience as an event during which the embodied corporeality of a person and an artwork came into contact. From this perspective, art and literature were phenomena realized as dynamic interactions among nerves, muscles, stone, and ink.[46]

In *Timoleon*, Melville offers up a collection of poems that inquire into the material basis of aesthetic experience and display all the beauty that did not, in fact, die out with the passing of the ancients.

The Art and Philosophy of Mixture

In the ancient world, Melville encountered mixtures of almost every imaginable type. Ancient artists routinely experimented with various media, and almost every story was retold in numerous ways and in numerous forms—in plays and oral tales; vases and pots; epics and lyrics; in philosophical dialogs; and in shrines, statues, and triglyphs. Each of those forms, in turn, was endlessly modified, changing and evolving over the course of centuries and across multiple places and cultures. As Ruskin writes,

> all European architecture, bad and good, old and new, is derived from Greece through Rome, and coloured and perfected from the East...Those old Greeks gave the shaft; Rome gave the arch; the Arabs pointed and foliated the arch... [and] there is high probability that the Greek received his shaft system from Egypt.[47]

Melville's understanding of mixture was also influenced by Renaissance art, especially Claude Lorrain's paintings of Greece and Italy. As Arthur Stedman noted in his obituary for Melville,

> In addition to his philosophical studies, [he] was much interested in all matters relating to the fine arts, and devoted most of his leisure hours to the two subjects. A notable collection of etchings and engravings from the old masters was gradually made by him, those from Claude's paintings being a specialty.

Robert K. Wallace points out that "Sixteen of Melville's Italianate engravings are of works by Claude Lorrain," and each of those works "expresses pictorially the exact quality that Melville expressed in words after visiting the Bay of Baiae and its environs in 1857: 'a singular melting together of art in ruins and nature in vigor.'"[48]

Melville was likely drawn to the graceful mixtures in Lorrain's paintings. Lorrain's *Morning in the Harbor* (Figure 10), for example, folds together a remarkable range of contrasts—in setting, color, tone, and brush strokes. On the right side of the image, Doric and Ionian columns, still standing after all these years, are topped with vegetation (which mirrors the swirling, vine-like volutes). On the left side—our eyes are invited to sweep back and forth across the painting—there are elegant wooden ships. In the background, castles and a pyramid seem to rise out of the ancient sea; while in the foreground, people talk, work, and wait on a Roman portico. Thousands of years of history are encapsulated in this single image. But Lorrain's soft brush strokes and use of light and color blend everything together, making these disparate elements seem to be part of a harmonious whole, as natural as the ebb and tide of the sea or the rising and falling of the sun.

Two of the books that Melville read about Lorrain, Owen Dullea's *Claude Gelée le Lorrain* (1887) and Hazlitt's *Criticisms on Art* (1844), highlight Lorrain's ability to paint unity out of disunity and weave together "magical combinations" out of

Figure 10. Claude Lorrain, *Morning in the Harbor* (1637). Oil on canvas. Courtesy of the State Hermitage Museum.

unlike parts. Dullea observes that Lorrain's landscapes feature recurring "fragments of various scenes, in which such subjects as the Coliseum, the arches of Constantine and of Septimus Severus, the temples of Vesta and the Sibyl," reappear again and again. He also quotes the painter Samuel Palmer, who, after seeing several of Lorrain's paintings in person, remarked: "miles apart I found the disjointed members, some of them most lovely, which he had 'suited to the desires of his mind'; there were the beauties, but the beautiful, the ideal Helen, was his own."[49] Hazlitt, with his characteristic wit and tendency for exaggeration, put it this way when discussing the allure of Lorrain's paintings:

> No one ever felt a longing, a sickness of the heart, to see a Dutch landscape twice; but those of Claude, after an absence of years, have this effect, and produce a kind of calenture. The reason of the difference is that, in mere literal copies from nature, where the objects are not interesting in themselves, the only attraction is to see the felicity of the execution; and, having once witnessed this, we are satisfied. But there is nothing to stir the fancy, to keep alive the yearnings of passion... Nature contains both large and small parts, both masses and details; and the same may be said of the most perfect works of art. The union of both

kinds of excellence, of strength with delicacy, as far as the limits of human capacity and the shortness of human life would permit, is that which has established the reputation of the most successful imitations of nature.[50]

Lorrain's paintings are not "mere... copies from nature," according to Hazlitt, but attempts to depict nature in all of its living dynamism and diversity. In his copy Melville underlined the word "calenture" and placed a checkmark next to it in the margins. *Calenture* (from the Latin *calere*, or "to be warm"), as Melville knew, is a disorder that sometimes afflicts sailors in the tropics: a "heat or stroke" in which "a stricken sailor pictures the sea as grassy meadows and wishes to dive overboard into them." Such is the sublime beauty of Lorrain's "soft, curled, hermaphroditical Italian pictures."[51]

Timoleon, which partly evolved out of Melville's earlier travels ("Fruit of Travel Long Ago"), is just as mixed as Lorrain's paintings. Even calling *Timoleon* a "volume" of poetry (a term that implies a single, overarching unity) understates the degree to which the poems are structured around contrasts and comparisons. *Timoleon* sweeps across thousands of years of history: the first poem, for example, is set in 394 BC; the final poem is dated "A.D. 16—"; and one of the poems is titled "Fragments of a Lost Gnostic Poem from the 12th Century." The poems feature a chorus of voices and perspectives (an apostate, an elderly rover, a scientist, a hermit, a suffering traveler, Samuel Taylor Coleridge, Percy Bysshe Shelley, the inebriates in David Teniers's tavern paintings); address a range of ideas, impressions, and subjects; and use an eclectic set of rhymes, oftentimes to pair unlike things or to suggest hidden possibilities ("state"/"abate"; "gods"/"rods").[52] Many of the poems not only incorporate such contrasts but also actively reflect on them: "Herba Santa" and "The Margrave's Birth Night" are meditations on pain suddenly giving way to peace, while "C—'s Lament" and "Shelley's Vision" (a diptych, they are meant to be read alongside one another) are about loss, affirmation, and the relation between them.

This keen attention to mixture plays an important role in *Timoleon*'s aesthetic and philosophical exploration of beauty. One of the lessons Melville learned from the ancients—a lesson that mirrored his own experiences as a writer—is that beauty has less to do with purity than with combination. The poem "Art" makes this aesthetic principle explicit:

> In placid hours well-pleased we dream
> Of many a brave unbodied scheme.
> But form to lend, pulsed life create,
> What unlike things must meet and mate:
> A flame to melt—a wind to freeze;
> Sad patience—joyous energies;
> Humility—yet pride and scorn;

> Instinct and study; love and hate;
> Audacity—reverence. These must mate,
> And fuse with Jacob's mystic heart,
> To wrestle with the angel–Art.[53]

The poem presents the act of creation as an act of blending—not invention *ex nihilo* but making "unlike things...meet and mate." The lines play with formlessness (flames, winds, passions, unbodied schemes) but Melville does in fact "lend" a form to this "pulsed life": it is similar to a Pindaric ode, a form that originated around the era of Timoleon and Timophanes. That ancient form is remade here, as Melville fills the lines with dyads, natural elements, and a Biblical parable about suffering, struggle, and divinity.[54] In the context of *Timoleon*, "Art" is not a staid reflection on the difficulty of creating great art but a meditation on the dynamic power of "pulsed life" writ large, which exceeds the bounds of any poem, statue, or work of art. If the ancients teach us anything, it is that pulsed life is omnipresent in the natural world.

The poems overflow with such fusions. "After the Pleasure Party" makes nature, art, love, and sex "meet and mate" as the speaker struggles with desire. "Pan's paramount mystery" is not, as *Billy Budd*'s narrator would have it, "Natural Depravity," but the injustice of bisexual division: "Why hast thou made us but in halves— / Co-relatives? This makes us slaves."[55] Some of the poems unfold as poetic pairs, clusters, and sequences (e.g. "The Night March" and "The Ravaged Villa," "Lone Founts" and "The New Zealot to the Sun"), while others flow between text and context (e.g. "Timoleon," "The Age of the Antonines"), or text and image (e.g. "The Bench of Boors," "The Marchioness of Brinvilliers"). In "Fruit of Travel Long Ago," the present gives way to the shoals of memory, and the human and non-human slide into each other with abandon: Venice's palaces become coral-like "reefs"; worms and men share the same "Pantheist energy of will"; the Church of Padua is like the human mind ("[a] vaulted place where shadows flit"); and Pisa's famous leaning tower is a work of earthen art made out of stony "tiers of architraves, / Fair circle over cirque," which induces the feeling of "Hovering, shivering on the verge."[56]

Melville considers not only the aesthetics of such mixtures but also their effects on the self. Several of the poems blend identities and perspectives in ways that undercut the very notion of individuated existence. The speaker of "Lone Founts" is unnamed but the poem expresses a view of science (i.e. it allows us to catch up to the ancients) that resembles Melville's, and, in an early draft, it was modeled on Giordano Bruno, an Italian scientist who viewed the cosmos as centerless, infinite, and beautiful.[57] "The Enthusiast" inhabits the mind of Achillas; "In the Desert" gives us the voice of Horace; while "The New Zealot to the Sun" (previously titled "The Scientist") echoes Omar Khayyám, the great Persian poet-scientist. In a letter to John C. Hoadley, Melville claimed he had just stumbled across the poem "Age of the Antonines," as if it were written by someone else at some other time: "In return for your M.S. favors I send you something I found the other day – came across it – in a lot of papers." "The Garden of Metrodorus," a poem ostensibly about nature and stillness, is also a poem about multiplicity and non-individuation. As Melville knew, there were two philosophers named Metrodorus, and one of them, Metrodorus of Lampsacus, was a close friend of Epicurus and a fervent advocate of Epicureanism. One of the prints Melville owned, a sketch by George Cooke of an ancient bust, depicted Epicurus and Metrodorus as twinned figures whose heads and perspectives are literally joined together (Figure 11).[58] Even the poems that *seem* to offer individual reflections on the ancient world frequently turn out to be intersubjective meditations on beauty. "Pausillippo," for example, is roughly drawn from Melville's visit to Italy but the poem centers on a fictional character named "Silvio" who, in turn, may or may not be the historical Silvio Pellico (an Italian poet and revolutionary who spent fifteen years in prison).

Such entanglements are one of beauty's primary effects. Every time we happen upon beauty, it makes us suddenly and intensely aware of something or someone

Figure 11. *Bust of Epicurus and Metrodorus* (second century CE). Photograph (2011) by Carole Raddato.

beyond the self's previously narrow purview—some corresponding vibrancy that had previously gone unnoticed. Such moments of recognition carry an ethical charge, since they spark an awareness of one's alterity. As Nancy Fredricks points out, Melville lays "the groundwork for a feeling of respect for ourselves and others." The sense of awe occasioned by beauty, Elaine Scarry reminds us, is what ties it to justice, since each experience with beauty brings with it the realization that beauty "does not [actually] depend on human beings to bring it about: though human beings have created much of the beauty of the world, they are only collaborators in a much vaster project."[59] In that regard, *Timoleon* is a collaborative creation, one that draws on ancient beauty to pull us into the vastness beyond ourselves.

The Beauty of the Everyday

One never knows what will have that impact—what particular line, shape, or flash of experience will quietly attach itself to you (or what you previously considered to be you), as though the self were a prosthetic formation acquiring some new extension. Oftentimes in Melville's writing it is the simplest and most unanticipated experiences that impart a sense of beauty—chancing upon a face in a crowd, lighting upon a crop of stones, seeing a tree in the desert. Beauty for Melville is not a rarefied essence but a common force that tends to appear when one least expects it.

That idea is powerfully conveyed in one of *Timoleon*'s clusters, a group of poems that runs from "Pausilippo" to "The Attic Landscape" and "The Same," leading up to "The Parthenon." These poems reflect on where beauty does and does not reside, and that reflection begins with "Pausilippo," a poem about a famous area of Naples renowned for its beauty. For centuries, wealthy Romans vacationed in this gorgeous villa surrounded by the rolling blue of the Mediterranean. Travel books celebrated Posillipo's unparalleled elegance and an international crew of artists, from J.M.W. Turner to Antonie Pitloo, depicted it in vivid, dramatic colors. In the eighteenth century the villa even gave rise to an entire "School of Posillipo," a group of landscape painters who trained their eyes and brushes on the area's buildings, cliffs, and waterways.[60] When the poem's speaker approaches the villa after years of feverish anticipation, his head is swirling with romantic ideas and grand expectations. He has visions of heavenly hills that wash their "feet / In Naples' bay" and lift their "head / In jovial season, curled with vines"—an unparalleled "charm of beauty" recognized by the first settlers who called it *Pausilypon*, or "respite from worry."[61] The speaker (the aforementioned Silvio) is desperate for such relief: he has been imprisoned without trial for years on end before finally, mercifully being released. The idea

Figure 12. John "Warwick" Smith, *Entrance to the Grotto of Posillipo, Naples.* Watercolor over graphite (1778–9). Courtesy of the Metropolitan Museum of Art.

of Posillipo, the tantalizing fantasy of this perfect place, was one of the things that kept him going in the darkest moments of his imprisonment. When it felt like the walls were closing in and his soul was as tortured as his body, Silvio would dream of this peerless place and the serenity it induces, the sense of unalloyed "Fulfillment and fruition" promised by everything that had been said, written, sketched, rumored, and painted (Figure 12).

Silvio's visit ends in bitter disappointment. The grottoes do not delight, the mountains do not make his heart leap, and none of the villa's famous beauty can mend his broken soul. "It unravels not the pain," he laments, "Pausilippo, Pausilippo, / Named benignly if in vain!" The poem could certainly be read as evidence of Melville's preference for the sublime over the beautiful, or as a reflection on the inability of beauty to curb suffering. Yet the poem is as much about the mind as it is about aesthetics, and its underlying suggestion is that beauty is not some discrete quality that has been meagerly and selectively parceled out. It is not contained solely in the Posillipos of the world. Instead, it is an exceedingly common element, an aesthetic substratum like Spinoza's monadological conception of matter—something that is everywhere woven into the fabric of the cosmos, often appearing in simple forms and combinations. It may not reside in Posillipo's famous grotto, but it is in the "tideless ripple" that passes by Silvio unnoticed at the end of the poem, and it is in everything he has overlooked on his dejected voyage to the coast.[62]

That idea is likewise conveyed in the pair of poems that follow "Pausilippo": "The Attic Landscape" and "The Same." Rather than focusing on the famous or the grand, these poems attend to simple yet astounding manifestations of earthly beauty. "Tourist," Melville admonishes, as if addressing people like Silvio who assume that beauty is limited to a small set of elite sites and works:

> spare the avid glance
> That greedy roves the sight to see:
> Little here of "Old Romance,"
> Or Picturesque of Tivoli.

One of Melville's recurring themes—one might even say the warning lodged in almost all of his works—is that expectations will mess you up. It is what blinds Amasa Delano as well as Bartleby's employer, and it is what makes *Battle-Pieces* so undeniably tragic. If one looks for beauty where one expects to find it—in the places the artists tell you to look, or philosophers claim it is lodged—you will fail to see what's right in front of you: the charm and grace of the world in its sheer simplicity. The poem continues,

> No flushful tint the sense to warm—
> Pure outline pale, a linear charm.
> The clear-cut hills carved temples face,
> Respond, and share their sculptural grace.
> 'Tis Art and Nature lodged together,
> Sister by sister, cheek to cheek;
> Such Art, such Nature, and such weather,
> The All-in-All seems here a Greek.[63]

The poem praises the Greeks' relationship to nature, a relationship defined not by power or domination but by a loving and egalitarian connection like "Sister by sister, cheek to cheek." The "carved temples" mirror the "clear-cut hills," sharing a common configuration and energy, as though "respond[ing]" to each other. The impact has nothing to do with the sublime, the picturesque, or any other tradition invented by human beings. It is instead a quiet magic that simultaneously resists expectations and encircles everything that exists:

> A circumambient spell it is,
> Pellucid on these scenes that waits,
> Repose that does of Plato tell-
> Charm that his style authenticates.[64]

Figure 13. Jiugang Wang, *Milan Cathedral from Piazza del Duomo* (2010). Photograph. Creative Commons.

If beauty is a "spell," it is cast not by people but by the everyday world in all of its "sculptural grace." The best works of art, like the carved temples of ancient Greece, simply respond to this pellucid charm.

Another work of art that approaches nature as a sibling is the Milan Cathedral (Figure 13). By the time Melville wrote about the Duomo di Milano, it had become a lightning rod of praise as well as criticism. After the foundations were laid in 1386, the Milan Cathedral was continually constructed, then reconstructed, until the mid-twentieth century. Through that long swath of time, scores of artists and architects participated in the cathedral's creation, adding new features and adjusting the style. Commentators tended to disagree vehemently about whether or not the results were successful. Most genteel observers considered the Milan Cathedral to be an aesthetic failure, an ugly blot on Europe's artistic landscape. Henry James declared the Duomo di Milan to be "not logical, not... commandingly beautiful, but grandly curious." It has "every style in the world," another visitor declared, "and every style spoiled." Others called it an "ugly staring thing," an "imitation" that "falls short of its model," and a "stupid failure."[65]

In *Timoleon*, the Milan Cathedral is anything but an "ugly staring thing":

> Through light green haze, a rolling sea
> Over gardens where redundance flows,

> The fat old plain of Lombardy,
> The White Cathedral shows.
> Of Art the miracles
> Its tribes of pinnacles
> Gleam like to ice-peaks snowed; and higher,
> Erect upon each airy spire
> In concourse without end,
> Statues of saints over saints ascend
> Like multitudinous forks of fire.
> What motive was the master-builder's here?
> Why these synodic hierarchies given,
> Sublimely ranked in marble sessions clear,
> Except to signify the host of heaven.

Melville is captivated by the duomo's gleaming marble, but the poem is primarily about the Milan Cathedral's elemental lines and shapes.[66] Surrounded by the "rolling sea" and "hazy" sky, the great spires look like a beautiful set of "ice-peaks" rising out of the earth. *Timoleon*, as we have seen, is fascinated by phases of matter, and that is certainly the case in these lines, as Melville turns our attention from the theurgic functions of the church to the natural structures that compose it, capped by the play with "synodic" in line 14, a word that denotes both an ecclesiastical assembly and a conjunction of astronomical objects—a set of icy planets or fiery stars, for example, that have the same elliptical longitude when observed from the earth.[67] The poem subtly enters the dialog about the aesthetics of the Milan Cathedral by saying yes, it is beautiful—one of art's "miracles," in fact—but only because it is exquisitely crafted out of nature's elements (earth, water, air, fire), which appear breathtaking in these sculpted forms.

That is the overwhelming implication of poems such as "Milan Cathedral," "The Attic Landscape," "Greek Masonry," and "The Marchioness of Brinvilliers": beauty is a widespread force that manifests in a multitude of patterns, actions, and sensations. It is on conspicuous display in great temples, statues, poems, and paintings, but what gives these objects their power has to do with their elemental forms and textures—icicles, for instance, or "the sprightly beam of morning." Such manifestations of beauty join us to the world, enriching our attachments and invigorating our sense of connection. According to Leo Bersani and Ulysses Dutoit, that is precisely what aesthetic experience tends to produce—not a "monumentalizing of the self" but a "renewable retreat from the seriousness of stable identities and settled being."[68] Melville's explorations of the beauty of water, light, stones, and other parts of the earth are thus exercises in "ornamentation," as Theo Davis defines it: aesthetic and phenomenological efforts to pay "a laudatory and attentive relation to the world."[69] *Timoleon* encourages us to pay attention to the simple beauty of what exists. The ancients remind us of that truth, even if the moderns have forgotten it.

Melville's writing undoubtedly delves into the "abyss of the impersonal within us," a sense of absence that proceeds from the inviolability of "the human" as a stable, knowable category.[70] However, in *Timoleon* that sense is counter-balanced—not negated by any means, but certainly attenuated and adjusted—by the convergence of nature and art. "In a Bye-Canal" is a case in point. At the beginning of the poem, the speaker is as isolated and depressed as Ishmael in "Loomings." He may not be knocking people's hats off in the street but he is feeling lonesome and dejected in one of the most beautiful places in Europe, riding on a gondola through the canals of Venice. It's a gorgeous day, one of those serene afternoons when all of nature seems to be in a trance, but he is as walled off as the Captain of the *Pequod*, feeling "haunted" by the past (which "follow[s] me... noiselessly") and by his own morbid thoughts ("Of portents in nature and peril in man"). Then, suddenly, the speaker is awakened—brought back to life as it were—by a sound, when the gondolier accidentally scrapes the wall of a great Venetian palace.

> And, hark, response I hear!
> A lattice clicks; and lo, I see
> Between the slats, mute summoning me,
> What loveliest eyes of scintillation,
> What basilisk glance of conjuration!
> But at the latticed eye—
> "Hey! Gondolier, you sleep, my man;
> Wake up!" And, shooting by, we ran;
> The while I mused, This, surely now,
> Confutes the Naturalists, allow!
> Sirens, true sirens verily be,
> Sirens, waylayers in the sea.
> Well, wooed by these same deadly misses,
> Is it shame to run?
> No! flee them did divine Ulysses,
> Brave, wise, and Venus' son.[71]

Several shifts occur here—the lines pivot from silence to speech, from isolation to relation, and from death to life, concluding with the final line's invocation of Venus. So what happens? What accounts for this change?

Everything is altered by what the speaker sees. In Venice, many apertures—gates, windows, doors, etc.—are adorned with intricate latticework: criss-crossing strips of metal, stone, or wood arranged in pleasing geometrical patterns. These lattices are often associated with Gothic architecture, but they cannot be attributed

Figure 14. *Gothic Window on the Basilica di S. Marco, Venice.* Photograph (2004) by Nino Barbieri.

"to any practice of any school" because they are "eternal forms, based on laws of gravity and cohesion."[72] In the poem, it is a beautiful Venetian lattice that unwittingly draws the speaker out of his stupor (Figure 14).

It is hard to discern where lattices begin or end, both within and outside of the poem. What is a poem but a type of verbal lattice? The human face shares similar features, too: "The latticed eye" refers to the aperture of the woven grid as well as the "magic glass" of the gondolier. When he says "A lattice clicks," it is as if the mind itself is a Venetian grid, the criss-crossing structure of which is evident throughout the city's waterways.

The lattice thus "confute[s] the Naturalists" in two different ways. A "Naturalist," in the classic, eighteenth-century sense of that term, would have no way of accounting for aesthetic experiences like the one conveyed in "In a Bye-Canal." But the same could be said of Melville's contemporary "Naturalists," writers such as Émile Zola, Frank Norris, and Theodor Dreiser who tended to see human actions as biologically and sociologically preconditioned. Beauty has a way of breaking up thoughts and shattering one's sense of isolation. Even when one is mired in dejection and worrying about "Envy and Slander," even when one is ensnared in what Walt Whitman called "the dark patches," something as basic but astounding as an arrangement of shapes can pull one back into the world, criss-crossing one's being with other modes of life. That is what happens in the poem as the previously morose speaker speaks to the gondolier (and according to Melville's journal, he got along famously with his young, handsome Italian guide, whom he nicknamed "Antonio the Merry").[73]

The poem's shifts lend support to Timothy Marr's observation that Melville must be read through a dual lens. "Melville's writings," Marr observes, "oscillate between a pantheistic merging with the cosmos and a fatal encounter with forces of heartless materialism," but Melville "also found through his writing a repose centered in a sustaining connection with the vital energies embodied by the capacity of material forms to regenerate and evolve new life."[74] *Timoleon* reveals that material forms are immediately and invariably aesthetic (and vice versa). That lesson about the materiality of beauty, as well as the beauty of matter, is something Melville learned from the ancients.

His many invocations of antiquity are thus an integral part of Melville's aesthetics. But that ancient turn of mind is hardly the only philosophico-aesthetic mode that Melville embraced. As we will see, these same aesthetic and philosophical concerns also carried him elsewhere, turning his attention to roses, daisies, and other types of organic beauty that—like a human life—effloresce even as they fade away.

2
Floral Beauty in *Weeds and Wildings*

Weeds and Wildings, the final set of poems that Melville wrote before his death, is a bit strange. Unlike many of Melville's works, *Weeds and Wildings* contains no voyages. There are no explicit reflections on race, democracy, or the United States. Nor are there oceans, deserts, or acts of resistance. Instead, one finds flowers upon flowers—bluebells, clovers, roses, and daisies, sometimes sprouting alone, sometimes growing in wild fields. One of the poems is about a chipmunk, and another poem is about a crow. Yet for the most part, *Weeds and Wildings* is—as the title implies—a series of poems about floral beauty.

The flowers on display in *Weeds and Wildings* evoke the varieties and possibilities of non-sovereignty. That driving interest in collectivity is evident on the very first page. "With you and me," he writes, ostensibly to his wife Elizabeth Melville (though as we will see, Nathaniel Hawthorne looms over the second half of the book), "Red Clover has always been one of the dearest flowers of the field." But that particular attachment

> implies no undelight as to this ruddy young brother's demure little half-sister, White Clover. Our feeling for both sorts originates in no fanciful associations egotistic in kind. It is not, for example, because in any exceptional way we have verified in experience the aptness of that pleasant figure of speech, *Living in clover*—not for this do we so take to the Ruddy One, for all that we once dwelt annually surrounded by flushed acres of it. Neither have we, jointly or severally, so frequently lighted upon that rare four-leaved variety accounted of happy augury to the finder; though, to be sure, on my part, I yearly remind you of the coincidence in my chancing on such a specimen by the wayside on the early forenoon of the fourth day of a certain bridal month, now four years more than four times ten years ago. But, tell, do we not take to this flower—for flower it is, though with the florist hardly ranking with the floral clans—not alone that in itself it is a thing of freshness and beauty, but also that being no delicate foster-child of the nurseryman, but a hardy little creature of out-of-doors accessible and familiar to every one, no one can monopolize its charm. Yes, we are communists here.[1]

In adoring clover, the Melvilles adore something that is exceedingly common. This "dearest flower of the field," *Trifolium*, grows everywhere, yielding crop upon crop of soft, sweet-smelling flowers that range in color from deep purple to yellow, crimson, and pale white.² Melville's point is that clover's incalculable value has nothing to do with rareness, exception, or singularity. Clover is beautiful not because it occasionally sprouts four leaves, or because the Melvilles take personal pleasure in it. Rather, clover is "a thing of freshness and beauty" to *all* living creatures:

> [It is] sweet in the mouth of that brindled heifer, whose breath you so loved to inhale, and doubtless pleasant to her nostril and eye; sweet as well to the like senses in ourselves, prized by that most radical of men, the farmer, to whom wild amaranths in a pasture, though emblems of immortality, are but weeds and anathema; finding favour even with so peevish a busybody as the bee.³

With its tripartite leaves and series of floral spikes, clover is a symbol of multiplicity, a reminder of nature's indifference to all "associations egotistic in kind."

For Melville, clover's beauty clues us in to the communal dimensions of being. From beginning to end, *Weeds and Wildings* is intricately trellised—like so many flower-like growths—around non-selfhood. The title page blurs Melville's identity, first by reducing his name to initials ("H.M."), then by quietly challenging the notion of authorship altogether, attributing Melville's sentence "Yes, decay is often a gardener" to "Anonymous" and leaving the quote "Alms for oblivion" similarly unattributed, just floating on the page like white clover. Many of the poems *seem* to come from the point of view of a couple (an "I" and "you"), but their experiences are the opposite of private property. They share ideas, sensations, and memories, and their interactions are intermingled with the environment. Art, we learn, is arboreal ("In season the leafage will tell"); people are "shades" and "lilacs"; chipmunks feel "glee"; and the dawn "flushes" like a reddened face. Such interlacing of the human and non-human is encapsulated in impossible figures: "heart-flowers" that "confess," "trumpet-flowers" that "proclaim," and roses that are "Queens" of the earth "blown thro' Ariel's clime."⁴

Across its pages, *Weeds and Wildings* both represents and reproduces what Herbert Marcuse calls "desublimation," an aesthetic experience that temporarily liberates us from the ego. As Marcuse writes, "The encounter with the truth of art happens in the estranging language and images which make perceptible, visible, and audible that which is no longer, or not yet, perceived, said, and heard in everyday life... [Art makes] the petrified world speak, sing, perhaps dance."⁵ For Melville, that dancing is most conspicuous in the innumerable flowers that adorn the earth, and he is not particularly choosey about what counts as a flower. The poems find as much beauty in a weed by the side of the road as they do in a brilliant rose in full bloom. That "way-side weed," Melville says, is just as "divine."⁶ *Weeds and Wildings* of course exults in the crowning glories of floral beauty: red roses, pink lilacs, and purple violets. But there are also dandelions, buttercups, strawberries, larkspurs, wildflowers, sweet-briar, syringe, aloe, flowering vines, and fields of maize, all of which come together in *Weeds and Wildings* to create a veritable rainbow of colors, smells, and pleasures. Melville even reclaims the beauty and significance of field asters. Although they are frequently overlooked, field asters take their name from the stars and, in their sun-like structure, resemble those luminous spheres which provide light and heat to the cosmos: "Like the stars in commons blue / Peep their namesakes, Asters here, / Wild ones every autumn seen."[7] (Figure 15).

Melville's conceit—that flowers are as important as the stars, including the one that makes life on earth possible—is not merely a conceit. He is making a rather strong claim for the lived significance of beauty. In *Weeds and Wildings*, flowers are not simple adornments that please the senses but vital mediums for understanding everything from aesthetics to love, memory, nature, and community. Composed while Melville suffered from congestive heart failure, slowly losing the ability to breathe and move—or even see, after years of ocular degeneration—*Weeds and Wildings* is a final embrace of the world shortly before death's arrival.[8] In these poems of praise, Melville provides a vision of life's gifts, documenting the myriad ways in which "Without movement of speech / Day deepens its sweetness."[9]

Given the subject matter, it is tempting to view *Weeds and Wildings* as an exercise in literary escapism. From a certain perspective, Melville seems to have gone from writing complex stories about some of the most pressing issues of the day to writing private poems about a bunch of plants. (This interpretation dovetails with readings of *Billy Budd* that view the novella as either a "testament of acceptance" or a commitment-free drama about irony and language.[10]) Nonetheless, *Weeds and Wildings* has much to say about time, passion, aesthetics, community, and the environment. Moreover, scholars "fit ... though few" have identified a distinct set of literary and biographical influences. Martin Kevorkian notes that *Weeds and Wildings* represents Melville's turn away from Shakespearean and Wordsworthian models in favor of a poetry of "imagistic urgency more clearly connected to Keats, Tennyson, Rossetti, and Swinburne."[11] That turn back is also a turn forward. In fact, it is possible to read *Weeds and Wildings* as an anticipation of Imagism, an early experiment with the types of compact verbal representation that later emerged in the poetry of H.D. and Ezra Pound. The palpable sense of urgency in *Weeds and Wildings* is also decidedly erotic, as John Bryant and Gillian Osborne have demonstrated. Bryant and Osborne provide contrasting accounts of Melville's intended subject (for Bryant, it is a volume for Elizabeth Shaw Melville, whereas Osborne views it as a belated memorial to Nathaniel Hawthorne), but they both emphasize the poems' intense interest in the body and its aesthetics (in the ancient sense of that term).[12]

The poems' commitment to life and beauty has a marked philosophical edge. Every elegant rose, every daisy and butterfly, indeed every expression of delight in *Weeds and Wildings* is shadowed by the sorrow that haunted so much of Melville's

FLORAL BEAUTY IN *WEEDS AND WILDINGS* 55

Figure 15. Jacob Vosmaer, *A Vase With Flowers* (1613). Oil on wood. Courtesy of the Metropolitan Museum of Art.

life and work. In his seventy-plus years on earth, Melville knew little sustained happiness, and even less tranquility. Biographical and contextual evidence indicate that Melville struggled repeatedly with depression, sinking into a pit of sadness again and again—when his early novels failed to secure him sustained success, when his marriage nearly unraveled, and when his son committed suicide. "Though I wrote the Gospels in this century," he lamented, "I [will] die in the gutter."[13] At one point, after his son Malcolm shot himself, his state of mind was apparently so fragile that his in-laws contemplated intervening.[14] The merriment that resounds in *Weeds and Wildings* is a return to life after decades of psychic conflict.[15]

Considering Melville's literary track record, this dialectical quality is not surprising. The poems may strike a very light tone, but this is still Melville, who conceives of literature and philosophy as paired endeavors. *Weeds and Wildings* is fueled by a distinct set of philosophical concerns, including (but not limited to) Schopenhauerian skepticism, Buddhist ideas of non-selfhood, and the metaphysical implications of floral poetry. What ties these poems together, anchoring Melville's poetry and philosophy alike, is an interest in the property-less nature of the cosmos. *Weeds and Wildings* suggests that nothing—not a flower in the field, not even one's feelings or memories—can really be owned. Everyone and everything is evanescent and floral beauty attunes us to this basic truth, reminding us that impermanence and non-individuation are fundamental to life itself.

In that regard, *Weeds and Wildings* grows out of a philosophico-aesthetic mode that Melville developed over the course of several decades. Sometimes encounters with beauty spark an exchange of experience, a blissful communalizing of the senses and scattering of the self. Such encounters tend to elicit a feeling of blithesome exuberance, and Melville explores that feeling in many different stories and poems, from "Cock-A-Doodle-Do!" to *Mardi* and *John Marr and Other Sailors*. However, it is in *Weeds and Wildings* that this type of beauty, and the sense of elation it produces, resonates most fully. To better understand this mode, I will take a cue from Melville and look at *Weeds and Wildings* from several perspectives. First, I will reconstruct the volume's floral aesthetics by zooming in and out of the individual poems. I will then consider some of the major philosophical questions raised by *Weeds and Wildings*, moving from Melville's engagements with Buddhism and Schopenhauer to the collective forms and sensations that emerge in the final section of the volume, "A Rose or Two: As They Fell."

Clover, Daisies, and Other Common Delights

If *Weeds and Wildings* is a celebration of life, it is also a celebration of the common. Time and time again, Melville emphasizes beauty's surprising ubiquity. In the poem "Madcaps," Melville links "Roses and Clover"—flowers renowned for their crimson and ivory hues—to a multitude of other reds and whites, underscoring just how widespread this merry-making combination tends to be. Other poems linger on mosses wrapping around stones, birds that sing, bees that dance, gusts of wind that roll across the grass, "white corals in green sea," weeds that spring from the soil, and the everyday lives of mice, crows, chipmunks, moles, and trees. Nearly every poem is shot through with a sense of exhilaration, a joyous discovery of beauty's plenitude. In the "heart of autumn!," Melville exclaims, all of this life "Flit[s] ... from our hearth!" He marvels at "Files on files of prairie maize: / On hosts of spears the morning plays!" and exclaims, "Thro' the heaven of summer we'll flee / And tipple the light!" In this philosophico-aesthetic mode, Melville's style is quite exuberant, and in *Weeds and Wildings* that exuberance proceeds from recognitions of common beauty.[16]

The poems conceive of commonness in several ways. For Melville, commonness is partly a matter of representation, and *Weeds and Wildings* finds floral beauty in a diverse set of forms. In "The Avatar," Melville positions "Sweet-Briar, a wilding weed" as the epitome of roses despite its "humbler look." Commonness in the poems also has to do with the senses—the countless ways in which hues, textures, sounds, and other types of sensorial phenomena organize lived experience. "The Dairyman's Child" sees "softness" not merely in objects that are gentle to the touch but in all sorts of natural and artistic life, from orchards to opal and frescoes.[17] *Weeds and Wildings* also views commonness in terms of property and ownership. The poems repeatedly light upon an idea that could not be less escapist: possession—the theory and practice of private ownership, which governs so much of the world—is a misleading and dangerous fiction. *Weeds and Wildings* suggests that nothing we typically consider to be our own—what we feel or conceive, what we touch or see—is really ours, and never can be. Every experience is shared with a frequency and variety that outstrip the imagination.

In both their form and content, the poems continually depict the limits of possession. To read *Weeds and Wildings* is to be immersed in a world of blended memories, joint sensations, and ambiguous voices. Many of the poems also insist on their own impermanence and unpossessability, in ways that echo the poem "Inscription":

> *For a boulder near the spot where the last hardhack was laid low by the new proprietor of the Hill of Arrowhead.*
> A weed grew here. Exempt from use,
> Weeds turn no wheel, nor run;
> Radiance pure or redolence
> Some have, but this had none,
> And yet heaven gave it leave to live
> And idle it in the sun.[18]

Nothing here is lasting or discrete enough to truly own. That allows "Inscription" to work on several levels: as a reminiscence about Melville's old home in Pittsfield, a meditation on nature writ large, and a meta-reflection on *Weeds and Wildings*. Weeds, like poems, make "nothing happen" (as Auden would have it): they "turn no wheel, nor run," and whatever "radiance" they have is almost accidental, occurring by the sheer luck of being lit by the sun or read by the eye. The weed does not own the sunlight any more than the "new proprietor" (who goes unnamed) possesses the weed, and the weed, in turn, does not possess any "redolence" on its own. As if this weren't enough, the poem is dedicated to a boulder. Not only is it unclear who made this inscription; the inscription is merely an act of the imagination, written not in stone but in a private manuscript that was never even published in Melville's lifetime, a manuscript that is itself dedicated to "oblivion."[19]

What and where is the self in such poems? To the degree that it endures at all (and that is very much in question), it exists as a loose assortment of willed and unwilled experiences that are shared among living beings. The mutable sense of selfhood that is on display in *Weeds and Wildings* thus resembles the way that "character" works in *The Confidence-Man*, recurring and reappearing in myriad forms and combinations. As Rachel Cole posits, "stable identity breaks down" in *The Confidence-Man*, as characters proliferate and assume a shared set of traits, revealing "the possibility that personhood might be" formed by one's milieu.[20] That conception of the self as fluid, communal, and contingent differs quite radically from mainstream American ideas of selfhood, which in Melville's day and our own put a premium on individual difference. From Ahab's possessive individualism to Emerson's self-reliance, Ayn Rand's objectivism, and twenty-first-century notions of genetic identity, American ideas of the self are predicated on resolute individuality.[21] Like a series of vines, the poems in *Weeds and Wildings* wrap around the idea that the self is a collective formation that inheres less in individualized thoughts than in shared experiences and entanglements.

That vision of collective being links *Weeds and Wildings* to Melville's earlier writings. Works like *Moby-Dick*, "Bartleby," and "Benito Cereno" reveal a writer who was deeply troubled by modernity and its numerous injustices. As Ishmael protests,

> Is it not a saying in every one's mouth, Possession is half of the law: that is, regardless of how the thing came into possession? But often possession is the whole of the law? What are the sinews and souls of Russian serfs and Republican slaves but Fast-Fish, ... [and] what is the great globe itself but a Loose-Fish?

Brian Yothers contends that Melville's career is marked by a fierce and sustained commitment to pacifism and egalitarianism, dual commitments that clash in his pained reaction to the Civil War, a violent attempt to enforce equality. Yothers' point is perceptive and illuminating. Those commitments indeed spark a majority of Melville's writings across the mid- to late nineteenth century, informing works as seemingly far apart as *Typee*, *Clarel*, and "The Bell-Tower."[22] Non-violence and egalitarianism, however, are almost never considered apart from nature in

Melville's writings. They are shared concerns, and in *Weeds and Wildings* Melville combines them in a rather distinct way, presenting beauty as so widely distributed and radically non-hierarchical that life itself has to be the basis for politics and aesthetics. *Weeds and Wildings* addresses the same questions Melville has always posed—Are we free or unfree? To what extent can we define who and what we are? What are the sources of power, beauty, and cosmic meaning?—but channels them into a floral poetry less interested in critique than in *affirmation*. And what gets affirmed is life's unpossessable plenitude.

To test out these ideas, Melville turns to multiple texts and traditions. In his final years, he read and reflected on Omar Khayyám's *Rubáiyát*, Sa'di's *The Gulistan* ("The Rose Garden"), James Thomson's *The City of Dreadful Night*, accounts of Siddhartha Ghautama, and the collected works of Arthur Schopenhauer.[23] All of these writings share an interest in the nature and significance of *anattā*, or "the non-self." *Anattā* implies that the notion of an individual self—an "I" with a distinct soul—is illusory and generates suffering. It is the attachment to *nattā* ("soul" in Pali, or what Schopenhauer dubs "the will") that blinds us to the world by wrapping us in an Ahabian fantasy of separateness. The term comes from early Buddhist texts, which present *anattā* as one of the three marks of existence. Melville's familiarity with the concept likely came from two philosophical sources: (1) Schopenhauer, who associates the self with the "will"; and (2) Pyrrhonism, which merged Buddhist views of non-selfhood into a skeptical tradition predicated on undecidability.

In *The World as Will and Idea*, Schopenhauer argues that "eager pursuit, anxiety, and suffering" are the offspring of a "hungry will" that falsely projects the individual self into the world. The "noblest" philosophical truth, according to Schopenhauer, is therefore contained in the Buddhist idea of Nirvana, "a state in which four things no longer exist—birth, age, sickness, and death." *Anattā* is also subtly woven into Pyrrhic skepticism. According to Christopher Beckwith, Pyrrho of Elis likely developed his understanding of *adiaphora* (the undecidability of phenomena) and *ataraxia* (tranquility) after meeting gymnosophists from India. *Adiaphora*, Beckwith notes, "is the negative of *diaphora*... and literally means... 'without a logical self-identity,'" paralleling Early Buddhist understandings of "*anātman* (Pali *anattā*), [which] means no (innate) self...and is applied to all dharmas."[24]

Weeds and Wildings offers a poetic vision of *anattā*, suggesting that what matters most—the countless flashes of experience that make life meaningful—is not exceptional but utterly common. "Hearth-Roses," for example, begins with a simple image—roses adorning a bedside—only to expand outward and evoke other, similar manifestations of fiery love and beauty:

>The Sugar-Maple embers in bed
>Here fended in Garden of Fire,

> Like the Roses yield musk,
> Like the Roses are Red,
> Like the Roses expire
> Lamented when low;
> But excelling the flower,
> Are odorous in ashes
> As e'en in their glow.
> Ah, Love, when life closes,
> Dying the death of the just,
> May we vie with Hearth-Roses,
> Smelling sweet in our dust.[25]

What happens to a life after it is gone? Something between "nothing" and "transcendence," it would seem. Roses yield a sweet and airy musk, while a felled maple becomes tinder for a fire, providing light, warmth, and fragrant smells for a loving couple. In short, earth becomes fire and air: a natural transformation that has occurred, and will keep occurring, again and again—not unlike the recycling of a poetic cliché ("Roses are Red"). Melville finds beauty as well as pleasure in this repetition of the common.[26] That is why there are no names, or even discernible human selves here: these "embers" of love are emblematic of many other abiding attachments and altered states.

Throughout *Weeds and Wildings*, Melville repeatedly disperses and democratizes experience in this manner. The poems indicate that nearly every organism, from birds and moles to grass and flowers, experiences beauty. The poems' interest in commonness and non-possession also extends to their form. Not only are they pitched as voices coming from multiple authors; they also offer themselves up as so many evanescent flowers, fit for taking in with the eye and the heart, but only for a moment. This fleeting sensation is part of Melville's interest in flowers more broadly. What is more impermanent than flowers? And what is more common—even clichéd—than poetry *about* flowers? These questions frame Melville's engagement with beauty, commonness, and the relation between them.

The tradition of floral poetry, of which *Weeds and Wildings* is undoubtedly an expression, stretches back to antiquity and forward through a veritable "panorama of empires," manifesting in everything from the poetry of Khayyám and Sa'di to the floral poems of the nineteenth century, many of which were written by women who depicted flowers as complex symbols and communicative media.[27] In Melville's day, poets such as Sarah Josepha Buell Hale, Caroline Kirkland, and Sarah Mayo (among others) saw flowers as living referents of a vast symbolic language, the syntax of which was inscribed in flowers' colors, types, and arrangements. In *The Flower Vase* (1844), for example, Mayo depicted asters as symbols of "Beauty in Retirement" and foxgloves as a way of saying "I am not ambitious for myself, but for you."[28]

Gillian Osborne asserts that *Weeds and Wildings* extends and mimics this floriographic tradition in two different ways: by discerning particular meanings in particular flowers, and by using this symbolic language to say things that would otherwise be very difficult to say. As Osborne puts it, this mimicry enables Melville to effectively "cross-dress" as a writer and turn part II of Weeds and Wildings ("A Rose or Two") into "a collection of love poems for Hawthorne."[29] If Osborne is right (and I think she is), and part II is addressed to Hawthorne—long since dead but still very much in Melville's heart—it would explain a great deal about the volume, such as its formal partitioning and its marked interest in paired dualities (e.g. summer and winter, sunlight and moonlight, clover and roses) which evoke the experiences he shared with Elizabeth and Nathaniel, respectively. As the poems unfold, types of love—like types of flowers—mix and remix, and so do erotic experiences:

> Meek crossing of the bosom's lawn
> Averted scenery veil-like drawn,
> Well beseem thee, nor obtrude
> The cloister of thy virginhood,
> And yet, white ruin, that seemly dress
> Of purity pale passionless,
> A May-snow is; for fleeting term,
> Custodian of love's lumbering germ—
> Nay, nurtures it, till time disclose
> Now frost-fed Amor's burning rose.[30]

None of these sensations are singular or sovereign. Sex, like poetry, dissolves boundaries between ostensibly particularized selves. Like so many poems in part II, this seems to be about Hawthorne and Melville, but both men remain unnamed and unidentified, as though they have melted into this frosty paradise. That is one of the effects of "Amor's burning rose": pleasure, like a floral poem, becomes boundless and unowned.

Beauty and Suffering: Melville vis-à-vis Schopenhauer

Weeds and Wildings is not entirely about beauty and pleasure, however. It is also about the suffering that provides beauty and pleasure with weight, specificity, and meaning. That dialectic runs through *Weeds and Wildings*, turning even the most lighthearted poems into refracted meditations on pain and loss.

Melville's understanding of this dialectic was impacted by his reading of Schopenhauer. Toward the end of his life Melville read and thought a lot about Schopenhauer, working his way through the philosopher's magnum opus, *The*

World as Will and Idea, as well as Schopenhauer's writings about love, aesthetics, acoustics, faith versus reason, optimism versus pessimism, and the human mind. In his final years, Melville pored over his personal copies of *Counsels and Maxims*, *Studies in Pessimism*, *The Wisdom of Life*, and *Religion: A Dialogue, and Other Essays*.

Some of Schopenhauer's defining ideas, and Melville's engagements with them, are well known. Scholars such as Sharon Cameron, William B. Dillingham, Paul Hurh, and Michael Jonik have retraced Melville's intertextual dialogs with Schopenhauer and examined the metaphysical nuances of Melville's Schopenhauerian turn.[31] Melville was drawn to Pessimism late in life for many of the same reasons he was drawn to Pyrrhonism decades earlier: both philosophies prioritize knowledge over belief and find doubt to be a positive rather than a negative means of apprehending the world, indeed a veritable starting-point for wisdom, ethics, and decision-making. According to Schopenhauer, doubt must ground our understanding of life: to the extent that we can, we must accept the fact that suffering can never be expunged—only delayed. Suffering is inevitably and inescapably a part of existence, so the most we can hope for, as Ishmael might put it, are interregnums in pain:

> *Brahma* is said to have produced the world by a kind of fall or mistake; and in order to atone for his folly, he is bound to remain in it himself until he works out his redemption. As an account of the origin of things, that is admirable! According to the doctrines of *Buddhism*, the world came into being as the result of some inexplicable disturbance in the heavenly calm of Nirvana, that blessed state obtained by expiation, which had endured so long a time—the change taking place by a kind of fatality. This explanation must be understood as having at bottom some moral bearing; although it is illustrated by an exactly parallel theory in the domain of physical science, which places the origin of the sun in a primitive streak of mist, formed one knows not how. Subsequently, by a series of moral errors, the world became gradually worse and worse—true of the physical orders as well—until it assumed the dismal aspect it wears to-day.[32]

Though Schopenhauer approvingly recites these Hindu and Buddhist creation stories, he also departs from them by suggesting that suffering is not imposed from the outside. Rather, it is the inevitable result of the human will, each action of which—indeed, every decision we make and every wish we have—sets suffering into motion.

These ideas might have been especially appealing for Melville in light of his own sorrows. His failure as a commercial writer, his struggles with his sexuality, and his son's suicide, William B. Dillingham claims, led him to seek "psychological protection from...devastating blows."[33] It is impossible to exactly know why Melville turned to Schopenhauer, but it is certainly possible to understand the consequences and implications of that turn. Scholars have made significant progress in that regard by reexamining Melville's life and circumstances and by rereading his later writings, especially *Billy Budd (An Inside Narrative)*, the poem-turned-novella that Melville penned more or less contemporaneously with *Weeds and Wildings*. Melville's fervent interest in Schopenhauer is born out, critics have demonstrated, not only in the ethical philosophy on display in *Billy Budd* but also in the novella's reflections on innocence versus experience; artful play with Schopenhauerian terms ("What testimony to the force lodged in will-power"; "But Claggart's conscience but being the lawyer to his will"); and tendency to question "individuality, rendering everything in essence like every other thing."[34]

All of which implies that Melville did not suddenly put Schopenhauer down when he turned to *Weeds and Wildings*. *Billy Budd* and *Weeds and Wildings* are joint meditations on beauty and suffering composed around the same time, and they both revolve around considerations that are central to Schopenhauer's philosophy. In *Weeds and Wildings*, however, the terms of Melville's engagement with Schopenhauer are decidedly different, and so is the version of Schopenhauer that gets presented. The Schopenhauer of *Weeds and Wildings* is not the dark, brooding, proto-existentialist of *The World as Will and Idea*, but the funny, sly philosopher who also wrote about flowers, trees, and beauty. Melville was drawn not just to Schopenhauer's thoroughgoing skepticism but to the ways in which skepticism could recast and reframe the most positive parts of life—art and beauty, love and friendship, peace and balance. In short, if *Billy Budd* grows out of Melville's interest in Schopenhauer's ideas about pain and willpower, *Weeds and Wildings* grows out of Melville's interest this more life-giving side of Schopenhauer, the ever-moving dawn in his dark philosophy.

Schopenhauer was very fond of flowers, for example, and considered them to be invaluable. *Studies in Pessimism* features a parable along these lines that would have fascinated Melville:

> In a field of ripening corn I came to a place which had been trampled down by some ruthless foot; and as I glanced amongst the countless stalks, every one of them alike, standing there so erect and bearing the full weight of the ear, I saw a multitude of different flowers, red and blue and violet. How pretty they looked as they grew there so naturally with their little foliage! But, thought I, they are quite useless; they bear no fruit; they are mere weeds, suffered to remain only because there is no getting rid of them. And yet, but for these flowers, there would be nothing to charm the eye in that wilderness of stalks. They are emblematic of poetry and art, which, in civic life—so severe, but still useful and not without its fruit—play the same part as flowers in the corn.[35]

Melville echoes this parable in *Weeds and Wildings*, emphasizing the non-utilitarian beauty of flowers and viewing all types of floral growth as symbols of art and literature. So the poems themselves become floral offerings and the volume, Melville reiterates, has no purpose. Melville, though, is far more enthusiastic about weeds than Schopenhauer, and tends to democratize what the philosopher calls "poetry and art," seeing it as laced throughout the human and non-human world.

Similar echoes, anticipations, and parallels recur across Schopenhauer's writings. Wisdom, Schopenhauer claims, is a kind of rose: "Wisdom which is only theoretical and never put into practice, is like a double rose; its color and perfume are delightful, but it withers away and leaves no seed. No rose without a thorn. Yes, but many a thorn without a rose." Elsewhere, Schopenhauer imagines that he speaks to trees:

> Once, as I was botanizing under an oak, I found amongst a number of other plants of similar height one that was dark in color, with tightly closed leaves and a stalk that was very straight and stiff. When I touched it, it said to me in firm tones: *Let me alone; I am not for your collection, like these plants to which Nature has given only a single year of life. I am a little oak.*

And when Schopenhauer wants to illustrate the negative power of the will (as well as the peace that comes from the will's suspension) he turns to plants, which are "much more content with mere existence than man." Unlike people, who tend to ruminate on the past and plan incessantly for the future, plants take in the "quiet, placid enjoyment of the present moment."[36]

Weeds and Wildings, of course, is not *about* Schopenhauer. But it *is* an act of co-creation, a book composed out of the whirling amalgam of words, ideas, impressions, feelings, and images that crop up in Schopenhauer and find their way into *Weeds and Wildings* alongside experiences from the many different sides of Melville's life, connecting Schopenhauer to Elizabeth Melville, Nathaniel Hawthorne, and a host of flowers, trees, and animals. Schopenhauer's role in this drama pivots on a single, animating question: in a world filled with suffering (and perhaps co-extensive with it), how does one achieve tranquility? All of the metaphysical "deserts" through which Melville wandered—from Gnosticism to Stoicism, Pyrrhonism, and, now, Pessimism—sought an answer to that question.[37] For Schopenhauer, suffering's inexorability means that life's aim should not be happiness but equanimity, which arrives when the will is suspended and suffering is temporarily paused. In such moments, "we are no longer the individual," we are "only that one eye of the world which looks out from all knowing creatures": an ego-less condition that can be provoked by nature, art, music, and other manifestations of life.[38]

Collectivity blooms throughout *Weeds and Wildings*. Melville's multihued crop of daisies, moss-roses, dandelions, and other flowers solicit our regard for the world and help us reevaluate the here and now, or what Maurice Merleau-Ponty dubs the "extraordinary overlapping" of phenomenological existence. "Without Price," Melville writes,

> Have the Roses. Needs no pelf
> The blooms to buy,
> Nor any rose-bed to thyself
> Thy skill to try:
> But live up to the Rose's light,
> Thy meat shall turn to roses red,
> Thy bread to roses white.[39]

This poem traffics in the metaphor of transubstantiation, but no deity guides this change. Death is indeed a process of transforming, not from matter into spirit but from "meat" into the chemical building-blocks of life. If one "Needs no pelf / The blooms to buy," that is because this precious cycle is both priceless and totally commonplace. In that respect the poem reiterates Schopenhauer's claim that beauty is but a "general conception of nature, is, in fact, her thought of a species. This is why beauty is so captivating: it is a fundamental thought of nature: whereas the individual is only a by-thought, a corollary."[40]

Weeds and Wildings is a final, resounding recognition of life's beauty before Melville too becomes dust and roses. And one of the recurring themes of this recognition is the illusoriness of the sovereign self, that inner Ahab we tend to carry around inside of our heads ("[I] stand alone among the millions of the peopled earth!")[41] The poems attempt to speak from a point of view liberated from the fiction of individuality that reigns over so much of human life. When Melville read Schopenhauer's *The World as Will and Representation*, he scored the following passage: "All virtue proceeds from the immediate and intuitive knowledge of the metaphysical identity of all beings.... Even the weakest intellect is sufficient to see through the *principium individuationis*."[42] If such knowledge is both "immediate and intuitive," that is because it is inscribed in nature. For Melville as for Schopenhauer, the truth of the *principium communis*—that "We are only that one eye of the world which looks out from all knowing creatures"—is all around us. *Weeds and Wildings* accordingly draws attention to open and decentered experiences, as well as the many objects and organisms that occasion them.

"The Blue Bird," for example, begins by describing a single, simple bird, then morphs into a meditation on the color blue:

> Beneath yon Larkspur's azure bells
> That sun their bees in balmy air
> In mould no more the Blue-Bird dwells
> Tho' late he found interment there.
> All stiff he lay beneath the Fir

> When shrill the March piped overhead,
> And Pity gave him sepulchre
> Within the Garden's sheltered bed.
> And soft she sighed—Too soon he came;
> On wings of hope he met the knell;
> His heavenly tint the dust shall tame;
> Ah, some misgiving had been well!
> But, look, the clear ethereal hue
> In June it makes the Larkspur's dower;
> It is the self-same welkin-blue
> The Bird's transfigured in the Flower.[43]

Melville again secularizes the idea of the afterlife while retaining a sense of awe. The larkspur and the bluebird share a similar hue, not a deep blue—the blue of the Pacific—but a "clear ethereal" version of the color, the "heavenly tint" of the sky. After the bird dies, the "shrill Spring"—not with any volition but simply by unfolding—covers the Larkspur in a natural "sepulcher," and the bird, in turn, provides sustenance for other lifeforms. Nature's intricacy is symbolized by the various shades of blue, related wavelengths of light that link everything from plants to birds to the sky. In Melville's time, color tended to be conceived in relational terms, and the poem both begins and ends with a comparison, tying the blue of the bird to the blue of the flower.[44] (The ancient Greeks called it *delphinium*, or "dolphin."[45]) And where is Melville here? He is absent altogether, part of the very *principus communis* he is describing. Maybe that commonality only becomes truly visible in the "clear ethereal" light of imminent death, which for Melville was turning out to be very different from what he'd imagined, like a gorgeous but deadly flower: the Larkspur (*delphinium*) is toxic (Figure 16).

Such poems might also be in dialog with Schopenhauer's color theory. In *On Vision and Colors* (1816), Schopenhauer updated Sextus Empiricus (one of Melville's favorite philosophers) "who had already explained [color perception] clearly and in detail, and even went so far as to prove that we do not know the things for what they may be by themselves, but only according to their appearances." Melville is less interested in the mind's processing of particular colors than in the fact that "we do not know the things for what they may be by themselves," which is one of the cornerstones of Melville's philosophy.[46] *Weeds and Wildings* apprehends the world by comparing and connecting; the poems fuse birds with flowers, beauty with memory, and life with death. It is less of a collection of discrete poems than a series of related images, repeated actions, and shared experiences. Nor is it clear where these poems originate. *Weeds and Wildings* routinely crosses in and out of multiple perspectives, migrating from the transposition of bodily forms in "The Blue Bird" to poems that seem to anthropomorphize nature but in fact possess no distinctly human point of view, focusing

Figure 16. *Delphinium.* From John Lindley, ed., *Ornamental Garden and Shrubbery*, Vol. 1 (1838).

instead on wheat spears that "dance," flowers that "revel," etc.[47] This is one of the reasons the volume continues to be something of a curiosity even for Melville's most seasoned readers: *Weeds and Wildings* frequently doesn't read like it was written by a single, identifiable person.

The idea that nothing is self-identical informs the poems in other ways as well. Considered as a genre, flower poems are written be given away. Attached to stems, tucked into letters, and presented as gifts, flower poems by definition reach outside of the self. Then there is the *principus communis* of the lines themselves, which typically unfold in metric beats of two and four, seemingly pairing off only to pose further, internal comparisons. Here, again, is "Clover":

> The June day dawns, the joy-winds rush,
> Your jovial fields are dressed;
> Rosier for thee the Dawn's red flush,
> Ruddier the Ruddock's breast.

As the sun hovers over the horizon, shedding its red light on the world, it illuminates numerous patterns. Several pairs and exchanges emerge almost all at once: in the meter (four lines with two couplets), rhymes ("rush"/"flush," "dress"/"breast"/"dressed"), alliterations ("day dawns," "June," "joy," "jovial"), and even *within* some of those pairs, like the internal rhyme in "Ruddier the Ruddock's breast," or the poem's evocation of blushing and nakedness.[48] In the manuscript, "Clover" follows "Clover Dedication" like a flower after a note, and it functions simultaneously as a poem for Elizabeth Melville, a meditation on red, and a poem about beauty, birds, bodies, blood, and wakefulness.

Floral beauty similarly ties us to communal being in "Rip Van Winkle's Lilac." In Melville's retelling of Washington Irving's story, Rip is still a bumbler who wakes up after a long sleep, but almost everything else is different. Rip sleeps much longer—decades upon decades, it seems—and when he awakes, he discovers that everyone he has known and loved is gone. His wife is nowhere to be found and their cottage has turned into a moss-covered ruin. The roof is caved in, crushed by a fallen willow tree—the very tree that Rip tried and failed to prune ("[a] monument of the negative victory of stubborn inertia over spasmodic activity and an ineffectual implement"). Rip then notices what has happened in his absence, indeed *because* of his absence: all of this loss and decay has yielded new life. The dead tree is

> tenderly dressed by the Spring; an umber-lined mount of mellow punk, mossed in spots, with wild violets springingt from it here and there, attesting the place of the departed, even the same place where it fell. But, behold; shooting up above the low, dilapidated eaves, the lilacs now laughed where the inconsolable willow had wept. Lightly it dropt upon the green roof the pink little bells from its bunched blossoms in place of the old willow's yellowed leaves.

Rip is bewildered by this beauty. Then, finally, he speaks—"half-consciously," Melville adds—and describes a future in which everyone finds "joyance" in the tree and its pink blossoms, the "reaking wafture" of which creates a community as people flock to this gorgeous abode of flowers and fungi, this "Lilac Land" where Rip's "heart-flowers out confessed":

Despite its slant ungainly trunk
Atwist and black like strands in junk,
Annual yet it flowered aloft
In juvenile pink, complexion soft.
That owner hale, long past his May,
His children's children—every one
Like those Rip romped with in the sun—
Merrily plucked the clusters gay.
The place a stranger scented out
By Boniface told in vinous way—
"Follow the fragrance!"
. . .
[N]eighbors, unconcerned before
When bloomed the tree by lowly door,
Craved now one little slip to train;
Neighbor from neighbor begged again.
On every hand stem shot from slip,
Till, lo, that region now is dowered
Like the first Paradise embowered,
Thanks to poor good-for-nothing Rip!
Some think those parts should bear his name;
But no—the blossoms take the fame.
Slant finger-posts by horsemen scanned
Point the green miles—To Lilac Land.
Go ride there down one charmful lane,
O reader mine, when June's at best,
A dream of Rip shall slack the rein,
For there his heart flowers out confessed.
And there you'll say,—O, hard ones, trude!
See, where man finds in man no ruse,
Boon Nature finds one—Heaven be blest![49]

The beauty of this scene derives from organic processes. The dead wood becomes food for mushrooms and the moss-covered trunk provides flowers with nutrients. The "slant, ungainly trunk, / Atwist and black" gives way to vivid pinks, greens, and whites, illustrating the way that life, death, and beauty are intertwined. No wonder Emily Dickinson dubbed the mushroom "the elf of plants"![50]

This flower-filled sketch tends to erase individual selves or blend them together. The author is never named and the story is addressed to an unidentified "Happy Shade" (a hazy shadow of a former person). Only the pink flowers ever acquire any significant fame ("Some think those parts should bear his name; / But no—the blossoms take the fame"), and the sketch continually appeals to the senses, dipping the reader into an immersive set of smells, forms, and colors. "Rip Van Winkle" is exceedingly atmospheric. It is not the "heart-flowers" alone that excrete a powerful fragrance; so does the sketch itself, which offers up a literary tincture. There's a blurriness to the landscape and the characters, a cloudy quality that is very much in keeping with Rip's dream-like state of mind. It is as if the self, too, is atmospheric—less of a discrete possession than a set of characteristics that waft like air, or spread like mist. Perhaps that is the most apt thing Melville could compose late in life, shortly before he too became dust: "For what is your life? It is even a vapour that appeareth for a little time and then vanisheth away."[51]

Beauty, Death, and the Aesthetics of Negation

The volume, however, ends not with a dreamy story about lilacs, but with "A Rose or Two: As They Fell." This concluding section is Melville's final creative release, and it is "devoted" (a supplication repeated across the poems) to the beauty of roses. For "fair you are," Melville crows, "Nor heaven reserves a fairer thing."[52] The fair flowers planted here include not only red roses (*rosa kordesii*) or show roses (though they are prevalent too, in all their splendor), but *all* roses: hearth-roses and moss-roses, sweet-briar and clovers, as well as everything else that might be called rose-like, from love and art to the human body. The symbolic pliability of the rose fascinates Melville, but so too does the sheer, life-giving power of its beauty. Roses allure because of their ability to spark joy, solicit awe, or invite silence. The poems describe that power in numerous ways, but they almost always invoke the language of sovereignty: "the flower-gods"; "The Queen of the Flowers"; "Reign endless, Rose!"[53] Monarchs or gods, roses seem to be endowed with otherworldly power.

Nonetheless, all of the qualities traditionally associated with sovereignty are inverted by roses. Instead of consolidating power, they spread it out; instead of dominating, they disseminate love, beauty, and delight. Whatever rule they have is over the senses, and that reign reattaches us to the natural world. If Timothy Morton is right, and at some point long ago there was a "Severing" of humanity from nature—a fatal division that occurred with the rise of civilization—then roses are beautiful reminders of what's been lost.[54] Their graceful symmetry, their brilliant shades of color, their thorny beauty (as if suffering were written into the rose's DNA), their rhizomatic roots—almost every quality of roses makes them conduits of connection and vehicles of meaning.

"A Rose or Two" is utterly communal. The poems in this final section laud the rose-like intertwinings that define earthly life: "O Rose, we plants are all akin, / Our roots enlock." Sometimes Melville's language scrambles categories, loosening the boundary between plant and animal, material and immaterial: "bell-flowers," "flower-gods," "trumpet-flowers." Elsewhere, the poems describe groups of like-minded devotees ("The New Rosicrucians," "We...natives of Eden," etc.), or evoke the atmospheric beauty of roses—the way they grab the eye, or fill a room both visually and somatically. Roses seem to "chime" their "beauty," as if they were natural bells, and their sweet "attar" still carries memories of "the bloom."[55] The poem "Hearth-Roses" uses the smell of roses to reflect on the relationship between love and light:

> The Sugar-Maple embers in bed
> Here fended in Garden of Fire,
> Like the Roses yield musk,
> Like the Roses are Red,
> Like the Roses expire
> Lamented when low;
> But excelling the flowers,
> Are odorous in ashes
> As e'en in their glow.
> Ah, Love, when life closes,
> Dying the death of the just,
> May we vie with Hearth-Roses,
> Smelling sweet in our dust.[56]

The poem interlaces three things: the life and death of roses, the passage from love to love's memory, and the transformation of fire into ambers and ash. As I mentioned earlier, *Weeds and Wildings* repeatedly asks the question, "What happens to a life after it is gone?" "Hearth-Roses" reframes that query, turning it into a question about love's afterlife. In that regard the poem is another testament to the permanence of impermanence and the inexorability of suffering, but the poem also reflects back on prior pleasure, suggesting that we should embrace love's sweetness while it lasts. "Hedge well thy Roses" indeed.

Many of the poems in "A Rose or Two" are also about Nathaniel Hawthorne. When Melville invokes love here, it takes on several connotations: love for the world (Shelley's definition); love as a cosmic force (à la Rumi); romantic love in general; and Melville's love, in particular, for Hawthorne, which continues to burn like the smoldering embers of a fire. That is why the section begins with the pairing of an Owl and a Meadowlark; it is why the poems play, almost obsessively, with vines and vine-like metaphors (in *Clarel* the character named "Vine" is based on Hawthorne, who wrote a famous book about "mosses"); and it is why Melville furtively invokes Hawthorne's name. As Osborne points out, "the hawthorn shrub (Genus *Crataégus*) belongs to the Rose family."[57] And in *The Scarlet Letter* (1850), Hester—following Hawthorne's intense identification with her in "The Custom House"—is associated with a "wild rose bush."[58] Hawthorne's afterglow is particularly bright in the subsection "Under the Snow," which features several poems bound together like a bouquet: "Amoroso," "Under the Snow," "The Ambuscade," "The Rose Window," and "The Devotion of the Flowers to Their Lady." These are the most erotic poems Melville wrote, his version of *Calamus*:

> Rosamond, my Rosamond
> Of roses is the rose;
> Her bloom belongs to summer
> Nor less in winter glows,
> When, mossed in furs all cosy,
> We speed it o'er the snows
> By ice-bound streams enchanted,
> While red Arcturus, he
> A huntsman ever ruddy
> Sees a ruddier star by me.
>
> O Rosamond, Rose Rosamond,
> Is yonder Dian's reign?
> Look, the icicles despond
> Chill drooping from her fane!
> But Rosamond, Rose Rosamond,
> In us, a plighted pair,
> First makes with flame a bond—
> One purity they share.
> To feel your cheek like ice,
> While snug the furs enclose—
> This is spousal love's device
> This is Arctic Paradise,
> And wooing in the snows!
> Rosamond, my Rosamond,
> Rose Rosamond, Moss-Rose![59]

These lines are about consummation. A set of opposites—colors (red and white), forms (roses, fire, and ice), seasons (summer and winter), people (Melville and Hawthorne)—all come together in this moment of bliss, this brief passage into paradise.[60] That consummation also involves naked bodies locked together. As Christopher Looby has argued, Melville tends to see aesthetics through the body and vice versa, linking "erotics" to "aesthetics" and "dramatiz[ing] their cognate status." The poem overflows with such corporealized aesthetics, as the feel of the furs blend with the feel of the moss, much like the beginning of "The Counterpane" in *Moby-Dick*: "partly lying on it as the arm did when I first awoke, I could hardly tell it from the quilt, they so blended their hues together; and it was only by the sense of weight and pressure that I could tell that Queequeg was hugging me."[61] In remembrance of Hawthorne, Melville also collected moss from Salem (Hawthorne's birthplace), which he kept "all cosy" in his personal copy of *Mosses from an Old Manse* (see Figure 17). Even years later, that moss still resembles a flame.

Melville might be speaking in a "closeted style" by making Hawthorne the secret subject of these poems, but the effect of that anonymity is to communalize the experiences the poems describe.[62] Everyone who has felt "love's device" has had a version of this same experience repeated in a different form. Even here, in this most Hawthorne-centric section, there is a kind of erasure of the self, a repeated passing into *anattā*. Most of the poems have little to no trace of authorship or identity. They sound like voices from nowhere, speakers of a language that emerges from nature itself. Whenever an "I" does appear in these poems, it is remarkably fluid. Sometimes the "I" is ancient, reaching back to bygone eras, ambiguously placed between "a garden and old tomb," or hailing from another perspective altogether ("Attributed to Clement Dronon, monk, a Provencal of noble birth in the eleventh century, in early life a troubadour, a devotee of Love and the Rose"). Occasionally, humans become flowers ("We are natives of Eden"), or morph into identityless observers:

> I woke, the great Rose-Window high,
> A mullioned wheel in gable set,
> Suffused with rich and soft in dye
> Where Iris and Aurora met;
> Aslant in sheaf of rays it threw
> From all its foliate round of panes
> Transfiguring light on dingy stains,
> While danced the motes in dusty pew.[63]

Although focused on a "great Rose-Window," this octet is really about change and relation, moving from a heightened state of self-awareness ("I woke") to an egoless evocation of dust motes "dancing" in red light. Yet the poem's perspective is hardly the only thing that is "transfigured." The window is rose-like in its structure ("foliate round of panes"). The light does not simply shine; it casts forth rays that resemble "sheaf[s]," or harvested stems. And the iris, too, is a "mullioned wheel" "suffused with rich and soft with dye." The interconnection at which the speaker arrives is already present in everything, and the mind is not so different from a ray of light, a rose, or a mote of dust. Maybe, the poem suggests, these are simply alternate modes of matter or related manifestations of life. Cast in a form typically reserved for love poems (like Donne's "Sweetest love, I do not goe"), the poem is an act of praise, but Melville's praise is directed at the natural world writ large, a world full of beauty and bereft of any self that can remain stable or solid.[64]

That praise resounds in "L'Envoi," the poem that concludes "A Rose or Two" as well as *Weeds and Wildings*:

Figure 17. Photograph of Melville's copy of *Mosses from an Old Manse*. Courtesy of the Houghton Library.

> Rosy dawns the morning Syrian,
> Youthful as in years of Noah:
> Why then aging at three-score?
> Do moths infect your mantle Tyrian?
> Shake it out where the sunbeams pour!

> Time, amigo, does not masque us—
> Boys in gray wigs, young at core.
> Look, what demigods of Damascus,
> Roses, lure to Pharpar's shore!
> Sigh not—Age, dull tranquilliser,
> And arid years that filed before,
> For flowers unfit us. Nay, be wiser:
> Wiser in relish, if sedate,
> Come graybeards to their roses late.[65]

As with almost everything Melville wrote, this poem could be read in a few different ways—as a meditation on old age, for example, or a final goodbye to his "amigo" Hawthorne. Nonetheless, the title suggests that something more is at stake in these lines. In Melville's era, the "L'Envoi" was considered a distinct poetic subgenre. Derived from the Old French word *envei*, or "to send one on one's way," a "L'Envoi" poem was where a poet was supposed to say a final word and reflect on his or her muse. Henry Wadsworth Longfellow's "L'Envoi" in *Voices of the Night* (1839) addresses the voices "that arose / After the Evening's close, / And whispered to my restless heart repose!," while James Russell Lowell's "L'Envoi" (subtitled "To the Muse") asks, "Whither? Albeit I follow fast, / In all life's circuit I but find, / Not where thou art, but where thou wast."[66]

Melville's "L'Envoi" similarly addresses his afflatus: "Time, amigo, does not masque us." But this is also a retrospective poem composed by an aged writer whose heart was slowly giving out and whose life was slipping away with each "Rosy dawn." It provides a retrospective account of all the earthly beauty that inspired Melville's writing through the years, from ships and friendship to light, landscapes, and the ancient world. To the degree that the poem has an underlying point, it is that old age allows one to "relish" the "roses" in a "wiser" way: death's arrival injects life with new verve and meaning. "L'Envoi" thus embodies a vital feature of late style, as Edward Said defines it, approaching life with a clarity that is possible only with "the decay of the body" and "the onset of ill health."[67]

Melville also fades away in the poem's misty revelation. This "L'Envoi," which concludes *Weeds and Wildings*, echoes the poem under the same title that concludes *Timoleon*. And that poem offers the chastened perspective of a seventeenth-century rover, "the Sire de Nesle," who "recoils" from the "terrible" earth and its "yearning infinite."[68] To further complicate matters, the section in which "L'Envoi" appears, "A Rose or Two," is mostly written to and for Hawthorne. The "amigo" addressed in these lines is at once Melville's afflatus and his long dead friend, whom the poem imagines as a fellow "graybeard"; and if this is Melville speaking, he of course goes unnamed and unidentified.

If we have learned anything from Melville's aesthetics, it is that these two dimensions of the poem—its mixing of identities and its investment in beauty—

are intimately linked. Beauty tends to dissolve the self and absorb us into what we previously considered to be outside or external. In that way it is like art, or as "L'Envoi" implies, like death. "Age," that "dull tranquilliser," may rob this experience of some of its elation, but there's clarity in that calmness. When "graybeards" come "to their roses late," they possess a keener sense of what matters and—as paradoxical as it may seem—an even fiercer attachment to this earth, this wonderous place "[y]outhful as in the days of Noah" where "the sunbeams pour."

3
Appalling Beauty in *Moby-Dick*

When the white whale finally appears in *Moby-Dick*, it is nothing short of a revelation.[1] The surprise is partly due to his late entrance. In a book that is literally named after him and is ardently interested in everything (and I mean *everything*) he represents, Moby Dick only emerges toward the very end, nearly 400 pages into the novel. However, the surprise is also due to the wild discrepancy between expectation and experience—between Moby Dick in myth and Moby Dick in reality. This is no mere whale, we repeatedly hear. He is a "murderous monster" responsible for untold funerals and amputations. He is a "deformed" thing of nightmares, a wicked creature full of "direful wrath." Ahab even seems to think that Moby Dick is so warped by his malevolence that he "spouts black blood."[2]

Yet when the whale finally surfaces off the coast of Japan, rising ever so gently out of the water, we discover that he is anything but the ugly monster he is reputed to be:

> As they neared him, the ocean ... seemed drawing a carpet over its waves; seemed a noon-meadow, so serenely it spread. At length the breathless hunter came so nigh his seemingly unsuspecting prey, that his entire dazzling hump was distinctly visible, sliding along the sea as if an isolated thing, and continually set in a revolving ring of finest, fleecy, greenish foam. He saw the vast, involved wrinkles of the slightly projecting head beyond. Before it, far out on the soft Turkish-rugged waters, went the glistening white shadow from his broad, milky forehead, a musical rippling playfully accompanying the shade; and behind, the blue waters interchangeably flowed over into the moving valley of his steady wake; and on either hand bright bubbles arose and danced by his side. But these were broken again by the light toes of hundreds of gay fowl softly feathering the sea, alternate with their fitful flight; and like to some flag-staff rising from the painted hull of an argosy, the tall but shattered pole of a recent lance projected from the white whale's back; and at intervals one of the cloud of soft-toed fowls hovering, and to and fro skimming like a canopy over the fish, silently perched and rocked on this pole, the long tail feathers streaming like pennons. A gentle joyousness—a mighty mildness of repose in swiftness, invested the gliding whale.[3]

Is the "breathless hunter" the whale, or is it Ishmael? As Christopher N. Phillips observes, Ishmael tends to slide from "the language of description and narration" to "narrating ... the act of perception [itself]," and here both levels of description underscore a distinct set of patterns.[4] Stunned by the beautiful colors and forms he beholds, Ishmael describes a symphony of circles. Waves, tipped by rings of foam, ripple around the whale's marbled body. Wrinkles curve across his "broad, milky forehead," and bubbles dance around his colossal back as it arches into the sky. These concentric circles impart a sense of connection between forms of life, blending sight, sound, and texture—the foam is "fleecy," the ocean becomes a carpet, a "cloud" of birds "feather" the sea. Melville's synaesthetic language plays with the eye and ear through tender vowels ("gentle joyousness," "soft-toed fowl") and rippling alliterations ("finest, fleecy, greenish foam," "so serenely it spread"). Even the birds partake in this joyous drama as they fly in circles through the air ("skimming like a canopy over the fish"), then light upon Moby Dick, becoming the "feathered pennons" of nature's flag. And that is the biggest surprise of all: Moby Dick is not a demon but part and parcel of nature's kaleidoscopic beauty.

How could we have been so terribly wrong about the white whale? As Elaine Scarry reminds us, beauty and reevaluation tend to go hand in hand: "The experience of 'being in error' so inevitably accompanies the perception of beauty that it ... [appears to be] one of its abiding structural features."[5] Ishmael's description of Moby Dick discloses two errors in particular. First, it soundly discredits what Ahab has been saying all along about the whale's monstrosity. Instead of a sinister aberration, we find a dance of colors and movements. Instead of an "intangible malignity," we find a whale gliding gracefully across the "wide-rolling watery prairies," a fellow creature driven not by evil but by all the things that define earthly life: the forging of bonds, the desire to test one's abilities, the impulse to move, think, and play.[6] That revelation points toward a second error, which has to do with the reason for Ahab's misinterpretation of Moby Dick: the moody captain of the *Pequod* has retreated so far into himself and shielded himself from beauty that he cannot apprehend the truth of the white whale. Ahab considers himself to be an avenging angel set apart and against the natural world, and that intellectual mistake is the root of his spiritual malady. As C.L. R. James words it, "Nature [for Melville] is not a background to men's activity or something to be conquered or used. It is part of [us], at every turn physically, intellectually, and emotionally."[7]

Moby-Dick is a book filled with juxtapositions, but this contrast between Ahab and nature plays a particularly important role.[8] In many respects it is the aesthetic and philosophical core of Melville's novel, the center of gravity around which the motley panoramas revolve. Ahab sees everyone and everything—captain and crew, humanity and nature, good and evil—as fundamentally separate and distinct, as if the wall rather than the atom were the universe's elemental building block.[9] *Moby-Dick* repeatedly distinguishes between Ahab's worldview, which is based on hierarchical division, and a more open, lateral, and loving viewpoint that sees human and non-human life as beautifully interwoven. From the wall-less intimacies of "A Squeeze of the Hand" to the "Siamese ligature[s]" of "The

Monkey-Rope" and Pip's vision of the "multitudinous, God-omnipresent" nature of the cosmos, *Moby-Dick* contains a host of other ways of valuing and experiencing life. These non-Ahabian parts of *Moby-Dick* invite us to conceive of beauty as something that is communal, non-possessive, and interdependent. Over and over in *Moby-Dick*, beauty swings open "the great flood-gates of the wonder-world," revealing affinities and intimacies that temporarily dissolve the little Ahab inside of us.

Moby-Dick may be a book about terror and death, but it is also a book about the opposite of existential dread. At their core, terror and beauty are different versions of the same experience: feeling the self dissolve as you come under the sway of someone or something else. *Moby-Dick* asks, What should one do with such experiences? One can certainly view the self's erosion, as Ahab does, as a threat to be repelled. That is what fuels Ahab's monomaniacal fire: a desire to piece the shattered self back together through violence. One can also view self-erasure, as Ishmael occasionally does, in nihilistic terms, as an "indefiniteness" that "shadows forth the heartless voids and immensities of the universe, and thus stabs us from behind with the thought of annihilation."[10] But moments in which the self fades away can sometimes be quite galvanizing. They can rouse the senses, create intimacies, and enable one to see life with fresh eyes. These multiple, overlapping possibilities are contained in the phrase Ishmael repeatedly uses to describe the white whale's appearance and effect: "appalling beauty." In Melville's era, the word *appalling* was less associated with disgust than it came to be later on. In the mid-nineteenth century, *appalling* still carried a semantic charge carried over from its etymological origins (in Old French, *apelir*, or "to be in consternation")—in short, to appall is to shock or stun. *Moby-Dick* is about experiences that appall you, in this older sense of the term.[11] Such experiences can either push you toward an existential abyss, or they can lead you out of it. As Simone Weil puts it, "The love of the beauty of the world ... [entails] the love of all the truly precious things that bad fortune can destroy. The truly precious things are those forming ladders reaching toward the beauty of the world."[12]

Beauty is thus an integral part of what has been variously called the "impersonal," "nonhuman," or "inhuman" element of Melville's writing.[13] To read Melville is to encounter a swirling vortex of surfaces and depths, parts and wholes, insides and outsides, which blur categorical distinctions. While reading *Moby-Dick*, it can be quite difficult to discern what, if anything, distinguishes someone from their environment. "Distinctly we see the difference of the colors," but "where exactly does the one first blendingly enter into the other?" As Ahab avers (in utter horror), even "the smallest atom [that] stirs or lives on in matter, ... has its cunning duplicate in [us]."[14] Two of the most compelling interpretations of *Moby-Dick*, Sharon Cameron's *The Corporeal Self* and Michael Jonik's *Melville and the Politics of the Inhuman*, demonstrate that Melville's entire philosophy is steeped in this playful subversion and redefinition of the "human." In Cameron's reading, *Moby-Dick* assiduously divides and distinguishes between persons in ways that resist the very process of personification. Melville, she notes, "seems to imagine his characters as part-people, people who only as complementarities comprise wholes." For Melville, this approach to characterization has ethical and philosophical consequences: "The characters, like ourselves, cannot see the whole world. They and we are a crew birthed from its navel and somehow related to it in an unfigurable connection that ceases to be problematic when the incomprehensible otherness that can neither be seen nor understood is absorbed into the self."[15]

How does that absorption work, and what enables it? Ahab offers us a clue: his rejection of his own "incomprehensible otherness" expresses itself as a rejection of the world's beauty. This link between beauty and personhood also enables us to extend Jonik's erudite reading of the novel's philosophy to a reading of the novel's aesthetics. Melville, Jonik posits, is fascinated by the "collocation of physical forces, agencies, and material processes" that seem to infringe upon the self from the outside but, in fact, "always already dwell within and act through [us]." These inhuman forces impact *Moby-Dick* in several ways, manifesting as "concatenation," "prosthetics," "immanent materiality," and "geometrics." Jonik frames his interpretation of the novel as an account of its materialist philosophy, and it is a very rich and compelling account. But what Jonik discloses is also immanently aesthetic: Melville's depiction of "characters and bodies as transindividual and relational" is bound up with Melville's engagements with beauty.[16] What is "concatenation" but a beautifully textured whole? What are "geometrics" but structures in which nature's beauty takes form?

Or to return to our earlier etymology: How does one think and feel one's way out of consternation, out of being appalled? To answer that question, I want to explore several interrelated ways in which *Moby-Dick* apprehends beauty. I will begin by examining the novel's artistic and spiritual depictions of whales, which associate whaling with warfare and beauty with the sacred. I will then look at the relationship between beauty and chance, which Melville addresses in chapters such as "The Pacific," "Moby Dick," and "The Symphony"; and interdependence, which acquires aesthetic dimensions in chapters like "The Counterpane," "The Monkey-Rope," and "The Mat-Maker." I will then turn to the novel's copious descriptions of weaving, through which Melville speculates about the patterned nature of beauty and the cosmos alike. As we will see, these engagements with beauty structure and inform the novel's ethical, metaphysical, and environmental ideas, providing a philosophico-aesthetic mode for *Moby-Dick* from beginning to end.

Whale Beauty

Moby-Dick is full of exuberant bursts, exquisite lines, and radiant surfaces. But few things are more striking than the whales that populate Melville's novel.

Ishmael is so stunned by the variety and magnitude of their beauty that he frequently finds himself at a loss, grasping for metaphor after metaphor to describe the indescribable. The sperm whale's colonnades of bones, he says, resemble a great pipe organ. As for its spout: "If you stand on its summit and look at these two ƒ-shaped spoutholes, you would take the whole head for an enormous bass-viol, and these spiracles, the apertures in its sounding-board." It is as though the whale were a musical instrument capable of sending gorgeous bass notes vibrating around the world. And when mist emerges out of that instrument, it creates a "canopy of vapor...glorified by a rainbow, as if Heaven itself had put its seal upon his thoughts." Their beauty may be musical, even divine, but it is also biological: as they swim, they form criss-crossing "veins," as though the earth were one vast heart and sperm whales the red blood cells. Or perhaps they are butterflies, since "the mere skeleton of the whale bears the same relation to the fully invested and padded animal as the insect does to the chrysalis that so roundingly envelops it." The sperm whale's very mouth—its much-feared jaw—is "beautiful," Ishmael asserts, since it is "lined, or rather papered with a glistening white membrane, glossy as bridal satins."[17]

Melville insists that if whales are like anything, they are like art—powerful, alluring, intricately patterned, and capable of eliciting a wide range of ideas and emotions. One can attempt to define it, but doing so is like "classify[ing] the constituents of a chaos."[18] So whales become nearly indistinguishable from books, paintings, songs, churches, arches, spires, sculptures, poems, myths, and other types of art that fill us with fear, joy, awe, pleasure, and mixtures thereof. That is why Ishmael has such trouble defining and distinguishing whales: their boundless beauty has less to do with conceptual categories than with flickerings of color, sound, texture, and sensation that exceed the bounds of language.[19] It also exceeds the bounds of print itself, as Melville struggles to contain his thoughts about whales within the material space of the novel ("Unconsciously my chirography expands into placard capitals. Give me a condor's quill! Give me Vesuvius' crater for an inkstand!"), evincing Katie McGettigan's insight that "in Melville's writing, the materiality of print...is a medium for aesthetic expression, literary representation, and philosophical inquiry."[20] As D.H. Lawrence remarks, one of the things that sets Melville apart is his "sheer vibrational sensitiveness": "like a marvelous wireless-station, he registers the effects of the outer world," writing in ways that mimic the "naked" movement of "bodily knowledge."[21] That "vibrational sensitiveness" is on display in *Moby-Dick*'s prismatic depiction of whales, as Melville attempts to express all the ways in which they are beautiful, from their biology to their symbolism.

Even the sperm whale's skin is a work of art. "Almost invariably," Ishmael says,

> it is all over obliquely crossed and re-crossed with numberless straight marks in thick array, something like those in the finest Italian line engravings. But these

marks do not seem to be impressed upon the isinglass substance above mentioned, but seem to be seen through it, as if they were engraved upon the body itself.

The whale's engraved skin proves to be quite generative for Ishmael, leading him not to conclusions but to a series of associations:

> In some instances, to the quick, observant eye, those linear marks, as in a veritable engraving, but afford the ground for far other delineations. These are hieroglyphical; that is, if you call those mysterious cyphers on the walls of pyramids hieroglyphics, then that is the proper word to use in the present connexion. By my retentive memory of the hieroglyphics upon one Sperm Whale in particular, I was much struck with a plate representing the old Indian characters chiselled on the famous hieroglyphic palisades on the banks of the Upper Mississippi. Like those mystic rocks, too, the mystic-marked whale remains undecipherable. This allusion to the Indian rocks reminds me of another thing. Besides all the other phenomena which the exterior of the Sperm Whale presents, he not seldom displays the back, and more especially his flanks, effaced in great part of the regular linear appearance, by reason of numerous rude scratches, altogether of an irregular, random aspect. I should say that those New England rocks on the sea-coast, which Agassiz imagines to bear the marks of violent scraping contact with vast floating icebergs—I should say, that those rocks must not a little resemble the Sperm Whale in this particular. It also seems to me that such scratches in the whale are probably made by hostile contact with other whales; for I have most remarked them in the large, full-grown bulls of the species.[22]

Rather than consisting in "disinterestedness" (as Kant averred), beauty forges connections. The intricate surface of the sperm whale's skin transports Ishmael, shuttling him from "Italian line engravings" to native "hieroglyphs" and the "mystic rocks" of New England. As Samuel Otter notes, Melville's phrase "obliquely crossed and re-crossed in thick array" refers to the intaglio print-making process that used metal plates to "create pattern, tone, and depth," a technique Melville associated with Giovanni Piranesi's hauntingly beautiful *Vedute di Roma*.[23] Ishmael's other references—native artists who chiseled meaning out of stone, and Louis Agassiz's discovery of continental glaciation—similarly underscore the power of beauty to inscribe and connect, or as Ishmael puts it, to crosshatch the world around us.

If *Moby-Dick* contains an anthropological insight, it is that we are pattern-making and pattern-seeking creatures, and this influences how we respond to beauty. Whenever one lights upon something beautiful, one almost instinctively seeks out sources and analogs. Thinking about beauty in this way, as Melville does, involves a significant departure from the possessive strains of Euro-American aesthetics, which tend to grasp beauty as a function and result of the ego's independence.[24] In *Moby-Dick*, beauty involves a motley host of attachments and associations that reveal the self to be prosthetic, aleatory, and deeply interdependent.[25] According to Alexander Nehamas, this is precisely why we can never adequately explain what we find beautiful:

> the judgment of taste is simply not a conclusion at all ... Beautiful things don't stand aloof, on their own, but direct our attention and our desire to everything we must learn and acquire in order to understand [them] ... They quicken the sense of life, giving it new shape and direction.[26]

It is this social, ego-less quality of beauty to which Ahab is so violently averse. But Ishmael is far more receptive to it, and that receptiveness leads him to sail from thought to thought, as the whales give his life "new shape and direction."

Reflecting on the sperm whale's skin, for example, inspires Ishmael to flip his thinking around. As if retracing the intricate lines on a Piranesi sketch, Ishmael moves from exteriority to interiority: "It is by reason of this cosy blanketing of his body, that the whale is enabled to keep himself comfortable in all weathers, in all seas, times, and tides." Ishmael can only marvel at that ability, given the mammalian similarities between humans and whales:

> like man, the whale has lungs and warm blood. Freeze his blood, and he dies. How wonderful is it then [that] ... he should be found at home, immersed to his lips for life in those Arctic waters! where, when seamen fall overboard, they are sometimes found, months afterwards, perpendicularly frozen into the hearts of fields of ice, as a fly is found glued in amber ... It does seem to me, that herein we see the rare virtue of ... thick walls, and the rare virtue of interior spaciousness. Oh, man! admire and model thyself after the whale! ... Like the great dome of St. Peter's, and like the great whale, retain, O man! in all seasons a temperature of thine own.[27]

If the skin allures and appalls because of its lineated intricacy, the whale's inner body is remarkable because of its "interior spaciousness" and balanced equilibrium. The passage revolves around two linked comparisons, likening the sperm whale to the human body and "the great dome of St. Peter's"—analogies that reveal beauty, corporeality, and sacredness to be conjoined, or as Ishmael might put it, "crossed and re-crossed" with one another. Our shared dependencies ("Like man, the whale has lungs and warm blood") enable us to appreciate the whale's "rare virtue": its ability to utterly be at home no matter the climate. What Melville is offering here—or drawing out, through comparative anatomy—is a broadened, biocentric worldview that sees life itself as both priceless and widely distributed.[28]

But why St. Peter's? It's a startling analogy that links whales to art, the Pacific to Rome, and the act of living to the act of worshipping. Melville's point partly has to do with analogy itself, which is integral to beauty and its concatenating effects. As Elizabeth Duquette contends, Melville is continually drawn to analogy because it enables verbal, philosophical, and heuristic insights.[29] There are also specific reasons why St. Peter's Basilica appears here. If anything is a marvel of "rare virtue," it is this massive, ornate, colonnaded shrine that required generations of artists to complete. Full of painted canopies and gorgeous sculptures, St. Peter's Basilica is the "gem" of the earth (as Emerson once put it), and its dome—designed by Michelangelo, who wanted to "raise the Pantheon in the air"—is its crowning glory.[30] In one of Melville's books about Italy, he read about the "unrivaled unity" of St. Peter's angles and portions, as well as the need to view the dome from several points of view: "The mind does not at once become conscious of its immensity, and it is only after its component parts have been examined, and perhaps only after several visits, that [it]...can be appreciated."[31]

Ishmael's description, which notes the ability of the dome and the sperm whale to regulate their temperature "in all seasons," also draws on Madame de Staël's *Corinne; or, Italy* (1800), which Melville purchased shortly before writing *Moby-Dick*. Architecture, de Staël suggests, is unique among the arts for its capacity to "awaken in our soul" multiple ideas without a single "determinate meaning,...so that we are seized, in contemplating it, with that kind of aimless reverie, which leads us into a boundless ocean of thought." If truth indeed resides "in landlessness alone," then architectural beauty is essential for voyaging through the world's "shoreless immensities." For de Staël, as for Melville, St. Peter's is a sacred space that reawakens one to the beauty of existence:

> This temple is like a world by itself; it...has its own peculiar season—a perpetual spring, which the external atmosphere can never change...I often come and walk here to restore to my soul that serenity which it sometimes loses: the sight of such a monument is like continual and sustained music, which waits to do you good when you approach.[32]

Melville picks up on that association with serenity, but he also turns St. Peter's into a symbol of beauty more broadly, and the beauty of that basilica arises out of its patterned connections. In *The Lives of Eminent Painters* (which Melville read with great interest), Giorgio Vasari noted the basilica's synthesizing power and attributed it to the elegance of Michelangelo's design: the grooved lines, raised ceilings, and receding walls all make it appear as though the church is being pulled upward by some vast, invisible force (Figure 18).[33]

This is the gravitational center of Melville's lectures about Italian art. Here, he declared, the self "is carried away with the very vastness": "The mind, instead of being bewildered within itself, is drawn out by the symmetry and beauty of the

Figure 18. George Cooke, *Interior of St. Peter's in Rome* (1847). Oil painting.

forms it beholds."[34] When St. Peter's appears in *Moby-Dick*, it encourages us to conceive of whales not merely as symbols of the sublime or ciphers of the indecipherable, but as fellow creatures in an intricate cosmos.[35] To assess the whale's meaning, it is necessary to treat a whale as one would treat Michelangelo's art, and what kind of response do works like the Sistine Chapel solicit? It is the same response that Ishmael has when he reflects, in sheer astonishment, on the whale's head (a "sanctuary"), skin ("like...the finest Italian line engravings"), or spermaceti ("beautiful crystalline shoots, as when...delicate ice is just forming in water").[36] *Moby-Dick* allows us to see and feel that whales are persons, and that nature is a complex system made up of innumerable crossings and combinations.

Some of the most insightful readings of the novel locate this biocentric viewpoint at the very heart of Melville's novel. John Levi Barnard posits that *Moby-Dick* not only traces the emergence of our present ecological era and its "extinction-producing economy" but also challenges the distinction between the edible and the exotic upon which "animal capitalism" conceptually depends. "On several occasions," Barnard points out, "Ishmael employs the term *murder*—typically applicable only to *homicide*—to signify the killing of nonhuman animals." This biocentric worldview, Colin Dayan argues, is expressed on every level of Melville's writing, from the language to the philosophy. If he sometimes "sacrificed the norms of style and expectations of polish," writes Dayan, Melville did so to reveal the "brutality and extermination" that undergirds people's daily lives: "[his] task was nothing less than to bring before his readers the meat—mutilated, bleeding, dead, rotting—that was as much a part of his surroundings as the glories of progress."[37]

This ethical vision would not be possible without the novel's reimagining of the self.[38] An expanded aesthetic and philosophical view of personhood shapes *Moby-Dick*, leading Ishmael to posit an almost endless series of parallels and affinities. Porpoises, we learn, feel joy. "Full of fine spirits," they enjoy swimming together "in hilarious shoals" and tossing "themselves to heaven like caps in a Fourth-of-July crowd." In "The Grand Armada," cetacean newborns suckle their mothers and look up as a human child does in peaceful wonderment. And when Queequeg dives headfirst into the head of a half-dissected whale to save "the Gay-Header," Tashtego, in chapter 78 (i.e. the chapter that follows "The Great Heidelburgh Tun," which considers the sperm whale's cranium), it is almost hilariously impossible to distinguish between the mélange of heads, bodies, and lives:

> Now, how had this noble rescue been accomplished? Why, diving after the slowly descending head, Queequeg with his keen sword had made side lunges near its bottom, so as to scuttle a large hole there; then dropping his sword, had thrust his long arm far inwards and upwards, and so hauled out poor Tash by the head. He averred, that upon first thrusting in for him, a leg was presented; but well knowing that that was not as it ought to be, and might occasion great trouble;—he had thrust back the leg, and by a dexterous heave and toss, had wrought a somerset upon the Indian; so that with the next trial, he came forth in the good old way—head foremost. As for the great head itself, that was doing as well as could be expected.[39]

It is in such passages that Melville's aesthetics and Melville's philosophy are most closely entwined. Queequeg's "noble rescue" reveals the thin line between life and death and the way they subtly reflect one another. That is the hopeful thread woven throughout *Moby-Dick*: this book that begins with depressive thoughts and ends with a suicidal hunt is also a celebration of life. The blurring of heads has a concerted effect, suggesting that it does not truly matter which brain belongs to which body: the will to live, or the will to die, matter far more than the particular vessel in which one does so. *Moby-Dick* challenges traditional conceptions of the ego, which emphasize separation and hierarchy, by prioritizing life itself in all of its appalling beauty.

Far from being a mere theme or stylistic flourish, beauty anchors the book's entire moral architecture.[40] If Ahab's "fiery hunt" is "demoniac" or the crew's abandonment of Pip is cruel, it is because these acts violate something that is sacred.[41] That sense of violation is underscored in Melville's numerous comparisons of whaling to human warfare, which spread and multiply until it is hard to tell where one ends and the other begins. In "The Advocate," Ishmael compares whaling captains to "Martial Commanders" and the ships' dirty decks to the "unspeakable carrion of... battle-fields." Whaling is just war by another name, and this slaughter literally lights the world: "for almost all the tapers, lamps, and candles that burn round the globe, burn, as before so many shrines, to [the whaling industry]." A similar, and equally disturbing, comparison appears in the seemingly innocuous "Cetology" chapter, under the heading "Book II (Octavo), Chapter IV (Killer)": "He is very savage... [Yet] exception might be taken to the name bestowed upon this whale, on the ground of its indistinctness. For we are all killers, on land and on sea; Bonapartes and Sharks included." Elsewhere, Melville ties warfare to whaling in other ways. The "American whale fishery," we learn, uses the same ranks as "the American navy," and sailors resemble medieval crusaders, pious warriors who traveled thousands of miles while "committing burglaries, picking pockets," and carrying out numerous other crimes. A "dead whale" resembles a "conquered fortress"; the "noble Sperm Whale's head" recalls "a Roman war-chariot"; and the list goes on.[42]

These comparisons could be seen as evidence of Melville's hopeless anthropomorphism or as attempts to naturalize the violence of whaling. But Melville was a pacifist, and his writings indicate that his commitment to "unconditional democracy on all sides" extended to his view of the environment and our place within it. This more unconditional understanding of life and beauty fuses the sequence of chapters that run from 61 ("Stubb Kills a Whale") to 66 ("The Shark Massacre"). Following the principle sketched out in chapter 60 ("The Line")—in short, that the entire world is "enveloped in whale-lines"—this sequence begins with a harpooning, then reels in the tragic consequences of sovereign selfhood. Stubb, the second mate who sees everyone and everything as intended for his personal use, takes the life of a whale. Armed with a sharp lance, he repeatedly and gleefully stabs the whale with all of his might, then does it again and again, until the blood begins to pour "like brooks down a hill," turning the ocean into a red tide. The whale, whose "tormented body rolled not in brine but in blood, which bubbled and seethed for furlongs behind in their wake," can barely breathe. His lungs begin to give out, as "jet after jet of white smoke was agonizingly shot from the spiracle of the whale, and vehement puff after puff from the mouth of the excited headsman." Then, to finish the kill, Stubb leans over the end of the bow and twists the blade of his crooked lance:

> Stubb slowly churned his long sharp lance into the fish, and kept it there, carefully churning and churning, as if cautiously seeking to feel after some gold watch that the whale might have swallowed, and which he was fearful of breaking ere he could hook it out. But that gold watch he sought was the innermost life of the fish. And now it is struck; for, starting from his trance into that unspeakable thing called his "flurry," the monster horribly wallowed in his blood, overwrapped himself in impenetrable, mad, boiling spray, so that the imperilled craft, instantly dropping astern, had much ado blindly to struggle out from

that phrensied twilight into the clear air of the day. And now abating in his flurry, the whale once more rolled out into view; surging from side to side; spasmodically dilating and contracting his spout-hole, with sharp, cracking, agonized respirations. At last, gush after gush of clotted red gore, as if it had been the purple lees of red wine, shot into the frighted air; and falling back again, ran dripping down his motionless flanks into the sea. His heart had burst![43]

Everything about this scene is profane.[44] The whale is in excruciating pain, gasping for life and wallowing in his own "clotted red gore," so that Stubb—the very definition of an asshole—can experience pleasure. The substitution of "blood" for "brine" is a twisted reversal of Jesus of Nazareth's transformation of water into wine, a not-so-subtle signal that something sacred is being defiled. Perhaps that is why Melville lingers on the breath, the incessant act that allows us to live and has long been associated with the divine. *Spirit* and *inspiration* share an etymological origin: this is the constant action through which we literally take in the world around us.[45] "Like man, the whale has lungs," and here they slowly give out, in spite of the whale's powerful will to live, as Stubb repeatedly sends the "crooked lance" into the hunted creature, until it releases a final, heartbreaking death-rattle.

When I say that this is profane, I mean that it desecrates something that is divine, a violation palpable in Stubb's desire to take "the innermost life of the fish" as if it were a "gold watch." For all of Melville's reputed fascination with the undecidability of meaning, he is quite clear here: this is nothing less than a murder. And the murderousness of Stubb's actions only reveal themselves—like the light around a dark silhouette—because of Melville's reflections on the beauty of whales. A living, breathing, fellow being full of "ethereal light," whose great head resembles the most breathtaking works of Michelangelo, has been killed. It is as if Stubb has smashed the dome of St. Peter's.

What is such a loss to Stubb, of course? It's nothing at all. He bears whales no particular ill will (unlike Flask, who considers them "a species of magnified… water rat[s]"), but he does view them as lesser, unequal beings—*animals*, in short—and that hierarchical view of life is precisely what's at stake. Like so many "concentric spiralizations," Stubb's diminishment of the whale gives way to other diminishments: the whale is sliced up and made into food—mere meat for the hungry sailors—and Stubb starts bossing around Fleece, the ship's black cook, as if *he* were subhuman too.[46] While Stubb chews out Fleece, the whale's carcass is consumed by sharks who occasionally miss their intended meal and bite each other, creating a pell-mell of unqualified "horror and diabolism": everyone and everything is cutting, eating, killing, or all three at once. As Ishmael remarks, "were you to turn the whole affair upside down, it would still be pretty much the same thing, that is to say, a shocking sharkish business enough for all parties." These sharks, we learn, are the very creatures that are also the invariable outriders of all slave ships crossing the Atlantic, systematically trotting alongside, to be handy in case a parcel is to be carried anywhere, or a dead slave to be decently buried... If you have never scene that sight, then suspend your decision about the impropriety of devil-worship, and the expediency of conciliating the devil.[47]

Rather than moving on, Melville heightens the horror and intensifies the diabolism. In "The Shark Massacre," Queequeg uses the whaling spade to carry out *more* violence, stabbing the sharks as they bite furiously at the whale and at each other, which sends them into a bloodied frenzy: "They viciously snapped, not only at each other's disembowlments, but like flexible bows, bent round, and bit their own; till those entrails seemed swallowed over and over again by the same mouth, to be oppositely voided by the gaping wound." And in "The Whale as a Dish," Ishmael reflects on the practice of eating a sperm whale's brains. Sometimes "hungry sailors crack open the skull with an axe," remove the "two plump, whitish lobes," doss them in flour, then fry them in a pan. This delicacy, he adds, is quite popular

> among some epicures; and every one knows that some young bucks among the epicures, by continually dining upon calves' brains, by and by get to have a little brains of their own, so as to be able to tell a calf's head from their own heads; which, indeed, requires uncommon discrimination. And that is the reason why a young buck with an intelligent looking calf's head before him, is somehow one of the saddest sights you can see. The head looks a sort of reproachfully at him, with an "Et tu Brute!" expression.

That discussion of meat-eating then segues into a meditation on murder and cannibalism:

> It is not, perhaps, entirely because the whale is so excessively unctuous that landsmen seem to regard the eating of him with abhorrence; that appears to result, in some way, from the consideration before mentioned: *i.e.* that a man should eat a newly murdered thing of the sea, and eat it too by its own light. But no doubt the first man that ever murdered an ox was regarded as a murderer; perhaps he was hung; and if he had been put on his trial by oxen, he certainly would have been; and he certainly deserved it if any murderer does. Go to the meat-market of a Saturday night and see the crowds of live bipeds staring up at the long rows of dead quadrupeds. Does not that sight take a tooth out of the cannibal's jaw? Cannibals? who is not a cannibal? I tell you it will be more tolerable for the Fejee that salted down a lean missionary in his cellar against a coming famine; it will be more tolerable for that provident Fejee, I say, in the day

of judgment, than for thee, civilized and enlightened gourmand, who nailest geese to the ground and feastest on their bloated livers in thy paté-de-foie-gras.

But Stubb, he eats the whale by its own light, does he? and that is adding insult to injury, is it? Look at your knife-handle, there, my civilized and enlightened gourmand dining off that roast beef, what is that handle made of?—what but the bones of the brother of the very ox you are eating? And what do you pick your teeth with, after devouring that fat goose? With a feather of the same fowl. And with what quill did the Secretary of the Society for the Suppression of Cruelty to Ganders formally indite his circulars? It is only within the last month or two that that society passed a resolution to patronize nothing but steel pens.[48]

If "uncommon discrimination" is required to distinguish a cow's head from a human's, that is because they are essentially the same. Melville plays up that sameness, referring to the epicures as "bucks," filling the sentences with ambiguous referents ("their heads," "brains of their own"), and describing meat-eating as indistinguishable from murder. The ambiguity and disgust continue to build until Melville returns to Stubb, whom he turns into a symbol of civilization's appetite for death. Ishmael said before that the whole world is enveloped in whale-lines, and here we see what he means: modernity depends on treating certain types of life as disposable. It is a "meat-market" writ large, a vast system premised on distinguishing persons from non-persons.[49] "Who is not a cannibal" indeed?

The disgust unloosed by this passage is only made possible by the beauty that precedes and follows it. This sequence is bookended by "The Line" (chapter 60) and "The Blanket" (chapter 67), which provide a robust aesthetic and ethical framework for assessing Stubbs's actions. Horror and beauty are entangled for Melville, like the "Indian-summer sunlight" and shrouded "blackness" he saw in Hawthorne's fiction. Such prodigious mixing formed the backbone of Melville's artistic ideal, as he described in his poem "Art": "But form to lend, / pulsed life create, / What unlike things must meet and mate."[50] This mating of "unlike things" is not simply a matter of balancing contradictions. It is a matter of determining how and why we value life. Beauty, as Melville understands it, is the opposite of Stubb's possessive, egocentric view of the world.[51]

This ethical and philosophical investment in beauty grounds Melville's treatment of the white whale. When Moby Dick spouts for a second time, it sends a thrill through Ishmael: "Moby Dick bodily burst into view!" Whereas Ahab hurtles his mortal self at the white whale as if his "heart had been a mortar," Ishmael's heart appears to burst with pleasure when Moby Dick breaches, leaping out of the water and carrying himself "salmon-like to Heaven":

> For not by any calm and indolent spoutings; not by the peaceable gush of that mystic fountain in his head, did the White Whale now reveal his vicinity; but by the far more wondrous phenomenon of breaching. Rising with his utmost

velocity from the furthest depths, the Sperm Whale thus booms his entire bulk into the pure element of air, and piling up a mountain of dazzling foam, shows his place to the distance of seven miles and more. In those moments, the torn, enraged waves he shakes off, seem his mane; in some cases, this breaching is his act of defiance. "There she breaches! there she breaches!" was the cry, as in his immeasurable bravadoes the White Whale tossed himself salmon-like to Heaven. So suddenly seen in the blue plain of the sea, and relieved against the still bluer margin of the sky, the spray that he raised, for the moment, intolerably glittered and glared like a glacier; and stood there gradually fading and fading away from its first sparkling intensity, to the dim mistiness of an advancing shower in a vale.[52]

This is not a whale, but a fellow being reaching up, like Michelangelo's dome, to the divine. And that "sparkling intensity" can be felt—if not entirely understood—in the beauty embodied and unleashed by the whale as it leaps bodily into the sky.

Ahab and the Elements

Ahab can apprehend none of this. When the white whale breaches, Ahab proclaims, "Aye, breach your last to the sun, Moby Dick!... [T]hy hour and thy harpoon are at hand!"[53] The more monomaniacally obsessed Ahab becomes, the more he blinds himself to beauty. *Moby-Dick* may be a book about everything, but one of its primary interests is the tension between Ahab's perspective and what lies outside of it: happiness, friendship, and everything else that beauty makes possible. Melville's book has long been construed as an ominous warning about American civilization plunging itself suicidally into the darkness.[54] Like every warning, though, it is also a missive of hope, a suggestion that the world would be more just, and more beautiful, if only we could destroy the Ahabs within us and grasp nature not as a separate agent to be used or destroyed but as ourselves laterally distributed.

These valences of the novel revolve around Ahab, and Ahab is defined by a contradiction. On the one hand, he sees himself as the ship's "supreme lord and dictator," separate from everyone and everything. As Ahab crows (his egotism sliding his speech into the third person), "Ahab stands alone among the millions of the peopled earth, nor gods nor men his neighbors!"[55] Neighborless, peerless, and unconnected, Ahab embodies what political philosophers call "possessive individualism." C.B. MacPherson, who coined the term, posited that possessive individualism is premised on the notion that an individual is "free inasmuch as he is proprietor of his person and his capacity. The human essence is freedom from dependence on the wills of others, and freedom is a function of possession."[56] Freedom, in other words, derives from one's power over nature and unfettered sovereignty from the will of others: it is hard to imagine a more apt description of Ahab's worldview. Ahab's elaborate fantasy of independence is costumed in a variety of analogies throughout *Moby-Dick*, as Melville compares Ahab to a Roman emperor, an Egyptian pharaoh, a Greek god, a Viking sea-king, a sultan, and a "khan of the plank." The moody captain of the *Pequod* sees his own body as a ruined possession—the "craven mate" of his "unconquerable" soul—and is attached to "little or nothing, out of himself" besides the white whale, which is mostly just a projection of his own diseased imagination.[57]

Moby-Dick casts considerable doubt on Ahab's grandiose self-assessment. Numerous characters make fun of him, every step he takes depends on his whale-bone prosthesis, and he fails at the one task that he has taken to be his life's sole, overriding purpose. The more one reads the novel the more difficult it becomes to say who, or what, Ahab really is. "Is Ahab, Ahab?" is not merely an existential question Ahab asks himself; it is one the novel incessantly poses and variously answers. At different moments in the novel, Ahab is described as a moose, a bear, a sea lion, a mountain, a baby chick, a storm, a wolf, a heron, an anaconda, a river, a tree, a bubble, and a piece of grass: figures drawn from nature and its intricate ecosystems.[58] Melville consistently blends Ahab into the environment in ways that underscore, in Elizabeth Schultz's words, an "irresistible interdependency" between the human and the non-human. As Michael Jonik remarks, "Ahab is not so much the epitome of ego or personhood that he is usually taken to be, but is...contrived through his prosthetic relationships with the inhuman, impersonal, and immaterial."[59] This interdependence, which cuts so sharply against Ahab's self-conception, is an intrinsic feature of Melville's philosophy of nature, as Schultz and Jonik remind us. But it is also an intrinsic feature of Melville's philosophy of beauty. Ahab might be a "heart-stricken moose," but his grief is fueled by his antipathy toward beauty and its ego-shattering effects.[60]

This is why the weather looms so large in the novel. *Moby-Dick* is full of winds, calms, storms, and other meteorological systems. As Eliza Richards points out, "Science of the period had recently come to understand weather as a global system, which meant that what goes around, comes around: what is elsewhere will eventually arrive here, perhaps in altered form." These manifestations of the weather become one of the main ways in which we apprehend Ahab, whose relationship to the world is mediated through his relationship to the elements. Melville is actually quite insistent about this. After the *Pequod* sets sail, Ahab exits his cabin only after they have sailed far enough south to escape the "biting Polar" air and "all its intolerable weather." When Ahab finally appears before the crew in "The Quarter-Deck," he is accompanied by a "fair wind" that propels the *Pequod* "through the water with a vindictive sort of leaping and melancholy rapidity." Ishmael picks up on the connection: "[apparently] nothing but the dead wintry bleakness of the sea had kept him so secluded." Throughout the novel, the boundary between Ahab and the weather thins and dissipates until he and the elements become interfused. As Melville writes, Ahab "was almost continually in the air," and seemed "branded" by "an elemental strife." Sometimes he is "charmed" by the weather, but more frequently he braces himself against it, as though the weather rather than the white whale is the evil force he desperately seeks to destroy.[61]

This connection is underscored in "The Pacific." The chapter begins with Ishmael marveling at everything that is joined together by the Pacific's rolling beauty:

> To any meditative Magian rover, this serene Pacific, once beheld, must ever after be the sea of his adoption. It rolls the midmost waters of the world, the Indian ocean and Atlantic being but its arms. The same waves wash the moles of the new-built Californian towns, but yesterday planted by the recentest race of men, and lave the faded but still gorgeous skirts of Asiatic lands, older than Abraham; while all between float milky-ways of coral isles, and low-lying, endless, unknown Archipelagoes, and impenetrable Japans. Thus this mysterious, divine Pacific zones the world's whole bulk about; makes all coasts one bay to it; seems the tide-beating heart of earth. Lifted by those eternal swells, you needs must own the seductive god, bowing your head to Pan.

Then Melville—as he so often does—offers us a contrast:

> But few thoughts of Pan stirred Ahab's brain, as standing like an iron statue at his accustomed place beside the mizen rigging, with one nostril he unthinkingly snuffed the sugary musk from the Bashee isles (in whose sweet woods mild lovers must be walking), and with the other consciously inhaled the salt breath of the new found sea; that sea in which the hated White Whale must even then be swimming. Launched at length upon these almost final waters, and gliding towards the Japanese cruising-ground, the old man's purpose intensified itself. His firm lips met like the lips of a vice; the Delta of his forehead's veins swelled like overladen brooks; in his very sleep, his ringing cry ran through the vaulted hull, "Stern all! the White Whale spouts thick blood!"[62]

These two passages are strung together through the metaphor of blood. The Pacific is the world's great "tide-beating heart," a vast pulsing sea that flows into everything, while Ahab's blood streams like a river rushing into the "Delta of his forehead" then swelling "like overladen brooks." And what defines the white whale for Ahab, in all of his intensified hatred? It is the creature's "thick blood," which he imagines will "spout" like oil. Even the passage's formal structure partakes in this bloody conceit, with the two paragraphs functioning like an artery and a vein. The first, arterial paragraph is about life, connection, and openness; the second, deoxygenated paragraph is about closure, death, and hatred.

This gorgeous circulation shows Ahab's "queenly" independence to be little more than a fiction. This self-avowed demigod cannot even smell something sweet without feeling threatened. He shuts his lips like a steel trap, then—as if his mouth were a blowhole and he's coming up for air—he spouts a vile oath. Ahab's reaction to sniffing the "sugary musk" makes one wonder: Why does Ahab respond as he does? The answer is not found here but in chapter 41, where Ishmael relays the origins of Ahab's malady.[63] Ishmael says one can only imagine the "inflamed, distracted fury" that overtook the minds of the whale's "more desperate hunters" when, "amid the chips of chewed boats, and the sinking limbs of torn comrades, they swam out of the white curds of the whale's direful wrath into the serene, exasperating sunlight, that smiled on, as if at a birth or a bridal." That view of nature's cruel indifference fuels Ahab's monomania, which did not take "its instant rise at the precise time of his bodily dismemberment," but later on, when Ahab, dismayed and "dismasted," lies in a whaling ship as it wheeled around the world in the middle of a brutal winter. For "long months of days and weeks," Melville writes,

> Ahab and anguish lay stretched together in one hammock, rounding in mid winter that dreary, howling Patagonian Cape; *then* it was, that his torn body and gashed soul bled into one another; and so interfusing, made him mad. That it was only then, on the homeward voyage, after the encounter, that the final monomania seized him, seems all but certain from the fact that, at intervals during the passage, he was a raving lunatic; and, though unlimbed of a leg, yet such vital strength yet lurked in his Egyptian chest, and was moreover intensified by his delirium, that his mates were forced to lace him fast, even there, as he sailed, raving in his hammock. In a strait-jacket, he swung to the mad rockings of the gales. And, when running into more sufferable latitudes, the ship, with mild stun'sails spread, floated across the tranquil tropics, and, to all appearances, the old man's delirium seemed left behind him with the Cape Horn swells, and he came forth from his dark den into the blessed light and air; even then, when he ... issued his calm orders once again; and his mates thanked God the direful madness was now gone; even then, Ahab, in his hidden self, raved on.[64]

Melville provides us with a tragedy within a tragedy. This is an origin story for Ahab's "direful madness," and what sets it into motion is Ahab's toxic, outsized sense of his own sovereignty, which is threatened and reduced by nature several times over—by the whale that takes his leg, the biting cold that freezes his body, and the violent winds that rock the ship, tossing him to and fro as he lies bound and immobilized in a hammock. To put this another way, what drives Ahab's violent fantasies—what he truly hates—is not nature as such but the truth that nature continually conveys: there is no such thing as a discrete, sovereign self.

The only moment in which Ahab opens himself to the world occurs in "The Symphony." This chapter, in which Ahab momentarily suspends his suicidal plan and instructs Starbuck to stay onboard the *Pequod*, is as much about aesthetics as it is about fate. The chapter begins with an extended description of a gorgeous day at sea. The "all-pervading azure" of the sky and the sea appear to be perfectly intermingled, "soft" and "robust" versions of the same lovely "firmaments." Though "contrasting within," Melville writes, "the contrast was only in shades and shadows without; the two seemed one." Playful birds glide through their air, gently lifted by the wind. Swordfish dart through the water. And the horizon itself "throb[s]" with the "soft and tremulous motion" of the waves, reminding Ishmael of the rhythm of sex.[65] Ahab, in spite of his himself, is deeply moved by all of this beauty:

> Tied up and twisted; gnarled and knotted with wrinkles; haggardly firm and unyielding; his eyes glowing like coals, that still glow in the ashes of ruin; untottering Ahab stood forth in the clearness of the morn; lifting his splintered helmet of a brow to the fair girl's forehead of heaven.
>
> Oh, immortal infancy, and innocency of the azure! Invisible winged creatures that frolic all round us! Sweet childhood of air and sky! how oblivious were ye of old Ahab's close-coiled woe! But so have I seen little Miriam and Martha, laughing-eyed elves, heedlessly gambol around their old sire; sporting with the circle of singed locks which grew on the marge of that burnt-out crater of his brain.
>
> Slowly crossing the deck from the scuttle, Ahab leaned over the side and watched how his shadow in the water sank and sank to his gaze, the more and the more that he strove to pierce the profundity. But the lovely aromas in that enchanted air did at last seem to dispel, for a moment, the cankerous thing in his soul. That glad, happy air, that winsome sky, did at last stroke and caress him; the step-mother world, so long cruel—forbidding—now threw affectionate arms round his stubborn neck, and did seem to joyously sob over him, as if over one, that however wilful and erring, she could yet find it in her heart to save and to bless. From beneath his slouched hat Ahab dropped a tear into the sea; nor did all the Pacific contain such wealth as that one wee drop.[66]

To "enchant" is to bewitch and delight.[67] It is one of the primary ways in which beauty is processed, and it moves Ahab, in spite of his long history of making "war on the horrors of the deep." The ecosystem in which he is suddenly immersed is open, flowing, and symphonic—the very opposite of the "tied up and twisted" Ahab, who has sealed himself in a "masoned, walled-town" of self-regard and isolation. (As Leslie E. Sheldon has documented, the chapter echoes *Paradise Lost*, intimating that Ahab's isolation has led to his fall.[68]) Yet after the "sweet childhood of air and sky" clears his mind, another source of beauty—human fellowship—moves Ahab to tears. Ishmael says he has seen Ahab's children "heedlessly gambol around their old sire; sporting with the circle of singed locks" on top of his head, and a similar uncoiling occurs when Ahab looks at Starbuck in the eye, that "magic glass."[69]

"The Symphony" thus illuminates two crucial aspects of beauty. First, it discloses the sheer variety of beauty's forms and sources. Beauty is not a rarefied property felt solely in the mind. The wind itself can strike one with its "sweetness," and so can the play of children, or the glance of a friend. Second, regardless of where it comes from, beauty tends to draw out and dissolve the ego. Even Ahab, this "untottering" czar of the sea and murderer-king of the deep, is moved by it, and it literally chases his shadow away.

What Ahab Cannot See

Ahab may reject nature's enchantments, but *Moby-Dick* offers numerous ways of valuing beauty and our chance encounters with it. The novel is as much a reflection on the beauty of friendship, language, sex, art, water, color, light, and movement as it is a meditation on terror. (Despite the novel's occasional morbidity, it is also quite funny. One of the chapters, "Leg and Arm," is crammed full of jokes that Ahab doesn't get.) Again and again, Melville tries to see the world in the way that whales do: through a kind of double vision that holds multiple "distinct picture[s]" in the mind's eye. And *Moby-Dick*'s dialectical treatment of nature—is it a source of beauty or terror?—functions like the book's central nervous system, threading through every chapter and triggering both pain and pleasure. Whatever hope there is in *Moby-Dick*, whatever sense of possibility the novel holds out for the world to come, derives from cultivating and supporting the non-Ahabian parts of ourselves. Melville might "say'st all of us are Ahabs," but the book also *resists* that charge, and this is why beauty is so important: it tears down the "walled-town[s]" we construct in our minds which often admits "but small entrance to any sympathy from the green country without."[70]

Beauty's power is on conspicuous display in the opening chapters, when Ishmael befriends Queequeg. Who can deny that Queequeg is astonishingly beautiful? Nobody, Ishmael says, could "show a cheek like Queequeg"—an erotic pun if ever there was one—and the beauty of Queequeg's backside (two cheeks separated by an elegant rift) reminds him of the beauty of "the Andes' western slope," which is "barred with various tinges" and perpetually open to the Pacific (whose waves shaped the mountains millennia ago).[71] Ishmael's response is at once sexual, aesthetic, and radically open-ended, linking land to ocean, skin to rock, Nantucket to South America, past to present, and himself to Queequeg. Not only is Queequeg's face exquisitely structured; the manner in which his forehead slopes gracefully away "from ... the brows"—the same S-shape that he notices in a sperm whale's flukes—makes Queequeg, in Ishmael's estimation, look like a more attractive version of George Washington.[72]

Although they hail from "contrasting climes," Ishmael and Queequeg become inseparable, and their relationship is like the threads of a beautiful quilt:

> Upon waking next morning about daylight, I found Queequeg's arm thrown over me in the most loving and affectionate manner. You had almost thought I had been his wife. The counterpane was of patchwork, full of odd little parti-coloured squares and triangles; and this arm of his tattooed all over with an interminable Cretan labyrinth of a figure, no two parts of which were of one precise shade—owing I suppose to his keeping his arm at sea unmethodically in sun and shade, his shirt sleeves irregularly rolled up at various times—this same arm of his, I say, looked for all the world like a strip of that same patchwork quilt. Indeed, partly lying on it as the arm did when I first awoke, I could hardly tell it from the quilt, they so blended their hues together; and it was only by the sense of weight and pressure that I could tell that Queequeg was hugging me.

As Christopher Looby notes, this passage intermingles "the categories of erotics and aesthetics into such intimate proximity that they can scarcely be told apart," as though Melville were drawing upon the corporeal origins of *Aisthesis* (which in ancient Greece connoted "knowledge through sensation").[73] To convey that sense of felt knowledge, Melville mixes seemingly disparate patterns, bodies, and sensations—intricate tattoos, multicolored "squares and triangles," night and day ("the next morning *about* daylight"), warmth and pressure—until their interdependence, or quiltedness (so to speak), becomes manifest. As Queequeg, Ishmael, and the world around them blend together, we find once again that the principle of separate selfhood—the principle embodied by Captain Ahab—cannot hold.

In that regard, the scene shades into the novel's other efforts to define Queequeg through Ahab, and vice versa. Throughout *Moby-Dick*, Ishmael compares Ahab to Queequeg, contrasting their actions, motivations, relationships, bodies, and uses of language. Their respective deaths (or in Queequeg's case, near-death) are especially telling. When Ahab dies, he is angry, lonely, and desperate to deal a fatal blow to nature. In his final act, he hurls a harpoon baptized in the blood of his "heathen" harpooners at the "damned whale," only to be snagged by the whale-line and shot into the sea. When Queequeg falls ill, not only is he surrounded by the crew and celebrated by Pip ("Let's make a General of him!" he exclaims); Queequeg spends what he assumes are his final moments using his harpoon to carve a beautiful canoe that will ferry him "out to the sea and floated away to the starry archipelagoes; for not only do they believe that the stars are isles, but that far beyond all visible horizons, their own mild, uncontinented seas, interflow with the blue heavens; and so form the white breakers of the milky way."

As if *that* weren't explicit enough, Melville adds (harkening back to chapter 41) that Queequeg "shuddered at the thought of being buried in his hammock, according to the usual sea-custom, tossed like something vile." Unlike Ahab (this really is quite on the nose), Queequeg "desired a canoe... that involved... uncertain steering, and much lee-way"—unlike, say, a track laid "with iron rails"—"adown the dim ages."[74]

Queequeg reveals the link between beauty and social bonds, vivifying the egoless pleasure sparked by love between equals. As Peter Coviello argues, Ishmael and Queequeg's relationship presents an "alternative to Ahab's destructive and terror-forged" worldview, and that alternative is clarified by Ishmael's previous isolation.[75] Before they met, Ishmael was contemplating suicide and weighed down by the "damp, drizzly November" in his soul; after they become "bosom friends," he feels awakened by "the sudden flame of friendship." Of course, this is also a book dedicated by one passionate friend to another, with the title page emblazoned with the words "To NATHANIEL HAWTHORNE," whom Melville loved for dropping "germinous seeds into [his] soul."[76] As he declared in a letter to Hawthorne, in true friendship there is no such thing as a sovereign self, no separate identity:

> Whence come you, Hawthorne? By what right do you drink from the flagon of my life? And when I put it to my lips—lo, they are yours and not mine. I feel that the Godhead is broken up like the bread at the Supper, and that we are the pieces. Hence this infinite fraternity of feeling.[77]

A friend takes one into the infinite, or, as Melville puts it, allows one to feel divinity "broken up" and consumed like communion. It is not a coincidence that the ecstatic joy of "A Squeeze of the Hand" involves a similar sociality, a co-working and co-feeling that yields a pleasing release: "I squeezed that sperm till I myself almost melted into it... and I found myself unwittingly squeezing my co-laborers' hands in it, mistaking their hands for the gentle globules."[78]

Even the parts of *Moby-Dick* that appear to be most skeptical about collectivity make a similar point. At the end of chapter 35 ("The Mast-Head"), Ishmael sits atop the masthead and recalls the story of a "young Platonist" who was "lulled... by the blending cadence of waves with thoughts" until he lost his identity:

> he takes the mystic ocean at his feet for the visible image of that deep, blue, bottomless soul, pervading mankind and nature; and every strange, half-seen, gliding, beautiful thing that eludes him; every dimly-discovered, uprising fin of some undiscernible form, seems to him the embodiment of those elusive thoughts that only people the soul by continually flitting through it. In this enchanted mood, thy spirit ebbs away to whence it came; becomes diffused

through time and space; like Cranmer's sprinkled Pantheistic ashes, forming at last a part of every shore the round globe over.

There is no life in thee, now, except that rocking life imparted by a gently rolling ship; by her, borrowed from the sea; by the sea, from the inscrutable tides of God. But while this sleep, this dream is on ye, move your foot or hand an inch; slip your hold at all; and your identity comes back in horror. Over Descartian vortices you hover.[79]

Melville seems to be offering a warning. As Richard Hardack observes, "Universal feelings and 'sociality' in nature are revealed as ephemeral, and each temporary felicity is inverted."[80] To be "diffused" is to be undone—to become ashes spread across the earth—and Melville says this selfless state is but a "dream." Nonetheless, the heart and soul of this warning has to do with the philosophical delusion of being disconnected from the world. Plato's *Phaedo*, which the "sunken-eyed young Platonist" has been reading, posits that the soul is separate from the body and independent of the material world, while René Descartes argues that we are immersed in a vast material substratum, an intricate and perhaps endless series of "large circling bands of material particles."[81] Melville's point is not that the loss of identity is an illusion but that identity is not an independent, spiritualized experience in the first place. Indeed if the world is composed of infinite rings of matter, then everyone and everything is literally connected on a microscopic level, and beauty allows us to sense those connections.

Beauty, of course, is notoriously unpredictable. Since you never know who or what will strike you as beautiful, encounters with beauty are indelible illustrations of the power of chance. This is one of the primary reasons why Ahab guards himself against beauty: his entire worldview is premised on fate. As Maurice Lee has demonstrated, *Moby-Dick* is a meditation on the role of accidents in earthly affairs. A great deal of the novel, from Ishmael's chance encounter with Queequeg to Ahab's chance encounter with the white whale, grew out of Melville's passionate interest in Pyrrhic skepticism, a philosophical tradition from ancient Greece that stressed the need to suspend judgment, particularly when it came to questions of causation.[82] As Ishmael remarks in chapter 72 ("The Monkey-Rope"), when he and Queequeg are literally tied together and on the edge between life and death, "my own individuality was now merged in a joint stock company of two," but this "interregnum in Providence" is the "precise situation of every mortal that breathes." In many respects, *Moby-Dick* is but "The Monkey-Rope" writ large: Melville spreads out this "interregnum in Providence" to show how entangled we are with a multitude of other lives, and this is the secret of Ahab's insanity. As Lee puts it, "Melville's topmost heresy does not only concern the mystery of iniquity. It also involves the almost unthinkable possibility that providence does not exist and that Ahab's insistent denial of chance is the maddest madness of all."[83]

When you are stunned by something and suddenly made aware of your interdependence, how do you respond? One can either embrace or refuse that experience, and *Moby-Dick* suggests that this decision is freighted with ethical consequences. This link between ethics and aesthetics frames the entire novel, but it plays an especially prominent role in chapter 47 ("The Mat-Maker"), in which Queequeg and Ishmael work together to create a sword-mat. At first, in the quiet act of looping the thread, it seems as though "each silent sailor... resolved into his own invisible self," but as they "pass and repass" the yarns between them, something far more selfless and cosmic comes into view:

> [I]t seemed as if this were the Loom of Time, and I myself were a shuttle mechanically weaving and weaving away at the Fates. There lay the fixed threads of the warp subject to but one single, ever returning, unchanging vibration, and that vibration merely enough to admit of the crosswise interblending of other threads with its own. This warp seemed necessity; and here, thought I, with my own hand I ply my own shuttle and weave my own destiny into these unalterable threads. Meantime, Queequeg's impulsive, indifferent sword, sometimes hitting the woof slantingly, or crookedly, or strongly, or weakly, as the case might be; and by this difference in the concluding blow producing a corresponding contrast in the final aspect of the completed fabric; this savage's sword, thought I, which thus finally shapes and fashions both warp and woof; this easy, indifferent sword must be chance—aye, chance, free will, and necessity—nowise incompatible—all interweavingly working together. The straight warp of necessity, not to be swerved from its ultimate course—its every alternating vibration, indeed, only tending to that; free will still free to ply her shuttle between given threads; and chance, though restrained in its play within the right lines of necessity, and sideways in its motions directed by free will, though thus prescribed to by both, chance by turns rules either, and has the last featuring blow at events.[84]

Scholars have construed this passage in different ways, reading it, for example, as an expression of Melville's "mysticism," or as a meditation on "the mind's ability to forge symbolic correspondences." But they have tended to agree that this passage is central to the novel's meaning.[85] There are ample reasons why: it synthesizes Ishmael's philosophy, provides a potent alternative to Ahab's vision of fate, and sets up the first lowering. But the passage is as much about aesthetics as it is about philosophy. Involving hundreds of overlapping threads trellised around a single rope and jointly constructed simultaneously by Ishmael (who "warps" with his needle) and Queequeg (who "woofs" with his sword), this swordmat is as intricately patterned as the surface of a sperm whale's skin. The lesson it imparts is a lesson about beauty as well as chance, suggesting that Pyrrhic skepticism has aesthetic consequences. If chance "has the last featuring blow," then beauty is equally causeless and inexorable. Whether we accept or deny it, whether we open ourselves to it or shut it out "like the lips of a vise," beauty is woven into the fabric of our world, "crosswise interblending" with our very being.

Woven Beauty

The intricate threading we encounter in "The Mat-Maker" is built into *Moby-Dick* from start to finish. The novel repeatedly apprehends beauty by focusing on lineated forms. The idea that beauty is essentially braided, like hair, quilts, or poetry, recurs again and again. "Etymology" and "Extracts" are laced together, inviting us to consider how one thread—a word, a quotation, or an entire language—loops into another. Whales, we learn, are "sinewy"—that is, full of fibrous cords (of muscle, nerves, and tissues) tightly bound together. And what does Ahab say right before he dies? "What breaks in me? Some sinew cracks!" (Ahab is also haunted by "all that cracks and sinews and cakes the brain," which he thinks the white whale embodies: "I see in him outrageous strength, with an inscrutable malice sinewing it"). Then there are the chapters themselves, which blend the act of writing with the act of weaving ("I shall...weave round them tragic graces") and are interwoven like the threads of a sword-mat, crossing over and under one another to construct a single, patterned whole. Or perhaps the chapters are "densely bedded 'sheaves'": literally, grooved wheels that hold ropes (or lines).[86] *Moby-Dick* may be a book about causality—a novel about why things do or do not happen—but Melville approaches such philosophical questions immanently, assessing meaning and beauty alike by foregrounding *how* they are constructed.

"There is an aesthetics in all things," Melville writes in "The Line," a chapter about the endlessly lineated nature of the world.[87] Three chapters in particular are woven together like a verbal quilt: "The Tail," "The Bower," and "The Gilder." "The Tail," of course, contains Melville's praise of the sperm whale's flukes, and that praise centers on beauty's threaded forms. The entire tail, he says, "seems a dense webbed bed of welded sinews" composed of "three distinct strata": "The fibres in the upper and lower layers, are long and horizontal; those of the middle one, very short, and running crosswise between the outside layers." Not only does this "triune structure" provide the tail with much of its power. "To the student of old Roman walls, the middle layer will furnish a curious parallel to the thin course of tiles always alternating with the stone in those wonderful relics of the antique, and which undoubtedly contribute so much to the great strength of the masonry."

As these fibrous threads run "crosswise," they spread outward, manifesting in everything from ancient walls to naked bodies, paintings, and gods:

> But as if this vast local power in the tendinous tail were not enough, the whole bulk of the leviathan is knit over with a warp and woof of muscular fibres and

filaments, which passing on either side the loins and running down into the flukes, insensibly blend with them, and largely contribute to their might; so that in the tail the confluent measureless force of the whole whale seems concentrated to a point. Could annihilation occur to matter, this were the thing to do it. Nor does this—its amazing strength, at all tend to cripple the graceful flexion of its motions; where infantileness of ease undulates through a Titanism of power. On the contrary, those motions derive their most appalling beauty from it. Real strength never impairs beauty or harmony, but it often bestows it; and in everything imposingly beautiful, strength has much to do with the magic. Take away the tied tendons that all over seem bursting from the marble in the carved Hercules, and its charm would be gone. As devout Eckerman lifted the linen sheet from the naked corpse of Goethe, he was overwhelmed with the massive chest of the man, that seemed as a Roman triumphal arch. When Angelo paints even God the Father in human form, mark what robustness is there. And whatever they may reveal of the divine love in the Son, the soft, curled, hermaphroditical Italian pictures, in which his idea has been most successfully embodied; these pictures, so destitute as they are of all brawniness, hint nothing of any power, but the mere negative, feminine one of submission and endurance, which on all hands it is conceded, form the peculiar practical virtues of his teachings. Such is the subtle elasticity of the organ I treat of, that whether wielded in sport, or in earnest, or in anger, whatever be the mood it be in, its flexions are invariably marked by exceeding grace. Therein no fairy's arm can transcend it.[88]

This is a meditation on a tail, of course. But it is also a rich, wide-ranging reflection on beauty more generally. What accounts for the ways in which we are pulled—as if by some quiet, irresistible force—toward a picture, a line, or a body, then toward other beautiful forms that seem to be utterly distinct yet uncannily familiar? Perhaps it is their "subtle elasticity": the ability of something statuesque to *move*, or to possess surprising strength or subtlety. Perhaps it is the way they mix and mingle types of pleasure, "running crosswise" between sight, sound, and feeling in ways that transform our sense of who, what, and where we are. Beauty appears to have less to do with fixed categories, such as "masculine" and "feminine" or "strength" and "harmony," than with the prodigious redrawing of those categories, "most successfully embodied" in Michelangelo's "hermaphroditical... pictures." Whatever the source of its power may be, beauty consists in an artful sinewing that rethreads the self into the broader world.

A similar glimpse of beauty occurs in "A Bower in the Arsicades." The chapter revolves around a fictional visit to the Solomon Islands, where a local king displayed the skeleton of a great sperm whale that had beached many years ago. Above everyone's heads the

> ribs were hung with trophies; the vertebræ were carved with Arsacidean annals, in strange hieroglyphics; in the skull, the priests kept up an unextinguished

aromatic flame, so that the mystic head again sent forth its vapory spout; while, suspended from a bough, the terrific lower jaw vibrated over all the devotees, like the hair-hung sword that so affrighted Damocles.

It was, Ishmael says, "a wondrous sight":

> The wood was green as mosses of the Icy Glen; the trees stood high and haughty, feeling their living sap; the industrious earth beneath was as a weaver's loom, with a gorgeous carpet on it, whereof the ground-vine tendrils formed the warp and woof, and the living flowers the figures. All the trees, with all their laden branches; all the shrubs, and ferns, and grasses; the message-carrying air; all these unceasingly were active.

That beauty leads to the chapter's central conceit:

> Through the lacings of the leaves, the great sun seemed a flying shuttle weaving the unwearied verdure. Oh, busy weaver! unseen weaver!—pause!—one word!—whither flows the fabric? what palace may it deck? wherefore all these ceaseless toilings? Speak, weaver!—stay thy hand!—but one single word with thee! Nay—the shuttle flies—the figures float from forth the loom; the freshet-rushing carpet for ever slides away. The weaver-god, he weaves; and by that weaving is he deafened, that he hears no mortal voice; and by that humming, we, too, who look on the loom are deafened; and only when we escape it shall we hear the thousand voices that speak through it. For even so it is in all material factories. The spoken words that are inaudible among the flying spindles; those same words are plainly heard without the walls, bursting from the opened casements. Thereby have villainies been detected. Ah, mortal! then, be heedful; for so, in all this din of the great world's loom, thy subtlest thinkings may be overheard afar. Now, amid the green, life-restless loom of that Arsacidean wood, the great, white, worshipped skeleton lay lounging—a gigantic idler! Yet, as the ever-woven verdant warp and woof intermixed and hummed around him, the mighty idler seemed the cunning weaver; himself all woven over with the vines; every month assuming greener, fresher verdure; but himself a skeleton. Life folded Death; Death trellised Life; the grim god wived with youthful Life, and begat him curly-headed glories.[89]

Ishmael, notes Illana Pardes, is assuming "Jonah's mantle once again, promising an even more penetrating representation of the 'interior structural features' of the whale."[90] The bones become vegetation, and vice versa, while fire, water, and air mix in the priests' "unextinguished aromatic flame," which enables the "vapory spout" of this long-dead whale to continue unabated. Hieroglyphs are inscribed in the bones, turning the skeleton into a kind of Rosetta Stone; the South Pacific blends into South Massachusetts ("Icy Glen"); and sights give way to sounds (spindles that "hum" and words that "burst"). It is as if the entire passage were a bough wrapped around with vine-line growths. Some of these growths are disturbing. If the universe was in fact created by a "weaver-god" who is "deafened" by his own loom, then no one can hear our prayers. The purpose of latticework, however, is to build and support, and Melville's sprouted lines all climb toward a conclusion: this dead whale, "all woven over with...vines," is a symbol of the "warp and woof" of existence. That is what this passage is ultimately about: the beautiful manner in which life and death are folded together—or to follow Ishmael's metaphor, *wedded* in ways that beget beauty and all of its "curly-headed glories." For all of *Moby-Dick*'s fascination with doom and darkness, it is hard to call passages such as this anything other than an embrace of existence, one that is neither foolhardy nor naive because it both recognizes and accepts the ways in which death trellises life, endowing it with structure, sense, and meaning.

That vision of ceaseless, interdependent growth finds its Ahabian dissent in "The Gilder," the third piece in Melville's triptych. "The Gilder" begins with yet another luxuriant ekphrasis of the weather at sea. After the *Pequod* has endured yet another storm, the swells subside, the winds die down, and the sun breaks out from behind the clouds. "At such times," Ishmael remarks, a sailor "seated in his boat, light as a bird canoe" and "floating upon a smooth sea," feels as though he is "sociably mixing with the soft waves themselves, that like hearth-stone cats... purr against the gunwale." Ahab, of course, *hates* these moments of "dreamy quietude" because they force him to behold "the tranquil beauty and brilliancy of the ocean." He steels himself against communal feeling, and the death-bound terms of his refusal recall "The Tail" and "A Bower," setting into relief their embrace of life. These "blessed calms," he declares, cannot last because the

> threads of life are woven by warp and woof: calms crossed by storms, a storm for every calm. There is no steady unretracing progress in this life; we do not advance through fixed gradations, and at the last one pause:—through infancy's unconscious spell, boyhood's thoughtless faith, adolescence's doubt (the common doom), then scepticism, then disbelief, resting at last in manhood's pondering repose of If. But once gone through, we trace the round again; and are infants, boys, and men, and Ifs eternally. Where lies the final harbor, whence we unmoor no more? In what rapt ether sails the world, of which the weariest will never weary? Where is the foundling's father hidden? Our souls are like those orphans whose unwedded mothers die in bearing them: the secret of our paternity lies in their grave, and we must there to learn it.[91]

This, too, is a storm, a squall that ensues after Ishmael's philosophical calm. For Ahab, life's warp and woof lead not to regrowth but to more death and decay. There is a loss at the origin of everything, Ahab suggests, and what are we but orphaned souls hopelessly searching for some sense of connection? Ahab's moroseness derives from his inability to reckon with chance: he simply cannot accept that calms and storms, in all their various forms, "cross" each other without end. But it also derives from his aversion to and rejection of beauty. To deny beauty is to deny life itself, and that is exactly what Ahab pledges to do by immolating himself in a "fiery hunt."

In that regard, *Moby-Dick* provides an expansive view of beauty's "mingled" and "mingling" qualities. The term Melville uses, "net-work," comes from sailing and the arts (the two realms where he felt most at home). "Net-work" originally referred to anything that was "like a net," but by Melville's time it also referred to a variety of other woven objects and thread-like forms. *Moby-Dick* extends this loose sense of "net-work" to discern the "patterns of interconnection and exchange" that define and organize beauty.[92] For Melville, beauty is found in networks far and wide, from art and language to friendship and weather systems. Beauty is not a set of features but a "co-operation of pleasures" that is co-extensive with life itself.[93]

Ishmael's reflections on this score lead him to a significant insight. Whales, he says, are not the only animals that spout:

> in any creature breathing is only a function indispensable to vitality, inasmuch as it withdraws from the air a certain element, which being subsequently brought into contact with the blood imparts to the blood its vivifying principle... [I]t follows that if all the blood in a man could be aerated with one breath, he might then seal up his nostrils and not fetch another for a considerable time.

This strange state of breathless life, Ishmael adds, is

> the case with the whale, who systematically lives, by intervals, his full hour and more (when at the bottom) without drawing a single breath, or so much as in any way inhaling a particle of air; for, remember, he has no gills. How is this? Between his ribs and on each side of his spine he is supplied with a remarkable involved Cretan labyrinth of vermicelli-like vessels, which vessels, when he quits the surface, are completely distended with oxygenated blood. So that for an hour or more, a thousand fathoms in the sea, he carries a surplus stock of vitality in him, just as the camel crossing the waterless desert carries a surplus supply of drink for future use in its four supplementary stomachs. The anatomical fact of this labyrinth is indisputable; and that the supposition founded upon it is reasonable and true, seems the more cogent to me, when I consider the otherwise inexplicable obstinacy of that leviathan in *having his spoutings out*, as the fishermen phrase it.[94]

Moby-Dick tends to do the same thing, plunging down to sunless depths on a breathless hunt only to rise up and have its spoutings out. That is the warp and woof the book, a whale-like movement between diving and breathing. Depending on one's mood, and what one wishes to get out of the novel, it is possible to follow Melville into the deep, where there is enough darkness and horror to drown the infinite of your soul. But *Moby-Dick* also breaches. And when it does, it is as if the whole terraqueous world has been tossed "salmon-like to Heaven." For all of its brooding about orphaned souls and nameless terrors, *Moby-Dick* is a life-affirming work of art, and that affirmation proceeds from and centers on its recognition of beauty.

Postscript
A Note on Method

An explanation is in order. This book is full of weeds, flowers, whales, tails, statues, and landscapes. It emphasizes texts such as *Timoleon* and *Weeds and Wildings*, which are relatively unbeloved even among Melvilleans. And it provides neither a chronological account of Melville's career nor a detailed cultural history of his writings. One might reasonably ask, Why did the book proceed in this manner?

There is a short answer and a long answer. The short answer: this book takes its methodological bearings from American Pragmatism and tries to interpret literature by prioritizing its effects, focusing on the aesthetic experiences elicited by Melville's writings. From beginning to end, I have been inspired by what William James dubbed "the pragmatist method," which involves construing "each notion by tracing its respective practical consequences."[1] The belief that literature, as W.H. Auden opined, "makes nothing happen," is simply untrue.[2] Literature inspires an astounding array of feelings, sensations, and ideas, many of which are quite intense and impactful. That makes it necessary to discover precisely what a piece of writing does. To be useful and accurate, criticism must concentrate not on *a priori* beliefs (whether the author's or the critic's) but on the distinct cluster of impressions produced by a work of literature. That is what I have attempted to do by reconstructing the philosophico-aesthetic experiences engendered by Melville's writings, and by exploring the meaning of those experiences.

In that regard, *Melville, Beauty, and American Literary Studies* responds to a pressing debate about the uses of literature and the purpose of literary criticism. For a rather long time now, literary studies has been defined by two paradoxical trends. On the one hand, the field has flowered methodologically, yielding a lively and eclectic range of interpretive approaches. These approaches run the gamut from new materialism to ecocriticism, historical poetics, animal studies, and methods variously inspired by feminism, Marxism, critical race theory, queer theory, and ethnic studies. There is probably no moment in the history of the field in which scholars have had a more diverse array of critical methods at their disposal. At the same time, nearly all of these approaches share a set of core assumptions. Instability, for example, is often valued as an end in itself, and unity—whether of time, space, genre, language, meaning, or identity—is often viewed with profound suspicion. As Hester Blum points out, all of the recent "shifts in the field, at once ideological, methodological, and dedicated to canon formation, are... invested in recognizing the artificiality and intellectual limitations of certain kinds of boundaries (whether national, political, linguistic, physiological, or temporal) in studying forms of literary and cultural influence and circulation."[3]

These different methods also tend to presume that literature is best understood as a cultural "text," the meaning of which is invariably tied to its context. That context is framed in a multitude of ways—as a story about the development of print culture, for example, or the evolution of ideas about gender—but the value of literature (and, thus, the purpose of literary studies) is often pitched in terms of sociological illumination. In other words, literature is broadly understood to be significant to the extent that it yields knowledge about the history of a given society. According to Joseph North, this implicit consensus can be traced back to the paradigm shift that occurred in the 1980s, after which most literary scholars have presumed "that, for academic purposes, works of literature are chiefly of interest as diagnostic instruments for determining the state of the cultures in which they were written and read."[4] Scholars' enduring investment in that diagnostic mode can be seen by glancing at the titles of recent monographs: *Reading for Reform: The Social Work of Literature in the Progressive Era*; *Reading Testimony, Witnessing Trauma: Confronting Race, Gender, and Violence in American Literature*; *Infrastructures of Apocalypse: American Literature and the Nuclear Complex*; *Black Queer Flesh: Rejecting Subjectivity in the African American Novel*; *Archives of Labor: Working-Class Women and Literary Culture in the Antebellum United States*.[5]

Most of this scholarship is deeply researched and finely executed. Numerous scholars, however, have expressed concerns about the field's methodological presuppositions. Stephen Best and Sharon Marcus contend that many of the ways in which contemporary critics read literature misrecognize the structure of literary works by assuming that the most important parts of a text are inevitably "hidden" or "repressed."[6] Bruno Latour posits that humanities scholarship has become increasingly redundant—indeed, it "has run out of steam"—because it is overinvested in disenchanting the world. According to Latour, most criticism amounts to an elaborate act of undeception, the point of which is to show how a certain history, system, or power structure subtly influences something that initially appears (erroneously, it turns out) to be independent or unique:

> Do you see... why it feels so good to be a critical mind? Why critique, this most ambiguous pharmakon, has become such a potent euphoric drug? You are always right! When naïve believers are clinging forcefully to their objects, claiming that they are made to do things because of their gods, their poetry, their cherished objects, you can turn all of those attachments into so many fetishes and humiliate all the believers by showing that it is nothing but their own projection, that you, and you alone, can see.[7]

Rita Felski has provided a thoughtful and thorough reconsideration of these methods. In a series of books and articles, including *The Limits of Critique* (2015) and *Critique and Postcritique* (2017), Felski has called for scholars to move beyond the "hermeneutics of suspicion" and develop new, alternative methods that prioritize "inspiration, invention, solace, recognition, reparation, or passion."[8] According to Felski, the notion that literature is defined by what it obscures—indeed, that its meaning can be fully understood only by a scholar who reads literature against the grain, applying the proper context or ideological lens—is so ubiquitous that it has become the discipline's operative mood. "Critique" is therefore not a method as much as a "sensibility" that informs and inflects the entire field of literary studies, in all of its methodological diversity. This groupthink, Felski argues, limits scholarship and pedagogy alike by undermining our ability to understand works of literature as works of art, and by making literary criticism quite dreary and depressing to read, since so much of it is characterized by the "kudzu-like proliferation of a hypercritical style of analysis that has crowded out alternative forms of intellectual life."[9]

Other problems abound. The "historicist/contextualist paradigm,"[10] as Joseph North calls it, depends on a philosophically dubious theory of experience. It is only possible to view literature as something that is determined by its preconditions—rather than by what it actually does—if one views experience itself as essentially mimetic. Richard Rorty argues that this is why most problems in philosophy are not capable of being solved: they mistakenly imply a strict dichotomy between the world and our perception of it. Most contemporary thought, Rorty contends, hinges on "the notion that human activity (and inquiry, the search for knowledge, in particular) takes place within a framework which can be isolated prior to the conclusion of inquiry—a set of presuppositions discoverable *a priori*."[11]

There is also the issue of evidence. If literature's value resides in the cultural or sociological knowledge that it yields, it is difficult to say why literature should be studied at all. Literary works, because they are so complex and polysemantic, tend to provide weak or ambiguous evidentiary support for broad cultural trends and historical patterns. Interpretations that heed Fredric Jameson's call to "Always historicize!"[12] are oftentimes almost impossible to verify. To cite one recent example: the language of *Moby-Dick* sometimes seems to echo the language of mid-nineteenth-century political Nativism, but it is very hard to discern whether this relationship is causal or coincidental.[13] Few if any answers can be found in Melville scholarship. As far as we know, Melville never borrowed, owned, or mentioned Nativist texts such as *Foreign Conspiracy against the Liberties of the United States* (1835) and *The Crisis! An Appeal to Our Countrymen on the Subject of Foreign Influence in the United States* (1844). And yet, as Kellen Bolt has compellingly argued, the attitudes, ideas, and sentiments of mid-century Nativism seem to play a major role in the novel, as "Melville casts xenophobia as an anti-American principle."[14] Is this happenstance, or is it part of the novel's design? There is no way to know for sure, and the field is full of questions that are similarly unanswerable, guaranteeing that any interpretive claim is tenuous at best.

The rapid proliferation of digital databases and online sources has compounded this problem. There is now an endless assortment of texts almost instantly available at one's fingertips. This vast expansion of the archive has been an unprecedented boon for teaching and scholarship, since it radically expands the range and type of texts that can be read, taught, and analyzed. Nonetheless, students and scholars alike are now swimming in a shoreless ocean of words and images, and this "textual superabundance" makes it very challenging (if not downright impossible) to conclude whether a claim is based on chance, evidence, or some unknowable combination thereof. Maurice Lee aptly summarizes this conundrum:

> Texts under theory became contingent and porous; multiculturalism opened the canon; and the New Historicism made any cultural discourse fair game for critical use. Interdisciplinarity further multiplied domains of possible evidence, as did the weakening of nation and period as bounding paradigms. Now the rise of digital archive has made an unimaginable quantity of evidence not only available but also searchable.... [Yet] claims about evidentiary relationships between texts are [increasingly] hard to falsify amid intertextual promiscuity, a dynamic that becomes increasingly irresistible as search engines make connections easier to claim.... [Indeed,] since the decline of formalism in the mid-twentieth century, major developments in literary theory and digital technology have moved in the direction of intertextuality, superabundance, and unfalsifiability.[15]

As a result, literary studies has morphed into mode of cultural diagnosis at the same time that it has become increasingly unverifiable.

I say all of this as someone who has both learned from and contributed to this type of diagnostic scholarship. My first book, *Nineteenth-Century American Literature and the Long Civil War* (2015), examined the ways in which writers such as Walt Whitman, Herman Melville, Frederick Douglass, and Emily Dickinson wrote about the Civil War for decades after 1865, depicting the war as a "transbellum" struggle. My next book, *Not Even Past: The Stories We Keep Telling about the Civil War* (2020), chronicled how and why American memories of the Civil War have gravitated toward particular narratives, such as the Family Tragedy and the Lost Cause.[16] While writing those books, I discovered that literature was an enticing and maddeningly elusive subject for cultural analysis. It is fairly easy to track the social and political influence of *Gone with the Wind*; it is nearly impossible to do the same for Sidney Lanier's *Tiger Lilies* or Nathaniel

Hawthorne's "Chiefly about War-Matters." As I continued to dive into the history of Civil War writing, I encountered a multitude of stories that were neither "hegemonic" nor "counter-hegemonic," and many texts that eschewed the Civil War altogether in creative and unexpected ways. It also became abundantly clear that this literature contained an array of aesthetic qualities that had no relationship to the politics of the Civil War. That is one of the main reasons I turned to Melville: to better understand the dynamic relationship between aesthetics, literature, and history, particularly when it comes to matters of beauty.

In that respect, this book joins a growing chorus of critics who have developed alternatives to the diagnostic method. Scholars such as Branka Arsić, Christopher Hanlon, Toril Moi, Jed Deppman, Michael Jonik, and Dominic Mastroianni have demonstrated the value of retracing the copious and circuitous ways in which literature "thinks," producing distinct patterns of philosophical thought and expression.[17] Caroline Levine, Benjamin Morgan, Cristanne Miller, and Samuel Otter, among others, have explored the astounding breadth and power of form, which shapes experience—both in and out of literary works—through particular "arrangement[s] of elements."[18] Other scholars have forged new paths by examining literature's spiritual and temporal dimensions, and by revealing the connections between art, literature, and sexuality.[19] These approaches go by different names and focus on different bodies of writing, but they are all, in effect, Pragmatist approaches to literature and the endeavor of literary criticism. I do not mean to suggest that they are, as Steven Knapp and Walter Benn Michaels implored in the 1980s, "Against Theory."[20] Rather, this scholarship *proceeds* Pragmatically, focusing on the affective, aesthetic, and intellectual dimensions of literature, then moves backwards to explain how it works.

We know that Pragmatism co-evolved with modern American literature, influencing everything from nineteenth-century writers' understanding of fate and free will to twentieth-century poets' uses of linguistic skepticism.[21] Yet very little attention has been paid to Pragmatism's aesthetic implications, particularly in regards to literature. As Christopher Looby and Cindy Weinstein point out, "It is curious that, even among scholars who are once again entertaining the possibility of examining the aesthetic dimension of art and experience,... there has been so little reference made to American pragmatism, which might very well provide valuable theoretical resources for a rematerialized aesthetic criticism."[22] Indeed, Pragmatism provides a robust methodological alternative, one that prioritizes experience, resists axiomatic interpretation, and emphasizes verifiability.

John Dewey's *Art as Experience* (1934) is a particularly rich resource for thinking about literature and aesthetics from a Pragmatist perspective. Although it has garnered little attention from literary scholars, *Art as Experience* provides a trenchant analysis of art, aesthetics, and the function of criticism. For Dewey, literature and art are significant not because of their discursive distinctness but because they are intimately tied to the panoply of aesthetic experiences that characterize everyday life. The world brims with aesthetic forms and sensations, and "in order to understand the aesthetic...one must begin with it in the raw; in the events that hold the attentive eye and ear": "the sights that hold the crowd—the fire-engine rushing by; the machines excavating enormous holes in the earth." The meaning of art, Dewey avers, is not contained between the walls of museums or the shelves of libraries; it is in "the tense grace of the ball-player... [and] the onlooking crowd," the "housewife...tending her plants," and "the zest of the spectator in poking the wood burning on the earth and in watching and darting flames and crumbling coals."[23] Literature and art grow directly out of these experiences and render them in altered form, often in ways that intensify the act of perception itself.

For Dewey, there is a crucial difference between the artistic object and aesthetic experience, and most of the failures of criticism are attributable to intellectuals' refusal to grasp that distinction. "When artistic objects," Dewey writes, are considered separate from the way they are experienced, "a wall is built around them that renders almost opaque their general significance.... Art is remitted to a separate realm, where it is cut off from that association with the materials and aims of every other form of human effort, undergoing, and achievement."[24] Dewey's book is a concerted attempt to recover these quotidian modes of aesthetic experience and reframe criticism as an endeavor grounded in the realities of everyday life. That effort involves viewing art as something that is rooted neither in a Cartesian model of reason nor in a Kantian theory of the imagination, but in biology itself. Bodies tend to experience the world aesthetically through the direct feedback of the senses, and through the flux of embodied consciousness. As Dewey writes,

> These biological commonplaces are something more than that; they reach to the roots of the aesthetic in experience. The world is full of things that are indifferent and even hostile to life; the very processes by which life is maintained tend to throw it out of gear with its surroundings. Nevertheless, if life continues and if in continuing it expands, there is an overcoming of factors of opposition and conflict; there is a transformation of them into differentiated aspects of a higher powered and more significant life.... Here in germ are balance and harmony attained through rhythm. Equilibrium comes about not mechanically and inertly but out of, and because of, tension.... Changes interlock and sustain one another. Wherever there is this coherence there is endurance.[25]

Dewey's reflections anticipate the insights of recent scholars who have revealed the biological roots of human artistry. Evolutionary psychologists, for example, have discovered that narrative art is "an intensified, functionally adaptive extension of mental qualities" which have played a fundamental role in the evolution of *homo sapiens*.[26] As Dennis Dutton observes, the evolution of our species is

> not just a history of how we came to have acute color vision, a taste for sweets, and an upright gait. It is also a story of how we became a species obsessed with creating artistic experiences with which to amuse, shock, titillate, and enrapture ourselves, from children's games to the quartets of Beethoven, from firelit caves to the continuous worldwide glow of television screens.[27]

According to Dewey, this commonality radically alters how we should understand literature and art, viewing them not as transcendent forms but as modes of experience that traffic in the same set of sensations and impressions that define organic life, recording "the energy of the things of the world." If Dewey is right, the enterprise of literary criticism is quite different from what many scholars have supposed. If literature is in fact something that "can only be felt, that is, immediately experienced," then criticism's chief purpose is not to impart a historical or sociological lesson, but to explain the particular ways in which literature "enlivens and animates."[28]

That effort is not without its pitfalls. "Every critic, like every artist," Dewey observes, has a bias, and when that bias is

> allowed to harden in a fixed mold, he becomes incapacitated for judging even the things to which his bias draws him. For they must be seen in the perspective of a world so mulitform and so full that it contains an infinite variety of other qualities that attract and of other ways of response.

It is also possible for a critic to err by overemphasizing the explanatory power of context. Literary works are undoubtedly connected to "the respective milieus in which they were produced," and "historical and cultural information may throw light on the causes of their production," but each work can only be experienced directly, in terms of "its own qualities and relations." The point of criticism, Dewey concludes, "is the reeducation of perception of works of art; it is an auxiliary in the process, a difficult process, of learning to see and hear."[29]

Pragmatist philosophy thus yields a loose set of interpretive principles which are particularly germane to considerations of aesthetics:

1. *A priori* assumptions tend to produce skewed readings and tenuous claims. Literature often turns out to be weirder, and wilder, than any political ideology or school of interpretation would assume.
2. Criticism is most useful and accurate when it attends to the effects of literary works. Cultural contexts and social conditions can be illuminating, but

criticism ultimately seeks to explain what a literary work (or genre, or movement) actually does—the particular set of impressions, responses, and felt ideas that it solicits.

Throughout this book, I have tried to proceed along these lines by reframing Melville's writings as vivid, complex engagements with beauty as both a concept and an experience. Yet my approach is one among a multitude of Pragmatist possibilities, and there are many different ways to experience these works. As Melville states in the poem "Art," literature depends not on discrete impressions ("love," "humility," etc.), but on the combining of those impressions into a collective whole. Criticism participates in that creation of "pulsed life" by recovering the myriad ways in which literature elicits curiosity, passion, recognition, joy, and surprise, thereby participating in the everyday drama of life itself.[30]

Notes

Preface

1. Herman Melville, "At the Hostelry," in the *Collected Poems of Herman Melville*, ed. Howard Vincent (Chicago, IL: Hendricks House, 1947), 319.
2. Michelle Neely, for example, has revealed numerous ways in which nineteenth-century American literature both records and contests ideas of environmental sustainability, and Maria A. Windell has documented how writers from the era both deployed and contested literary genres that circulated widely throughout the Americas. See Michelle Neely, *Against Sustainability: Reading Nineteenth-Century America in the Age of Climate Crisis* (New York: Fordham University Press, 2020) and Maria A. Windell, *Transamerican Sentimentalism and US Literary History* (New York: Oxford University Press, 2020). If recent literature is any indication, this dialectical quality of American literature subsists. In *Dead Pledges: Debt, Crisis, and Twenty-First Century Culture* (Stanford, CA: Stanford University Press, 2018), Annie McClanahan discloses how contemporary literature—whether in the form of novels, horror films, or photographs—tends to be structured around a shared grammar of debt and credit.
3. Joel Pfister, *Surveyors of Customs: American Literature as Cultural Analysis* (New York: Oxford University Press, 2016), 9.
4. This point has been compellingly argued by C.L.R. James and, more recently, by Edward Sugden. For James, Melville's prescience inheres in his ability to discern the defining features of an emerging capitalist modernity, which in the 1840s and 1850s was only beginning to take shape. Melville's writing, as James puts it, is "the grandest conception that has ever been made to see the modern world, our world, as it was, and the future that lay before it. The voyage of the Pequod is the voyage of modern civilization seeking its destiny" (C.L.R. James, *Mariners, Renegades, and Castaways: The Story of Herman Melville and the World We Live In* (New York: C.L.R. James, 1953), 19). Melville's discernment, though, is also a matter of timing. As Sugden points out, Melville wrote at the outset of a "new phase of capitalism" that transformed the world through international markets: "Herman Melville was simultaneously a product and the foremost observer and theorist of this transnational world." Edward Sugden, "Marginal States: Melville in the Marquesas, 1842," in *The New Melville Studies*, ed. Cody Marrs (New York: Cambridge University Press, 2019), 70.
5. *Chiaroscuro* (Italian for "light and dark") was a technique developed by Renaissance artists that employed stark contrasts, particularly in color. John Bryant explores Melville's interest in and use of chiaroscuro in *Melville and Repose: The Rhetoric of Humor in the American Renaissance* (New York: Oxford University Press, 1993), 18–19. On Melville's fascination with J.M.W. Turner, and the complex ways in which Melville engages with Turner's art and aesthetics, see Robert K. Wallace,

Melville and Turner: Spheres of Love and Fright (Athens, GA: University of Georgia Press, 1992).
6. Herman Melville, *Published Poems*, Vol. 11 of *The Writings of Herman Melville*, ed. Robert C. Ryan et al. (Evanston and Chicago, IL: Northwestern University Press and The Newberry Library, 2009), 56–7.
7. Herman Melville, *Moby-Dick*, Vol. 6 of *The Writings of Herman Melville*, ed. Harrison Hayford, Hershel Parker, and G. Thomas Tanselle (Evanston and Chicago, IL: Northwestern University Press and The Newberry Library, 1988), 123.
8. Herman Melville, *Clarel*, Vol. 12 of *The Writings of Herman Melville*, ed. Harrison Hayford, et al. (Evanston and Chicago, IL: Northwestern University Press and The Newberry Library, 1991), 208. Samuel Otter analyzes Melville's interest in Giovanni Piranesi in "Melville, Poetry, Prints," in *Melville's Philosophies*, ed. Branka Arsić and K.L. Evans (New York: Bloomsbury, 2017), 219–60.
9. Melville, *Published Poems*, 37, 86, 119, 106, 41–3.
10. Hsuan Hsu, "War, Ekphrasis, and Elliptical Form in Melville's *Battle-Pieces*," *Nineteenth-Century Studies* 16 (2002): 51–71; Timothy Sweet, "*Battle-Pieces* and Vernacular Poetics," *Leviathan* 17.3 (October 2015): 25–42 (26).
11. See Dennis Berthold, "Pictorial Intertexts for *Battle-Pieces*: Melville at the National Academy of Design, 1865," in *Melville as Poet: The Art of "Pulsed Life"*, ed. Sanford E. Marovitz (Kent, OH: Kent State University Press, 2013); Peter Coviello, "Battle Music: Melville and the Forms of War," in *Melville and Aesthetics*, ed. Samuel Otter and Geoffrey Sanborn (New York: Palgrave, 2011), 193–212 (195); and Jennifer Greiman, "Melville in the Dark Ages of Democracy," *Leviathan: A Journal of Melville Studies* 18.3 (October 2016): 11–30 (14).
12. Walter Benjamin, "The Work of Art in the Age of Mechanical Reproduction," in *Illuminations*, trans. Harry Zohn, ed. Hannah Arendt (Mariner Books, 2019), 195.
13. Benjamin, "The Work of Art."
14. As quoted by Elaine Scarry in *On Beauty and Being Just* (Chicago, IL: University of Chicago Press, 2007), 109.
15. Melville, *Published Poems*, 58.
16. Melville, *Published Poems*, 35–6.
17. Rosanna Warren, "Dark Knowledge: Melville's Poems of the Civil War," *Raritan* 19.1 (Summer 1999): 100–21. This ethical framework bears directly on *Battle-Pieces*' treatment of slavery. As Brian Yothers asserts, it is important not to let Melville "off the hook for his suggestion that whites are 'nearer in nature' to himself and his readership than African Americans," but it is also important to note "how deeply Melville was moved, and even changed by the injustice of slavery and the events of the Civil War and Emancipation when we consider that Melville found 'the erecting in our advanced century of an Anglo-American empire based on the systematic degradation of man' to be a sufficiently loathsome prospect that he was willing to abandon, or at least substantially modify, a lifetime of principled pacifism." In *Battle-Pieces*, Melville's ethical and aesthetic impulses thus resemble the wind in "The Conflict of Convictions": "It spins against the way it drives" (Melville, *Published Poems*, 10). See Brian Yothers, "Herman Melville," in *American Literature in Transition, 1851–1877*, ed. Cody Marrs (New York: Cambridge University Press, 2022), 58–73.

18. Melville, *Published Poems*, 108.
19. According to Sigmund Freud, one of the foremost features of human nature is the *Todestrieb*, or "death drive." See Sigmund Freud, *Beyond the Pleasure Principle*, trans. C.J.M Hubback (Vienna and London: The International Psycho-Analytical Press, 1922).
20. G. Striker outlines Empiricus's philosophy in "*Ataraxia*: Happiness as Tranquility," *The Monist* 73 (1996): 97–110. The quote comes from Empiricus's *Outlines of Pyrrhonism*, though Diogenes Laërtius clarifies that the claim first originated with Agrippa; William Smith, *A Dictionary of Greek and Roman Biography and Mythology* (London: John Murray, 1880), 77.
21. Kandice Chuh, *The Difference Aesthetics Makes: On the Humanities "After Man"* (Durham, NC: Duke University Press, 2019), 13. In *None Like Us: Blackness, Belonging, Aesthetic Life* (Durham, NC: Duke University Press, 2019), Stephen Best demonstrates that beauty is vital to the study of black history, black art, and the relationship between them. In *The Natural History of Sexuality in Early America* (Baltimore, MD: Johns Hopkins University Press, 2020), Greta LaFleur reframes the history of sexuality, pleasure, and aesthetics as part of the history of the environment (and evolving conceptions thereof). The aesthetics of revolution, as well as the revolutionary potential of aesthetic thought, are explored by Jacques Rancière in *The Politics of Aesthetics: The Distribution of the Sensible*, trans. Gabriel Rockhill (London and New York: Bloomsbury, 2004).
22. Melville, *Moby-Dick*, 37.

Introduction

1. Melville, *Moby-Dick*, 184; Melville, *Battle-Pieces*, 46.
2. Herman Melville, "Statues in Rome," in *The Piazza Tales and Uncollected Prose*, Vol. 9 of *The Writings of Herman Melville*, ed. Harrison Hayford, Hershel Parker, and G. Thomas Tanselle (Evanston and Chicago, IL: Northwestern University Press and The Newberry Library, 1987), 405.
3. Geoffrey Sanborn, "Melville and the Nonhuman World," in *The New Cambridge Companion to Herman Melville*, ed. Robert S. Levine (New York: Cambridge University Press, 2014), 13.
4. Herman Melville, *Timoleon*, in *Published Poems*, 291.
5. Melville, *Moby-Dick*, 456.
6. On "Venice," see also Michael Jonik, *Herman Melville and the Politics of the Inhuman* (New York: Cambridge University Press, 2018), 217–21. As Jonik observes, "The poem is an ode to the creative power of nonhuman life" and "it is not a question of mere resemblance. Rather [the poem] shows how both nonhuman and human agencies are functions of their capabilities to form conative assemblages, assemblages marked by their material relations, energies, and autopoietic capacities" (220).
7. Melville, "Statues in Rome," 406. On these lectures, see also Christopher Sten "Melville and the Visual Arts: An Overview," in *Savage Eye: Melville and the Visual Arts*, ed. Christopher Sten (Kent, OH: Kent State University Press, 1991), 21–4. For a thorough

and insightful examination of the role that Italian politics, art, and aesthetics play in Melville's writings, see Dennis Berthold, *American Risorgimento: Herman Melville and the Cultural Politics of Italy* (Columbus, OH: Ohio State University Press, 2009).

8. As Sanborn points out, "throughout Melville's nonfiction, fiction, and poetry—in, for example, the stories about a rooster, a chimney, and a beetle; the poems about a shark, a lilac tree, a sea hawk, a kitten, an iceberg, and a piece of kelp; the book of poetry that is chiefly about plants; and, of course, the novel about a whale—the difference between humans and nonhumans is less significant than the difference between isolation and response" (Sanborn, "Melville and the Nonhuman World," 11).

9. Percy Bysshe Shelley, "On Love," in *Shelley on Love*, ed. Richard Holmes (Berkeley, CA: University of California Press, 1980), 71; Melville, "Statues in Rome," 399.

10. Herman Melville, *Weeds and Wildings*, ed. Robert C. Ryan (Evanston, IL: Northwestern University Press, 1967), 34.

11. Some of the most important and insightful studies in this vein include: Branka Arsić, *Passive Constitutions, or 7 ½ Times Bartleby* (Stanford, CA: Stanford University Press, 2007); Elizabeth Duquette, "Speculative Cetology: Figuring Philosophy in *Moby-Dick*," *ESQ* 47.1 (2001): 33–57; Nancy Fredericks, *Melville's Art of Democracy* (Athens, GA: University of Georgia Press, 1995); Jennifer Greiman, "Melville and the Conceits of Theory," in *The New Melville Studies*, 138–50; Paul Hurh, *American Terror: The Feeling of Thinking in Edwards, Poe, and Melville* (Stanford, CA: Stanford University Press, 2015) and Paul Hurh, "*Billy Budd*: Pessimism for Post-Critique," in *The New Melville Studies*, 151–68; Jonik, *Herman Melville and the Politics of the Inhuman*; Maurice Lee, *Uncertain Chances: Science, Skepticism, and Belief in Nineteenth-Century American Literature* (New York: Oxford University Press, 2012), 47–88, and Maurice Lee, "Melville's Subversive Political Philosophy: 'Benito Cereno' and the Fate of Speech," *American Literature* 72.3 (September 2000): 495–519; Dominic Mastroianni, *Politics and Skepticism in Antebellum American Literature* (New York: Cambridge University Press, 2014), 61–82, and Dominic Mastroianni, "Perfectionist *Pierre*," in *The New Melville Studies*, 83–95; Edward Sugden, *Emergent Worlds: Alternative States in Nineteenth-Century American Culture* (New York: NYU Press, 2008), especially the coda; as well as the essays in *Melville's Philosophies*; and *Melville among the Philosophers*, ed. Tom Nurmi and Corey McCall (Lanham, MD: Lexington Books, 2017).

12. See, for example, Jennifer Baker, "Dead Bones and Honest Wonders: The Aesthetics of Natural Science in *Moby-Dick*," in *Melville and Aesthetics*, 85–101; Berthold, *American Risorgimento*; Bryant, *Melville and Repose*; William B. Dillingham, *An Artist in the Rigging: The Early Work of Herman Melville* (Athens, GA: University of Georgia Press, 2008); Sianne Ngai, *Ugly Feelings* (Cambridge, MA: Harvard University Press, 2008); Samuel Otter, *Melville's Forms* (forthcoming); Samuel Otter, "Melville's Style," in *The New Melville Studies*, 114–37; Samuel Otter, "An Aesthetics in All Things," *Representations* 104.1 (Fall 2008): 116–25; Douglas Robillard, *Melville and the Visual Arts: Ionian Form, Venetian Tint* (Kent, OH: Kent State University Press, 2007); Geoffrey Sanborn, *The Value of Herman Melville* (New York: Cambridge University Press, 2018); John Stauffer, "Interracial Friendship and the Aesthetics of Freedom," in *Melville and Douglass: Essays in Relation*, ed. Robert S. Levine and Samuel Otter

(Chapel Hill, NC: University of North Carolina Press, 2011), 134–58; Christopher Sten, *The Weaver-God, He Weaves: Melville and the Poetics of the Novel* (Kent, OH: Kent State University Press, 1996); Elisa Tamarkin, "A Final Appearance with Elihu Vedder: Melville's Visions," *Leviathan* 18.3 (2016): 68–111; Robert K. Wallace, *Melville & Turner: Spheres of Love and Fright* (Athens, GA: University of Georgia Press, 1992); and Robert K. Wallace, "'Unlike Things Must Meet and Mate': Melville and the Visual Arts," in *A Companion to Herman Melville*, ed. Wyn Kelley (London: Wiley, 2006); as well as the essays in *Melville and Aesthetics*; Sten, *Savage Eye*; and Daniel Hoffman-Schwartz, ed., *Handsomely Done: Aesthetics, Politics, and Media after Melville* (Evanston, IL: Northwestern University Press, 2019).

13. Ngai, *Ugly Feelings*, 56; Theo Davis, "Melville's Ornamentation," in *Melville and Aesthetics*.

14. Branka Arsić and K.L. Evans, "Introduction: Reconstructing Melville," in *Melville's Philosophies*, 3.

15. A brief word about the nomenclature used in this book. Scholars have made compelling arguments that, in order to decolonize the field, "American literature" should be reconceived and reframed as "U.S. literature." Although many of these arguments are sound, I refer throughout this book to American literature, American literary history, and American literary studies for a few reasons. First, the term "U.S. literature" implies a stable, identifiable set of national boundaries that are belied by the dynamic, ever-shifting borders of the nineteenth-century United States and by the transnational connections and exchanges that defined the literature and culture of this era. As Maria Windell's *Transnationalist Sentimentalism and Nineteenth-Century US Literary History* (New York: Oxford UP, 2020), Sugden's *Emergent Worlds*, and Raul Coronado's *A World Not to Come: A History of Latino Writing and Print Culture* (Cambridge, MA: Harvard University Press, 2016) have demonstrated, literature in this period had a very tenuous relation to almost every conceivable type of boundary—verbal, legal, and generic—and the term "American" better describes that kind of boundaryless formation. Moreover, Melville did not simply write about the United States: his work draws from literary, philosophical, and aesthetic traditions that long predate the U.S., and his writings—like the characters that populate them—are set across this "terraqueous globe."

16. The work I refer to includes Erica Fretwell, *Sensory Experiments: Psychophysics, Race, and the Aesthetics of Feeling* (Durham, NC: Duke University Press, 2020), Theo Davis, *Ornamental Aesthetics: The Poetry of Attending in Thoreau, Dickinson, and Whitman* (New York: Oxford University Press, 2016); Édouard Marsoin, *Melville et l'usage des plaisirs* (Paris: Presses Sorbonne Université, 2019); Russ Castronovo, *Beautiful Democracy: Aesthetics and Anarchy in a Global Era* (Chicago, IL: University of Chicago Press, 2007); Otter and Sanborn, *Melville and Aesthetics*; Christopher Looby and Cindy Weinstein, *American Literature's Aesthetic Dimensions* (New York: Columbia University Press, 2011); and Hoffman-Schwartz, *Handsomely Done*. The quote comes from Looby and Weinstein's insightful introduction (6). For other excellent work in this vein, see, for example, Caroline Levine, *Forms: Whole, Rhythm, Hierarchy, Network* (Princeton, NJ: Princeton University Press, 2015); Natalia Cecire, *Experimental: American Literature and the Aesthetics of Knowledge* (Baltimore, MD:

Johns Hopkins University Press, 2019); and Benjamin Morgan, *The Outward Mind: Materialist Aesthetics in Victorian Science and Literature* (Chicago, IL: University of Chicago Press, 2017).

17. Fretwell, *Sensory Experiments*, 4.
18. Melville, *Published Poems*, 46; Herman Melville, *Billy Budd, Sailor*, ed. Harrison Hayford and Merton M. Sealts (Chicago, IL: University of Chicago Press, 2001), 218; Melville, *Published Poems*, 236; Melville, *Moby-Dick*, 195.
19. See, respectively, Zachary Vernon, "'Being Myriad, One': Melville and the Ecological Sublime in Faulkner's *Go Down, Moses*," *Studies in the Novel* 46.1 (Spring 2014): 63–82; David E. Nye, *American Technological Sublime* (Cambridge, MA: MIT Press, 1994), 245–6; Harold Bloom, *The Daemon Knows: Literary Greatness and the American Sublime* (New York: Penguin, 2015); Bryan C. Short, "Multitudinous, God-omnipresent, Coral Insects: Pip, Isabel, and Melville's Miltonic Sublime," *Leviathan* 14.1–2 (March 2012): 17–28; and Fredericks, *Melville's Art of Democracy*. The Burkean resonances of Melville's works are also explored in Stauffer, "Interracial Friendship and the Aesthetics of Freedom," 134–58; Richard S. Moore, *That Cunning Alphabet: Melville's Aesthetics of Nature* (Amsterdam: Rodopi, 1982); Marvin Fisher, *Going Under: Melville's Short Fiction and the American 1850s* (Baton Rouge, LA: Louisiana State University Press, 1977); and Barbara Glenn, "Melville and the Sublime in *Moby-Dick*," *American Literature* 48.2 (May 1976): 165–82.
20. Some of the most fruitful inquiries into Melville's aesthetics have placed him within the tradition of the picturesque rather than the aesthetics of the sublime. See, for example, Tamarkin, "A Final Appearance with Elihu Vedder"; William B. Dillingham, *Melville and His Circle: The Last Years* (Athens, GA: University of Georgia Press, 2008), 7–10; Robillard, *Melville and the Visual Arts*; and Bryant, *Melville and Repose*, 16–17; and John Bryant, "Toning Down the Green," in *Savage Eye*, 145–61. My reading of Melville has been influenced by these studies, but my focus here is slightly different, since beauty for Melville often involves but is not co-extensive with the picturesque. To put this another way: the picturesque is one of beauty's major forms but it is not, for Melville, beauty's summation.
21. Glenn reads the novel as an "exhaustive catalog of 'what things they are that cause in us the affections of the sublime and beautiful'"—in short, a testing out of Burke's aesthetic philosophy in the realm of fiction. Even "the loose, episodic, digressive narrative," she writes, "may be seen ... as tightly ordered with respect to Burke's ideas of sublimity" (Glenn, "Melville and the Sublime in *Moby-Dick*," 165–6).
22. Melville, *Billy Budd, Sailor*, 62; Melville, *Moby-Dick*, 134. As John Milton remarked, "For Books are not absolutely dead things, but doe contain a potencie of Life in them to be as active as that Soule whose progeny they are; nay, they do preserve as in a violl the purest effiacie and extraction of that living intellect that bred them." John Milton, *Areopagitica: A Speech to The Parliament of England for the Liberty of Unlicensed Printing* (London: R. Hunter, 1819), 17.
23. Melville, "Statues in Rome," 399. My understanding of Melville's reading practices has been influenced by several studies, including Merton M. Sealts's *Melville's Reading* (Columbia, SC: University of South Carolina Press, 1988); Dillingham's *Melville and His Circle*; Robin Grey's (ed.) *Melville & Milton: An Edition and Analysis of Melville's*

Annotations on Milton (Duquesne, PA: Duquesne University Press, 2004); Brian Yothers's *Sacred Uncertainty: Religious Difference and the Shape of Melville's Career* (Evanston, IL: Northwestern University Press, 2016); Jonik, *Herman Melville and the Politics of the Inhuman*; Walter Bezanson, "Melville's Reading of Arnold's Poetry," *PMLA* 69.3 (June 1954): 365–91; and the essays by Charlene Avallone, Peter Balaam, Elizabeth Schultz, and Wyn Kelley in *Melville and Women*, ed. Elizabeth Schultz and Haskell Springer (Kent, OH: Kent State University Press, 2006). An indispensable resource for studying Melville's reading practices is Melville's Marginalia Online, ed. Steven Olsen-Smith and Peter Norberg: http://melvillesmarginalia.org/

24. These quotes come from Melville's marginalia in his copy of Ralph Waldo Emerson's *Essays* (4th edn; Boston, MA: Munroe, 1847): http://melvillesmarginalia.org/

25. In *Melville's Reading*, Sealts notes that Melville owned a personal copy of Edmund Burke's *A Philosophical Inquiry into the Origin of Our Ideas of the Sublime and Beautiful, with an Introductory Discourse Concerning Taste, and Several other Additions* (Philadelphia, PA: Printed for D. Johnson, Portland, by J. Watts, 1806). That copy is now housed at the Houghton Library.

26. Edmund Burke, *A Philosophical Enquiry into the Origin of our Ideas of the Sublime and the Beautiful* (London: J. Dodsley, 1767). According to Burke, desire and beauty are worlds apart: desire is "evident in brutes, whose passions are more unmixed, and which pursue their purposes more directly," while beauty manifests as a feeling of love (65). Elaine Scarry notes that such divisions have diminished beauty in the Western imagination: "Formerly capable of charming or astonishing, now beauty was the not-astonishing; as it was also the not-male, the not-mountainous, ... the not-night. Each attribute or illustration of the beautiful became one member of an oppositional pair, and because it was almost always the diminutive member, it was also the dismissable member" (Scarry, *On Beauty and Being Just*, 83–4).

27. Burke, *A Philosophical Enquiry*, 237–8. In *Melville and Repose*, Bryant similarly distances Melville from Burke, observing that Burke's ideas contrast wildly with writings such as "Rip Van Winkle's Lilac" and the Burgundy Club Sketches, "nor can an aesthetic of the sublime fully account for Melville's comic sensibility, or Coleridgean 'inverse sublimity'" (272, n. 35).

28. Ray B. Browne discusses Vere's Burkean qualities in *Melville's Drive to Humanism* (Lafayette, LA: Purdue University Press, 1971).

29. Herman Melville, letter to Nathaniel Hawthorne (July 1851), in *Correspondence*, Vol. 14 of *The Writings of Herman Melville*, ed. Lynn Horth (Evanston and Chicago, IL: Northwestern University Press and The Newberry Library, 1993), 190.

30. Melville, *Moby-Dick*, 375–6.

31. Melville, *Moby-Dick*, 375.

32. Melville, *Moby-Dick*, 377–8.

33. Melville, *Moby-Dick*; Friedrich Schiller, *On the Aesthetic Education of Man* (1794), trans. Keith Tribe, ed. Alexander Schmidt (New York: Penguin, 2016).

34. David Graeber, "What's the Point if We Can't Have Fun?," *The Baffler* 24 (January 2014): https://thebaffler.com/salvos/whats-the-point-if-we-cant-have-fun

35. Hurh, *American Terror*. As Hurh explains, "Melville frames the act of thinking as an affect" and the terrors of *Moby-Dick* tend to "arise not as against any particular

philosophical outlook but rather from the application of dialectical method to the problem of dialectical method itself" (29).

36. Melville, *Moby-Dick*, 73, 557; Melville, "Bartleby, the Scrivener: A Story of Wall-Street," in *The Piazza Tales*, 30.

37. William B. Dillingham situates Melville within the picturesque tradition that grew out of the late eighteenth century, a tradition that emphasized the balance of "contrasting elements": "roughness as well as smoothness, the bleak as well as the cheerful, irregularity as well as the seamless, and so forth." John Bryant likewise links Melville to Uvedale Price's theory of picturesque perspective and Nathaniel Hawthorne's view of the "moral picturesque." Melville, Bryant argues, shared this tradition's "view of the mind as blending light and dark moods, and of the chiaroscuro as a form of self-conscious restraint or 'toning down' of personality." Elisa Tamarkin points out that Melville's interest in the picturesque is political as well as aesthetic, since the tradition's "spirit of accommodation suggests a classical ideal of 'balanced interests' that might apply as much to the goals of a republican society as to its own heterogeneous aesthetic." See Dillingham, *Melville and His Circle*, 8; Bryant, *Melville and Repose*, 16; and Elisa Tamarkin, "Melville with Pictures," in *The New Cambridge Companion to Herman Melville*, 178.

38. Most strains of the picturesque tradition also eschewed questions about the origins of beauty. As William Gilpin writes in his *Three Essays on Picturesque Beauty* (London: R. Blamire, 1792), "We inquire not into the general sources of beauty... The question simply is, What is that quality in objects, which particularly marks them as picturesque?" (4).

39. Melville, *Moby-Dick*, 246; Herman Melville, *White-Jacket*, Vol. 5 of *The Writings of Herman Melville*, ed. Harrison Hayford, Hershel Parker, and G. Thomas Tanselle (Evanston and Chicago, IL: Northwestern University Press and The Newberry Library, 1970), 44; Herman Melville, *John Marr and Other Sailors*, in *The Poems of Herman Melville*, ed. Douglas Robillard (Kent, OH: Kent State University Press, 2000), 280.

40. Melville, "Benito Cereno," in *The Piazza Tales*, 68; Melville, *Battle-Pieces*, 42; Herman Melville, *Mardi and a Voyage Thither*, Vol. 3 of *The Writings of Herman Melville*, ed. Harrison Hayford, Hershel Parker, and G. Thomas Tanselle (Evanston and Chicago, IL: Northwestern University Press and The Newberry Library, 1970), 99.

41. John Ruskin, *Modern Painters*, Vol. 1 (New York: Wiley, 1860); Germaine de Staël, *Of Germany*, Vol. II (New York: Derby & Jackson, 1861), 169–70.

42. William Hazlitt, *Criticisms on Art: And Sketches of the Picture Galleries of England* (London: Templeman, 1843), 8. According to Melville's Marginalia Online, Melville marked this passage in his copy of the book.

43. James Jarves, *The Art Idea: Sculpture, Painting, and Architecture in America* (New York: Hurd and Houghton, 1864), 325. Douglas Robillard notes that "the volume was given to Melville in 1871 by his brother-in-law, J.C. Hoadley." Robillard, *Melville and the Visual Arts*, 49.

44. Dawn Coleman, "Mahomet's Gospel and Other Revelations: Discovering Melville's Hand in The Works of William E. Channing," *Leviathan: A Journal of Melville Studies* 17.2 (June 2015): 74–88.

45. William Ellery Channing, "Self-Culture," in *The Works of William Ellery Channing*, Vol. 2 (Boston, MA: George G. Channing, 1849), 365.
46. Herman Melville, "The Encantadas," in *The Piazza Tales*, 136; Melville, *White-Jacket*; Herman Melville, "The Piazza," in *The Piazza Tales*, 2.
47. John Wenke, *Melville's Muse: Literary Creation and the Forms of Philosophical Fiction* (Kent, OH: Kent State University Press, 1995), 15.
48. Thomas Nurmi and Corey McCall, "Introduction," in *Melville among the Philosophers*, vii. Recent work in this area has been inventive and robust. The power and range of Melville's philosophy are explored in Thomas Nurmi's *Magnificent Decay: Melville and Ecology* (Charlottesville, VA: University of Virginia Press, 2020) and Jonik's *Herman Melville and the Politics of the Inhuman*, which convincingly reframe Melville as a philosopher of the environment and the material world. Paul Downes provides a fruitful and intriguing account of Melville's philosophical and political engagements with Thomas Hobbes in "Melville's Leviathan," in *Melville's Philosophies*; and Duquette cogently examines Melville's dialogs with Plato and Locke in "Speculative Cetology," 33–57.
49. Melville, *Moby-Dick*, 376.
50. According to William Hogarth, nearly all sources of beauty shared something in common, a singular "line of beauty" which tended to take the form of a "waving" or "serpentine" undulation. William Hogarth, *The Analysis of Beauty; Written with a View of Fixing the Fluctuating Ideas of Taste* (London: W. Strahan, 1772), 38, 52.
51. Hogarth, *The Analysis of Beauty*, 375 (my emphasis), 378.
52. Hogarth, *The Analysis of Beauty*, 379, 378.
53. See Otter, *Melville's Forms*; and Otter, "Melville's Style," 114–37.
54. Otter, "Melville's Style," 117.
55. Nurmi, *Magnificent Decay*, 4.
56. Michael Snediker, "Melville and Queerness without Character," in *The New Cambridge Companion to Herman Melville*, 155–68; Jonik, *Herman Melville and the Politics of the Inhuman*, 10; Sharon Cameron, *Impersonality: Seven Essays* (Chicago, IL: University of Chicago, 2007), 182; Paul Hurh, "Clarel, Doubt, Delay," in *Melville's Philosophies*, 80. On Melville's anticipatory posthumanism, see also Thomas Nurmi, "Mineral Melville," *J19: The Journal of Nineteenth-Century Americanists* 7.1 (Spring 2019): 155–83; John Levi Barnard, "The Cod and the Whale: Melville in the Time of Extinction," *American Literature* 89.4 (2017): 851–79; and Matthew Rebhorn, "Billy's Fist: Neuroscience and Corporeal Reading in Melville's *Billy Budd*," *Nineteenth-Century Literature* 72.2 (September 2017): 218–44.
57. Jennifer Greiman, for example, examines the role of gravity in *Battle-Pieces*—wherein the Civil War is co-extensive with falling or dropping, in one form or another—while Paul Hurh underscores Melville's fervent interest in sounds, and Tom Nurmi links Melville to nineteenth-century geological science. See, respectively, Jennifer Greiman, "Circles Upon Circles: Tautology, Form, and the Shape of Democracy in Tocqueville and Melville," *J19: The Journal of Nineteenth-Century Americanists* 1.1 (Spring 2013): 121–46; Paul Hurh, "The Sound of Incest: Sympathetic Resonance in Melville's *Pierre*," *Novel: A Forum on Fiction* 44.2 (2011): 249–67; and Nurmi, "Mineral Melville."
58. Herman Melville, letter to Hawthorne (June 1851), in *Correspondence*, 193–4.

59. Jordan Alexander Stein, "History's Dick Jokes: On Melville and Hawthorne," *LA Review of Books* (2015): https://lareviewofbooks.org/article/historys-dick-jokes-on-melville-and-hawthorne/
60. *Oxford English Dictionary* online: https://www.oed.com/
61. According to R.P. Winnington-Ingram, mode in Greek sense refers to a pattern of tone within a particular piece of music. "Mode," he writes, "is essentially a question of the internal relationships of notes within a scale, especially of the predominance of one of them over the others as a tonic, its predominance being established in any or all of a number of ways: e.g. frequent recurrence, its appearance in a prominent position as the first note or the last, the delaying of its expected occurrence by some kind of embellishment" (2). Given Melville's tendency to see literature as subtly yet significantly connected to the other arts, we might fruitfully use the concept of "mode" to describe the various ways in which he frames his writing philosophically and aesthetically. R.P. Winnington-Ingram, *Mode in Ancient Greek Music* (Cambridge: Cambridge University Press, 2014), 2.
62. Winnington-Ingram, *Mode in Ancient Greek Music*, 397; Melville, *Weeds and Wildings*, 5.
63. Melville, *Moby-Dick*, 450.
64. On this partitioning of Melville's career, see my earlier book *Nineteenth-Century American Literature and the Long Civil War* (Cambridge and New York: Cambridge University Press, 2015), 90–2.
65. Gilles Deleuze and Felix Guattari, *A Thousand Plateaus: Capitalism and Schizophrenia*, trans. Brian Massumi (Minneapolis, MN: University of Minnesota Press, 1987), 118.
66. In the 1820s, *Blackwood's Edinburgh Magazine* opined: "We say most truly, that America has not hitherto produced great writers. Is not this a fact? It would better become those who lose their temper about it to endeavour to amend it." Americans bristled at such dismissals and made a case for "American literature" as a distinct and cogent tradition. John C. Gray, in his 1821 Phi Beta Kappa oration, posited that an American literature was just *about* to come into existence: "What we have already accomplished furnishes a ground of hope... There is doubtless yet much room for improvement, but we have [steadily] proceeded [and progressed...] We are [now] preparing to distinguish ourselves among nations by our writings as well as by our actions" (John C. Gray "America and England," *Blackwood's Edinburgh Magazine* 16 (July–December 1824): 476); John C. Gray, "An Oration, pronounced before the Society of Phi Beta Kappa, at Cambridge, August 30, 1821," *North American Review* 7.13 (1821): 478. John C. McCloskey provides a brief history of the term in "The Campaign of Periodicals after the War of 1812 for National American Literature," *PMLA* 50.1 (1935): 262–73.
67. Numerous nineteenth-century anthologies were constructed in this manner, including Evert Duyckinck and George Duyckinck's *Cyclopaedia of American Literature*, 2 vols. (New York: Charles Scribner, 1855) and Charles Cleveland's *A Compendium of American Literature: Chronologically Arranged, with Biographical Sketches of the Authors* (Philadelphia, PA: E.C. and J. Biddle, 1858). On the history of American literature anthologies and the development of a canon, see Nancy Glazener,

Literature in the Making: A History of U.S. Literary Culture in the Long Nineteenth Century (New York: Oxford University Press, 2016).
68. Duyckinck and Duyckinck, *Cyclopaedia of American Literature*, Vol. 1, 1 (emphasis mine).
69. Elizabeth Renker, *The Origins of American Literary Studies: An Institutional History* (New York: Cambridge University Press, 2007).
70. Dorri Beam, *Style, Gender, and Fantasy in Nineteenth-Century American Women's Writing* (New York: Cambridge University Press, 2010), 2.
71. John Crowe Ransom, "Criticism, Inc.," *Virginia Quarterly Review* (Autumn 1937).
72. William K. Wimsatt and Monroe Beardsley, "The Affective Fallacy" (1949), in *The Verbal Icon: Studies in The Meaning of Poetry* (Lexington, KY: University of Kentucky Press, 1954), 21.
73. R.P. Blackmur, "The Craft of Herman Melville," *The Virginia Quarterly Review* 14.2 (Spring 1938): 266–82; Milton R. Sterns, "Some Techniques of Melville's Perception," *PMLA* 73.3 (June 1958): 251–9; Walter Bezanson, Introduction to *Clarel: A Poem and Pilgrimmage in the Holy Land* (New York: Hendricks House, 1960).
74. William B. Cairns, *On the Development of American Literature from 1815 to 1833: With Special Reference to Periodicals* (Madison, WI: University of Wisconsin Press, 1898); W. Edward Farrison, "The Origins of Brown's *Clotel*," *Phylon* 15 (1954): 347–54; Gustav Gruener, "Poe's Knowledge of German," *Modern Philology* 2.1 (June 1904): 125–40; Brander Matthews, "The President's Address: The Economic Interpretation of Literary History," *PMLA* 25 (1910): lviii–lxxiii; Donald Davidson, "Regionalism and Nationalism in American Literature," *American Review* 5 (1935): 48–61; Fred Harvey Harrington, "Literary Aspects of American Anti-Imperialism, 1898-1902," *New England Quarterly* 10.4 (December 1937): 650–67; Clifton Furness, "Walt Whitman's Politics," *American Mercury* 16 (1929): 459–66; Randall Stewart, "Hawthorne and Politics: Unpublished Letters to William B. Pike," *New England Quarterly* 5.2 (April 1932): 237–63; Philip Graham, "Lanier and Science," *American Literature* 4.3 (1932): 288–92; Alain Locke, "The Negro's Contribution to American Art and Literature," *The Annals of the American Academy of Political and Social Science* 140.1 (1928): 234–47; W.S. Tryon, "Nationalism and International Copyright: Tennyson and Longfellow in America," *American Literature* 24.3 (1952): 301–9; Gregory Paine, "The Frontier in American Literature," *Sewanee Review* 36 (1928): 225–36.
75. Lyle H. Wright, "A Statistical Survey of American Fiction, 1774-1850," *Huntington Library Quarterly* (1939): 309–18; Robert H. Walker, Jr., "Social Themes in Late Nineteenth Century American Verse: A Quantitative Study," Ph.D. Dissertation (1955). As Maurice Lee argues, there was an "information revolution" long "before Big Data and Big Tech, before DH and the dominance of STEM fields," along with the resulting anxiety regarding the "fall of literature into information" (4). See Lee's illuminating study, *Overwhelmed: Literature, Aesthetics, and the Nineteenth-Century Information Revolution* (Princeton, NJ: Princeton University Press, 2019). On "distant reading," see Franco Moretti, *Distant Reading* (New York and London: Verso, 2013).
76. For examples of these early archival efforts, see John Howard Birss, "A Book Review by Herman Melville," *New England Quarterly* 5.2 (April 1932): 346–48, and John Howard Birss, "'Travelling': A New Lecture by Herman Melville," *New England Quarterly* 7.4

(December 1934): 725–8. For early interpretations of Melville's treatments of race, see James, *Mariners, Renegades, and Castaways*; Sidney Kaplan, "Herman Melville and the American National Sin: The Meaning of *Benito Cereno*," *The Journal of African American History* 41.4 (October 1956): 311–38, Robert M. Farnsworth, "Slavery and Innocence in *Benito Cereno*," *ESQ* 44 (1966): 94–6, and Priscilla Allen Zirker, "Evidence of the Slavery Dilemma in *White-Jacket*," *American Quarterly* 18 (1966): 477–92. For contextual accounts, see James D. Hart, "Melville and Dana," *American Literature* 9.1 (1937): 49–55, Robert S. Forsythe, "Herman Melville in Honolulu," *New England Quarterly* 8.1 (March 1935): 99–105, and O.W. Riegel, "The Anatomy of Melville's Fame," *American Literature* 3.2 (May 1931): 195–203. On Melville and science, see Elizabeth S. Foster, "Melville and Geology," *American Literature* 17.1 (March 1945): 50–65, and Tyrus Hillway, "Melville and the Spirit of Science," *South Atlantic Quarterly* 48 (1948): 77–88. On Melville and religion, see Paul W. Miller, "Sun and Fire in Melville's *Moby-Dick*," *Nineteenth-Century Fiction* 13.2 (September 1958): 139–44, H. Bruce Franklin, *The Wake of the Gods: Melville's Mythology* (Stanford, CA: Stanford University Press, 1963), and William Rosenfeld, "Uncertain Faith: Queequeg's Coffin and Melville's Uses of the Bible," *Texas Studies in Literature and Language* 7 (1966): 317–27. Brian Yothers provides an astute overview of this early scholarship in *Melville's Mirrors: Literary Criticism and America's Most Elusive Author* (Rochester, NY: Camden House, 2011). On postsecular approaches, see Jared Hickman and Peter Coviello's special issue of *American Literature*, "After the Postsecular" 86.4 (December 2014).

77. Wendy Steiner, *Venus in Exile: The Rejection of Beauty in Twentieth-Century Art* (Chicago, IL: University of Chicago Press, 2001), 1.
78. Pierre Bourdieu, *Distinction: A Social Critique of the Judgment of Taste*, trans. Richard Nice (Cambridge, MA: Harvard University Press, 1984), 6.
79. Raymond Williams, *Keywords: A Vocabulary of Culture and Society* (New York: Oxford University Press, 1976), 28.
80. Raymond Williams, *Marxism and Literature* (New York: Oxford University Press, 1977), 156.
81. Jane Tompkins, *Sensational Designs: The Cultural Work of American Fiction* (New York: Oxford University Press, 1986), 5; John Carlos Rowe, *Literary Culture and US Imperialism: From the Revolution to World War II* (New York: Oxford University Press, 2000), 249, 19; Janice Radway, *Reading the Romance: Women, Patriarchy, and Popular Culture* (Chapel Hill, NC: University of North Carolina Press, 1984); Sacvan Bercovitch and Myra Jehlen, eds., *Ideology and Classic American Literature* (New York: Cambridge University Press, 1986); Walter Benn Michaels and Donald E. Pease, eds., *The American Renaissance Reconsidered* (Baltimore, MD: Johns Hopkins University Press, 1985); David Lloyd, *Under Representation: The Racial Regime of Aesthetics* (New York: Fordham University Press, 2018), 8.
82. Burke, *A Philosophical Enquiry*, 267. Burke is paraphrasing William Cheselden, a British surgeon who recalled a blind boy who, years later, regained his sight: "Among many remarkable particulars that attended his first perceptions, and judgments of visual objects, Cheselden tells us, that... upon accidently seeing a negro woman, he was struck with great horror at the sight."

83. Johannes Blumenbach *On the Natural Varieties of Mankind* (1775), in *The Anthropological Treatises of Blumenbach and Hunter*, trans. Thomas Bendyshe (London: Longman, Green, Longman, Roberts, & Green, 1865), 269; Charles White, *An Account of the Regular Gradation in Man, and in Different animals and Vegetables* (London: C. Dilly, 1799), 134; Ralph Waldo Emerson, *English Traits* (1856), in *The Complete Works of Ralph Waldo Emerson*, Vol. 2 (London: Bell & Daldy, 1866), 30.
84. Melville, *Moby-Dick*, 189.
85. Melville, *Moby-Dick*, 278.
86. Henry David Thoreau, *Walden: A Fully Annotated Edition*, ed. Jeffrey S. Cramer (New Haven: Yale University Press), 11; Alexander Nehamas, *Only a Promise of Happiness: The Place of Beauty in a World of Art* (Princeton, NJ: Princeton University Press, 2007), 99.
87. See, for example, Angela M. Achorn and Gil G. Rosenthal, "It's Not About Him: Mismeasuring 'Good Genes' in Sexual Selection," *Trends in Ecology & Evolution* 35.3 (March 2020): 206–19; and Benedict G. Hogan and Mary Caswell Stoddard, "Synchronization of Speed, Sound, and Iridescent Color in a Hummingbird Aerial Courtship Dive," *Nature Communications* 9 (2018): https://doi.org/10.1038/s41467-018-07562-7.
88. Richard O. Prum, *The Evolution of Beauty: How Darwin's Forgotten Theory of Mate Choice Shapes the Animal World—and Us* (New York: Doubleday, 2017), 8.
89. Immanuel Kant, *Critique of Judgment*, trans. J.H. Bernard (London: Macmillan and Co., 1914), 59–60; Bourdieu, *Distinction*, 31–2.
90. Christopher Castiglia, *The Practices of Hope: Literary Criticism in Disenchanted Times* (New York: NYU Press, 2017), 4.
91. Melville, *Clarel*; Melville, *Moby-Dick*, 274; Melville, "At the Hostelry," 313.
92. Plato, *The Banquet*, trans. Percy Bysshe Shelley (London: Cassell & Co., 1893).

Chapter 1: Ancient Beauty in *Timoleon*

1. Charles Waldstein recounts and explores the discovery of this statue in "Praxiteles and the Hermes with the Infant Dionysos," in *Essays in the Art of Pheidias* (New York: Cambridge University Press, 1885), 373–93.
2. Melville, *Published Poems*, 312.
3. In that respect, the poem is part of Melville's career-long interest in comparative religion, from Zoroastrianism to esoteric Christianity. For a fuller account of Melville's engagements with various spiritual traditions, see William Potter, *Melville's Clarel and the Intersympathy of Creeds* (Kent, OH: Kent State University Press, 2004); Yothers, *Sacred Uncertainty*; and the essays in *Visionary of the Word: Melville and Religion*, ed. Brian Yothers and Jonathan A. Cook (Evanston, IL: Northwestern University Press, 2017).
4. *Pierre*, 180; *Typee*, 236; Melville, *Published Poems*, 236; Melville, *Published Poems*, 60; *Redburn*, 104; Melville, *Published Poems*, 236; Melville, *Billy Budd, Sailor*, 51, 64; Melville, *Moby-Dick*, 115, 73; and Melville, *Published Poems*, 64.

5. On nineteenth-century Americans' fascination with all things Greek and Roman, see Carl J. Richards, *The Golden Age of the Classics in America: Greece, Rome, and the Antebellum United States* (Cambridge, MA: Harvard University Press, 2009) and Caroline Winterer, *The Culture of Classicism: Ancient Greece and Rome in American Intellectual Life, 1780-1910* (Baltimore, MD: Johns Hopkins University Press, 2002). On the racial politics of this classical tradition, see John Levi Barnard, *Empire of Ruin: Black Classicism and American Imperial Culture* (New York: Oxford University Press, 2018).

6. In "Melville with Pictures," Tamarkin retraces Melville's interest in Claude Lorrain, positing that Melville "became increasingly obsessed" with Lorrain's art "in the last decades of the nineteenth century before he died" (175). In "From Ancient Rome to Modern Italy," *Leviathan* 15.3 (October 2013): 41–54, Robert K. Wallace situates Melville's fascination with Lorrain in relation to Melville's abiding fascination with Italian art. For a thoughtful assessment of Melville's response to Giovanni Piranesi, see Otter, "Melville, Poetry, Prints."

7. Arthur Schopenhauer, *Religion: A Dialogue, and Other Essays*, trans. T. Bailey Saunders (London: Swan Sonnenschein & Co., 1891), 36; Matthew Arnold, *"Culture and Anarchy" and Other Writings*, ed. Stefan Collini (Cambridge: Cambridge University Press, 1993), 67, 130.

8. Gail Cofflery makes a solid case that that Billy Budd is based on Antinous in "Classical Iconography in the Aesthetics of *Billy Budd, Sailor*," in *Savage Eye*, 257–76. For Melville, Cofflery writes, "the beauty of Antinous was 'pre-eminently Greek,' as he wrote beside a line of 'Laodamia' in his book of Wordsworth's poems. Like the god Apollo whom he resembles, Antinous symbolized the Greek idea of perfect male beauty" (257). She also suggests that Antinous "might have acquired deeper personal meaning" for Melville at this point in his life since "Antinous was that god worshipped by parents grieving for a son" (259).

9. Herman Melville, *Journals*, ed. Howard C. Horsford and Lynn Horth (Evanston and Chicago, IL: Northwestern University Press and the Newberry Library, 1989), , 90. In that same journal entry, Melville's initial disillusionment quickly gives way to humor. "To account for this abundance of stones," he writes, "many theories have been stated: *My* theory is that long ago, some whimsical King...took it into his head to pave all Judea, and entered into contracts to that effect; but the contractor becoming bankrupt mid-way in his business, the stones were only dumped on the ground, & there they lie to this day" (90).

10. Melville, *Journals*, 64.

11. Edward Sugden notes that Melville wrote amidst several large-scale transformations within capitalism, repeatedly "forcing as much history as possible into his works, reducing it to a chaotic, intense state, [and] taking it...to the brink of collapse before finding that it was his own form that would necessarily have to buckle first." For Cesare Casarino, Melville's writing is best apprehended as a series of meditations on the crises that define capitalist modernity—indeed, the only nineteenth-century rival to Marx in his apprehension of capitalism's inherent limits. See Sugden, *Emergent Worlds*; and Cesare Casarino, *Modernity at Sea: Melville, Marx, Conrad in Crisis* (Minneapolis, MN: University of Minnesota Press, 2002).

12. Melville, *Published Poems*, 266.
13. Melville, "Bartleby, the Scrivener," 23; Melville, *Moby-Dick*, 250; Melville, *Battle-Pieces*, 44; Melville, *Clarel*, 457.
14. Lewis Mumford, *Herman Melville: A Study of His Life and Vision* (New York: Literary Guild of America, 1929), 395, 397.
15. I am thinking, in particular, of the following interpretations of *Timoleon*, which have illuminated the volume's historical, aesthetic, and artistic dimensions: Tamarkin, "A Final Appearance with Elihu Vedder, and Tamarkin, "Melville with Pictures"; Edgar A. Dryden, *Monumental Melville: The Formation of a Literary Career* (Stanford, CA: Stanford University Press, 2004), 167–94, the quote is from 171; Jonik, *Herman Melville and the Politics of the Inhuman*, 215–24; Douglas Robillard, "Wrestling with the Angel: Melville's Use of the Visual Arts in *Timoleon*," in *Savage Eye*, 246–56; and Douglas Robillard, "'Magian Wine' and Melville's Art of Revision," *Leviathan* 3.1 (March 2001): 73–81; Wyn Kelly, *Herman Melville: An Introduction* (London: Blackwell, 2008), 166–75; Sanford E. Marovitz, "Connecting by Contrast: The 'Art' of *Timoleon, Etc.*," in *Melville as Poet*; and Daniel Clinton, "Line and Lineage: Visual Form in Herman Melville's *Pierre* and *Timoleon*," *Nineteenth-Century Literature* 73.1 (June 2018): 1–29.
16. Melville, *Published Poems*, 304, 305.
17. *Oxford English Dictionary* online: https://www.oed.com.
18. Melville, *Published Poems*, 280, 269.
19. Melville, *Published Poems*, 265, 274, 260, 276, 314, 315.
20. On Melville's oceanic style and imagination, see Hester Blum, *The View from the Masthead: Maritime Imagination and Antebellum America Sea Narratives* (Philadelphia, PA: University of Pennsylvania Press, 2012), as well as the essays in *"Whole Oceans Away": Melville and the Pacific*, ed. Jill Barnum, Wyn Kelly, and Christopher Sten (Kent, OH: Kent State University Press, 2007).
21. Ronan Ludot-Vlasak, *Essais sur Melville et l'Antiquité Classique* (Paris: Honoré Champion, 2018).
22. Melville, *Correspondence*, 193.
23. Plato, *Timaeus*, trans. Desmond Lee (New York: Penguin, 1977), 124; Lucretius, *On the Nature of Things*, trans. Frank O. Copley (New York: Norton, 1977), 1; Hesiod, *Theogeny*, as qtd. by Federico Vercellone in *Beyond Beauty*, trans. Sarah De Sanctis (Albany, NY: SUNY Press, 2017), 3. Hesiod is also mentioned by Shelley in his introduction to *Prometheus Unbound*. Melville's poem "Shelley's Vision" is partly based on his visit to the Baths of Caracalla, where Melville imagined Shelley wrote *Prometheus Unbound* (*Journals*, 106).
24. Rather than embracing science *tout court*, these poems partake in the broader project of synthesizing aesthetic and empirical thought. As Paul Hurh notes, "the concept of thinking had become, in the wake of Enlightenment empiricism, more and more coterminous with a set of austere mechanical processes, such as the scientific method or the denuded functions of analytical logic," so writers such as Melville sought to "give it feeling" (Hurh, *American Terror*, 247).
25. Nurmi, *Magnificent Decay*, 2.
26. Kant, *Critique of Judgment*, 38; Burke, *A Philosophical Enquiry*.

27. Tamarkin, "A Final Appearance with Elihu Vedder," 70, 93.
28. Melville, *Published Poems*, 281. The quote, of course, is taken from the Book of James. Brian Yothers suggests that the poem ties "the Buddhist doctrine of nirvana" to "the biblical passage's emphasis on evanescence," drawing out a "parallel between Christian doctrine and Buddhist philosophy." Yothers, "Melville after Secularism," in *The New Melville Studies*, 64.
29. Pierre Bayle, *A General Dictionary, Historical and Critical*, 10 vols., trans. John Peter Bernard, Thomas Birch and John Lockman (1734–41), vol. 7, 233.
30. Melville, *Published Poems*, 275.
31. Melville, *Moby-Dick*, 375.
32. John Ruskin, *The Stones of Venice*, Vol. 1: The Foundations (London: Smith, Elder, & Co., 1858), 223, 225, 228–333.
33. Samuel Otter and Geoffrey Sanborn, "Introduction: Aesthetics and Melville," in *Melville and Aesthetics*, 7.
34. John Onians recounts the temple's creation and design in *Classical Art and the Cultures of Greece and Rome* (New Haven: Yale University Press, 1999), 41–58. Joan Breton Connelly discusses the Parthenon's cosmological dimensions in *The Parthenon Enigma* (New York: Knopf, 2014).
35. Melville, *Published Poems*, 302.
36. Bryan C. Short, "'Like Bed of Asparagus': Melville and Architecture," in *Savage Eye*, 110.
37. Melville thus associates whiteness not with race—as many of his predecessors and contemporaries were wont to do—but with the intensities and qualities of light. As Nell Irvin Painter details in *The History of White People* (New York: Norton, 2010), many commentators, from Johann Joachim Winckelmann to Hiram Powers, saw the beauty of ancient art as a racial characteristic that revolved around "hard, white, young bodies" (62). In "The Parthenon," and in *Timoleon* more generally, whiteness is decoupled from individual bodies and reframed as both an aesthetic effect and a type of light. Melville's treatment of whiteness echoes Goethe's relational theory of color, according to which various hues are the result of dynamic interactions between light and shadow. See Johann Wolfgang von Goethe, *Theory of Colours*, trans. Charles Lock Eastlake (Cambridge, MA: MIT Press, 1982).
38. Melville, *Published Poems*, 302.
39. Bayle, *A General Dictionary*, Vol. 3, 271, 277. On Melville and Spinoza, see also Michael Jonik, *Melville and the Politics of the Inhuman*, 3–4 and 193–4. As Jonik contends, Spinoza "comes to signify for Melville a profoundly nonanthropocentric philosophy, one founded on the resolute inhumanness and impersonality of 'God, or Nature'" (4).
40. Melville, *Moby-Dick*, 195.
41. Melville, *Published Poems*, 303.
42. Flaxman, as quoted by Christopher Wordsworth in *Greece: Pictorial, Descriptive, and Historical* (London: John Murray, 1844), 57–8.
43. Ronan Ludot-Vlasak notes that such a comprehensive view can only happen in a poem since the ruins of the temple are broken up and scattered: "Dans un regard toujour mouvant, l'écriture poétique recompose un edifice qui n'existe plus que comme object discursif et le supplément" (217).

44. Charles W.J. Withers, *Zero Degrees: Geographies of the Prime Meridian* (Cambridge, MA: Harvard University Press, 2017), 18–19. Because of their investment in symmetry, aesthetics, and antiquity, poems such as "The Parthenon" echo several parts of *Billy Budd*. The narrator repeatedly, indeed almost exhaustively, describes Billy as beautiful. Not only is Billy disarmingly "handsome"; his "significant personal beauty" (137) is like that of a flower ("the lily was quite suppressed and the rose had some ado visibly to flush through the tan" (50)). Billy also hails from a "rustic" (50) world that passed away "before the time of steamships" (1). A "barbarian," the narrator declares, "Billy radically was—as much so, for all the costume, as his countrymen the British captives, living trophies, made to march in the Roman triumph of Germanicus" (120). These two qualities—Billy's historical backwardness and his personal beauty (and its effects)—are intimately linked: Billy embodies an ancient aesthetics predicated on symmetry (his inside and outside perfectly reflect one another), which contrasts with the way that form and content have become divorced from one another in modernity, for instance in Claggart's convoluted speech.

45. The poem is mostly interested in lines, light, and matter, but Melville may have also been aware of the fact that the Parthenon was not always so "gleaming" white. As Christopher Wordsworth notes in his 1844 travel guide *Greece* (a book Melville owned), "The Parthenon in its glory" was "enriched with a profusion of vivid colours, which throw around the fabric a jovial and festive beauty, admirably harmonizing with the brightness and transparency of the atmosphere which encircles it. The cornice of the pediments [was] decorated with painted ovoli and arrows; coloured meanders twine[d] along its annulets and beats;... the pediments [were] studded with disks of various hues; the triglphys of the frieze [were] streaked with tints which terminate in plate-bands and guttae of azure dye" (197). Such multichromatic ornamentation was central to ancient art, a fact lost during and after the Renaissance's neoclassical revival. Mark Abbe recovers this ancient interest in color in "The Polychromy of Roman Sculpture," in *The Oxford Handbook to Roman Sculpture*, ed. E. Friedland, M. G. Sobocinski, and E.K. Gazda (Oxford: Oxford University Press, 2015), 173–88. See also the essays in *The Polychromy of Ancient Sculpture and Architecture*, ed. P. Liverani and F. Paolucci (Florence: Galleria degli Uffizi / Universita degli Studi Firenze, 2020, and the work of the Ancient Polychromy Network: http://www.ancientpolychromynetwork.com

46. Morgan, *The Outward Mind*, 5.

47. Ruskin, *The Stones of Venice*, 13.

48. Arthur Stedman, "Introduction to the 1892 Edition [of *Typee*]," in *Melville in His Own Time: A Biographical Chronicle of His Life, Drawn from Recollections, Interviews, and Memoirs by Family Friends*, ed. Steven Olsen-Smith (Iowa City: University of Iowa Press, 2015), 167; Wallace, "From Ancient Rome to Modern Italy."

49. Owen Dullea, *Claude Gelée le Lorrain* (New York: Scribner, 1887).

50. Hazlitt, *Criticisms on Art*, 105–6, 209.

51. *Oxford English Dictionary* online: https://www.oed.com; Melville's Marginalia Online; Melville, *Moby-Dick*, 376. The quote about "hermaphroditical style" is about Michelangelo, of course, but Melville is also naming a certain Italian style of which Lorrain's paintings are undoubtedly a part. On Melville's Italian connections and

influences, see also Dennis Berthold, *American Risorgimento*; and Wallace, "From Ancient Rome to Modern Italy."
52. Melville, *Published Poems*, 284, 286.
53. Melville, *Published Poems*, 280.
54. S.F. Fogle and P.H. Fry, "Ode," in *The Princeton Encyclopedia of Poetry and Poetics*, ed. Roland Greene and Stephen Cushman (Princeton, NJ: Princeton University Press, 2012), 972.
55. Melville, *Billy Budd, Sailor*, 75; Melville, *Published Poems*, 262.
56. Melville, *Published Poems*, 291, 295, 294.
57. Melville, *Published Poems*, 792.
58. Herman Melville, Letter to Hoadley (1877) in *Correspondence*, 452; Bayle, *A General Dictionary*, Vol. 7. Hennig Cohen notes, "Melville owned an engraving by George Cooke from the *Historical Gallery of Portraits and Paintings*, Vol. 4 (London, 1807–11), showing four heads. In the margin he wrote the names 'Epicurus' and 'Metrodorus'" (Hennig Cohen, ed., *Selected Poems of Herman Melville* (New York: Doubleday/Anchor, 1964), 241).
59. Fredricks, *Melville's Art of Democracy*, 7; Scarry, *On Beauty and Being Just*, 110.
60. On the artistic history of Posillipo, see Albert Boime, *The Art of the Macchia and the Risorgimento: Representing Culture and Nationalism in Nineteenth-Century Italy* (Chicago, IL: University of Chicago Press, 1993), 78–82; Sylvian Bellenger, "The Scenography of the Neapolitan Crèche," in *The Neapolitan Crèche at the Art Institute of Chicago*, ed. Sylvain Bellenger and Carmine Romano (New Haven, NJ, and London: Yale University Press and the Art Institute of Chicago, 2016), 27–46; 78–82; and Rafaella Causa, *La Scuola di Posillipo* (Milan: Fratelli Fabbri Editori, 1967).
61. Melville, *Published Poems*, 297, 298.
62. Melville, *Published Poems*, 299.
63. Melville, *Published Poems*, 300.
64. Melville, *Published Poems*, 300.
65. John Ruskin, *The Works of John Ruskin*, Vol. 9 (London: George Allen, 1903), 469; Henry James, *Italian Hours* (Boston, MA, and New York: Houghton Mifflin, 1909), 126; Thomas White, *Fragments of Italy and the Rhineland* (London: William Pickering, 1841), 306; Antoine Valery, *Historical, Literary, and Artistic Travels in Italy* (Paris: Boudry's European Library, 1839), 38; William Rae Wilson, *Notes Abroad and Rhapsodies at Home*, Vol. 1 (London: Longman, Reeds, Orme, Brown, Green, & Longman, 1837), 190. Melville's view of the Milan Cathedral is closer to that of Mark Twain, who marveled: "What a wonder it is! So grand, so solemn, so vast! And yet so delicate, so airy, so graceful...I cannot understand how it can be 2nd to anything made by human hands." *Innocents Abroad, or The New Pilgrim's Progress*, Vol. 1 (New York: Houghton Mifflin, 1911), 170.
66. Melville, *Published Poems*, 296. In his *Journals*, Melville called the church "Glorious." It is "[m]ore satisfactory to me than St. Peters," he added, and possesses a "wonderful [sic] grandure. Effect of burning window at end of aisle...The group of angels on points of pinnacles & everywhere. Not the conception but execution" (121). The following day, he was impressed by the elemental dynamism of Titian's art: "4 fine allegorical paintings—Earth, Air, Fire, Water" (122).

67. Hanni Karttunen, et al., *Fundamental Astronomy* (London: Springer, 2017).
68. Melville, *Published Poems*, 285; Leo Bersani and Ulysses Dutoit, *Arts of Impoverishment: Beckett, Rothko, Resnais* (Cambridge, MA: Harvard University Press, 1993), 9.
69. Davis, *Ornamental Aesthetics*, 3.
70. Branka Arsić, *On Leaving: A Reading in Emerson* (Cambridge, MA: Harvard University Press, 2010), 15.
71. Melville, *Published Poems*, 292-3.
72. Ruskin, *The Stones of Venice*, 183.
73. Walt Whitman, "Crossing Brooklyn Ferry," in *Leaves of Grass* (1860), The Walt Whitman Archive: https://whitmanarchive.org/published/LG/1860/poems/122. As Melville wrote in his *Journals*, "Floating about philosophizing with Antonio the Merry... Rather be in Venice on rainy day, than in [any] other capital on a fine one" (120).
74. Timothy Marr, "Melville's Planetary Compass," in *The New Cambridge Companion to Herman Melville*, 189.

Chapter 2: Floral Beauty in *Weeds and Wildings*

1. Herman Melville, *Weeds and Wildings*, in *The Works of Herman Melville*, Vol. 16: Poems (New York: Russell & Russell, Inc., 1963), 303.
2. I am drawing upon Frederick Joseph Hermann's summary of these plants in *A Botanical Synopsis of the Cultivated Clovers* (Washington, D.C.: U.S. Department of Agriculture, 1953).
3. Melville, *Weeds and Wildings*, 303-4.
4. Melville, *Weeds and Wildings*, 299, 307-8, 314, 305, 333, 335, 334.
5. Herbert Marcuse, *The Aesthetic Dimension: Toward a Critique of Marxist Aesthetics* (Boston, MA: Beacon Press, 1978), 72-3.
6. Melville, *Weeds and Wildings*, 314.
7. Melville, *Weeds and Wildings*, 315.
8. "Heart failure" is listed as the cause of death in the *New York Times* obituary (October 2, 1891), which is reprinted in Watson G. Branch, ed., *Herman Melville: The Critical Heritage* (London and New York: Routledge, 1974), 418.
9. These lines are from Helen Dunmore, who wrote some of her most stunning poems while she was ill. Helen Dunmore, *Inside the Wave* (Hexmore: Bloodaxe Books, 2017).
10. See, for example, E.L. Grant Watson, "Melville's Testament of Acceptance," *New England Quarterly* 6 (1933): 319-27, and Barbara Johnson, "Melville's Fist: The Execution of Billy Budd," *Studies in Romanticism* 18 (Winter 1979): 567-99.
11. Martin Kevorkian, "Faith Among the Weeds: Melville's Religious Wildings Beyond These Deserts," in *Visionary of the Word*.
12. John Bryant, "Ordering the Rose: Melville's Poetic Revisions," *Melville Society Extracts* (July 1999); Gillian Osborne, "Melville and His Flowers," in *The New Melville Studies*, 27-42. My gloss on the ancient origins of aesthetics draws on Susan Buck-Morss's analysis in *Dreamworld and Catastrophe: The Passing of Mass Utopia in East and West*

(Cambridge, MA: MIT Press, 2002). As Buck-Morss notes, "*Aisthesis* is the sensory experience of perception [itself]. The original field of aesthetics is not art but reality—corporeal, material, nature...It is a form of cognition achieved through taste, touch, hearing, seeing, smell—the whole corporeal sensorium" (101).

13. Melville, *Correspondence*, 192. On Melville's battles with mental illness (and the consequences for his family), see Dillingham, *Melville and His Circle*, 65-7; Elizabeth Renker, "Herman Melville, Wife Beating, and the Written Page," *American Literature* 66.1 (March 1994): 123-50; and Eleanor Melville Metcalf, *Herman Melville: Cycle and Epicycle* (Cambridge, MA: Harvard University Press, 1953).

14. See Renker, "Herman Melville, Wife Beating, and the Written Page," as well as Robert S. Levine's discussion of Renker's article in "Afterword: 'New,' 'Old,' and 'With,'" in *The New Melville Studies*, 223-35.

15. My reading of *Weeds and Wildings* echoes Peter Riley's account of Melville's post-retirement career, which he explores in "Melville's Retirement," *Leviathan: A Journal of Melville Studies* 18.3 (October 2016): 112-28, and in *Whitman, Melville, Crane, and the Labors of Poetry: Against Vocation* (New York and Oxford: Oxford University Press, 2019), 108-26. Works such as *Weeds and Wildings*, Riley suggests, should be read in the context of Melville's retirement from the Customs House in 1885, after which Melville "approached literary composition and revision...as an extension of (rather than a release from) other forms of work, an approach that makes his [late] writings remarkably imbricated and coextensive with one another."

16. Melville, *Weeds and Wildings*, 311, 312, 313.

17. Melville, *Weeds and Wildings*, 335, 312.

18. Melville, *Weeds and Wildings*, 320.

19. Melville, *Weeds and Wildings*, 299; W.H. Auden, "In Memory of Y.B. Yeats," in *Another Time* (New York: Random House, 1940).

20. Michael Paul Rogin, *Subversive Genealogy: The Politics and Art of Herman Melville* (Berkeley and Los Angeles, CA: University of California Press, 1985), 244; Rachel Cole, "At the Limits of Identity: Realism and American Personhood in Melville's *The Confidence-Man*," *NOVEL: A Forum on Fiction* 39.3 (Summer 2006): 385-6. Critics may disagree about the genre and politics of *The Confidence-Man*, but they have tended to agree about slipperiness of identity in the novel. See Jennifer Greiman's *Democracy's Spectacle: Sovereignty and Public Life in Antebellum American Writing* (New York: Fordham University Press, 2011); Mark Noble, "Reading Melville Reading Character," *J19: The Journal of Nineteenth-Century Americanists* 4.2 (Fall 2016): 237-47; and Justine Murison, "Paranoid Reading, Surface Pleasures, and Deadpan Humor in *The Confidence-Man*," in *The New Melville Studies*, 13-26.

21. As you might imagine, there is a massive amount of scholarship on American individualism. Two of the most perceptive commentators, to my mind, are Alexis de Tocqueville and Sacvan Berkovitch, both of whom explore the origins, allures, and limitations of American individualism. See Alexis de Tocqueville, *Democracy in America* (New York: Library of America, 2004), and Sacvan Bercovitch, *The Puritan Origins of the American Self* (New Haven: Yale University Press, 1975).

22. Melville, *Moby-Dick*, 398; Yothers, "Herman Melville."

23. Dillingham, *Melville and His Circle*, 66.

24. Arthur Schopenhauer, *The World as Will and Idea*, trans. R.B. Haldane and J. Kemp (7th ed., London: Kegan Paul, Trench, Trubner & Co., 1909), Vol. 1, 213, 460; Christopher Beckwith, *Greek Buddha: Pyrrho's Encounter with Early Buddhism in Central Asia* (Princeton, NJ: Princeton University Press, 2015), 26, 30.
25. Melville, *Weeds and Wildings*, 336.
26. Because it traffics in such clichés, *Weeds and Wildings* chafes against standard ways of evaluating literary works, which tend to elevate exceptionality over commonness. As Claudia Stokes posits, that way of reading literature overlooks the "scope and uses of poetic conventionality" (32) as well as the range of effects and ideas that such conventions could provoke, especially in the hands of adept poets. Stokes, "The Poetics of Unoriginality: The Case of Lucretia Davidson," *Legacy* 32.1 (2015): 31–52.
27. Eliza Richards provides a fuller account of this floral tradition in "The Civil War Language of Flowers," in *A History of Nineteenth-Century American Women's Poetry*, ed. Jennifer Putzi and Alexandra Socarides (New York: Cambridge University Press, 2017), 248–63.
28. Sarah Carter Edgarton Mao, *The Flower Vase: Containing the Language of Flowers, and Their Poetic Sentiments* (Lowell: Joshua Merrill, 1850), 55.
29. Osborne, "Melville and His Flowers," 29.
30. Melville, *Weeds and Wildings*, 338.
31. See Sharon Cameron, "'Lines of Stones': The Unpersonified Impersonal in Melville's *Billy Budd*," in *Impersonality*, 180–204; Hurh, "*Billy Budd*: Pessimism for Post-Critique," 151–68; Dillingham, *Melville and His Circle* (especially chapter 2); and Jonik, *Herman Melville and the Politics of the Inhuman*, 231–2.
32. Arthur Schopenhauer, *Studies in Pessimism: A Series of Essays*, trans. T. Bailey Saunders (London: Swan Sonnenschein & Co., 1891), 22–3.
33. Dillingham, *Melville and His Circle*, 65.
34. Hurh provides an especially compelling account of the novella's Schopenhauerian resonances in "*Billy Budd*," 151–68. Extending and updating Cameron's reading of *Billy Budd* as a dialog with Schopenhauer's theory of will and world-making, Hurh argues that Melville was particularly influenced by Schopenhauer's thoroughgoing pessimism: "For if, as Cameron points out, *Billy Budd* attempts to portray a state of undifferentiated, characterless being as any way desirable, that is because the very conditions of differentiation that create the physical world are also responsible for the suffering suffusing it" (162).
35. Schopenhauer, *Studies in Pessimism*, 137.
36. Schopenhauer, *Studies in Pessimism*, 138; Arthur Schopenhauer, *Essays*, trans. T. Bailey Saunders (New York: L. Burt, 1891), 453; Schopenhauer, *Studies in Pessimism*, 19.
37. Nathaniel Hawthorne, *The English Note-Books* (1870).
38. Schopenhauer, *The World as Will and Idea*, Vol. 3. In *Counsels and Maxims*, another book by Schopenhauer that Melville owned, Schopenhauer claimed that the highest goal is "freedom from pain": "The truth of this remark turns upon the negative character of happiness—the fact that pleasure is only the negation of pain, and that pain is the positive element in life." Yet, Schopenhauer adds, we only grow aware of this fact as we grow old: "We are all born, as Schiller says, in Arcadia. In other words, we come into the world full of claims to happiness and pleasure, and we cherish the fond

hope of making them good. But, as a rule, Fate soon teaches us, in a rough and ready way, that we really possess nothing at all, but that everything in the world is at its command, in virtue of an unassailable right, not only to all we have or acquire... but even to our very limbs, our arms, legs, eyes, and ears, nay, even to the nose in the middle of our face." Arthur Schopenhauer, *Counsels and Maxims*, trans. T. Bailey Saunders (London: Swan Sonnenschein & Co., 1890), 3, 8.

39. Maurice Merleau-Ponty, "Eye and Mind," in *The Primacy of Perception*, trans. James M. Edie (Evanston, IL: Northwestern University Press, 1964), 162; Melville, *Weeds and Wildings*, 336.
40. Schopenhauer, *Religion*, 76.
41. I have, of course, slightly altered the original declaration, which is "Ahab stands alone among the millions of the peopled earth, nor gods nor men his neighbors!" (Melville, *Moby-Dick*, 553).
42. Schopenhauer, *The World as Will and Idea*, Vol. 2. "For Schopenhauer," Cameron explains, "individuality is only phenomenal—manifested in time and space—but not manifested in the realm of the noumenal to which persons have access through the body as will" (*Impersonality*, 197).
43. Melville, *Weeds and Wildings*, 311–12.
44. Nicholas Gaskill, *Chromographia: American Literature and the Modernization of Color* (Minneapolis, MN: University of Minnesota Press, 2018), 10–14.
45. Louis Pammel, *A Manual of Poisonous Plants* (New York: Torch Press, 1910), 84.
46. Arthur Schopenhauer, *On Vision and Colors*, trans. Georg Stahl (New York: Princeton Architectural Press, 2010), 47.
47. Melville, *Weeds and Wildings*, 313, 342.
48. Melville, *Weeds and Wildings*, 305.
49. Melville, *Weeds and Wildings*, 322–33.
50. Emily Dickinson, "The Mushroom is the elf of plants," in *The Gorgeous Nothings*, ed. Marta Werner and Jen Bervin (New York: New Directions, 2013).
51. Melville, *Weeds and Wildings*, 322; Melville, *Published Poems*, 281.
52. Melville, *Weeds and Wildings*, 334.
53. Melville, *Weeds and Wildings*, 335, 334.
54. Timothy Morton, *Humankind: Solidarity With Nonhuman People* (London and New York: Verso, 2017). This "Severing," Morton adds, is a "catastrophe" that "does not take place 'at' a certain 'point' in linear time, but a wave that ripples out in many dimensions, in whose waves we are caught." However, James C. Scott's history of early *homo sapiens* suggests that these ripples might have begun with the advent of agriculture and the accompanying rise of the state. See James C. Scott, *Against the Grain: A Deep History of the Earliest States* (New Haven, NJ: Yale University Press, 2017).
55. Melville, *Weeds and Wildings*, 334, 335, 337, 341, 337.
56. Melville, *Weeds and Wildings*, 336.
57. Osborne, "Melville and His Flowers," 32.
58. Nathaniel Hawthorne, *The Scarlet Letter*, ed. Leland S. Person (New York: Norton Critical Edition, 2017), 1.
59. Melville, *Weeds and Wildings*, 338–9.

NOTES 137

60. According to Jack Goody, this connection between flowers and sexuality has a long history, and it is not merely symbolic: "From the botanical standpoint, flowers represent a method of continuing the life of plants.... The end of the Age of Reptiles saw the appearance of angiosperms, the 'encased seeds' of the flowering plants emerging out of pollen-disseminating varieties.... Reproduction [thenceforward] depended on the flower attracting other species, by its colour, its odour, its sweetness and its shape, all of which developed during the Cretaceous period. Sexuality lies at the core of the flower's existence and played a prominent part when it was taken up in human life." Jack Goody, *The Culture of Flowers* (Cambridge: Cambridge University Press, 1993), 3–4.
61. Christopher Looby, "Strange Sensations: Sex and Aesthetics in 'The Counterpane,'" in *Melville and Aesthetics*; Melville, *Moby-Dick*, 25.
62. James Creech proposes that many of the peculiarities of Melville's style—the complex syntax, emphasis on secrecy and revelation, etc.—are best understood as byproducts of Melville's sexual self-repression. See James Creech, *Closet Writing/Gay Reading: The Case of Melville's Pierre* (Chicago, IL: University of Chicago Press, 1993).
63. Melville, *Weeds and Wildings*, 338–9, 341, 340–1.
64. John Donne, "Song: Sweetest Love, I Do Not Go," in *The Love Songs of John Donne* (New York: Macmillan, 1982), 12.
65. Melville, *Weeds and Wildings*, 349.
66. Henry Wadsworth Longfellow, "L'Envoi," in *Voices of the Night* (London: Edward Moxon, 1843), 143; James Russell Lowell, "L'Envoi," in *The Poetical Words of James Russell Lowell*, Vol. 1 (Boston, MA: Ticknor and Fields, 1863), 298.
67. Edward Said, *Late Style: Music and Literature Against the Grain* (New York: Pantheon Books, 2006), 6.
68. Melville, *Published Poems*, 317.

Chapter 3: Appalling Beauty in *Moby-Dick*

1. As Franklin observes, this is "one of the great moments of revelation in literature" (*The Wake of the Gods*, 64).
2. Melville, *Moby-Dick*, 179, 183, 184, 163.
3. Melville, *Moby-Dick*, 546–7.
4. Christopher N. Phillips, *Epic in American Culture: Settlement to Reconstruction* (Baltimore, MD: Johns Hopkins, 2012), 264.
5. Scarry, *On Beauty and Being Just*, 28.
6. Melville, *Moby-Dick*, 184, 482.
7. James, *Mariners, Renegades, and Castaways*, 86.
8. Critics have consistently made this point. Margaret Atwood, in her wonderful story "Hello, Martians. Let *Moby-Dick* Explain" (*New York Times*, 2012) presents Ahab's antipathy toward nature as so blindingly obvious that even an extraterrestrial lifeform can immediately understand it. After feeding the novel into translate.google.com, the aliens exclaim "Holy crap!," then and offer the following interpretation: "'*Moby-Dick*' is about the oil industry... And the Ship of American State. The owners of the Pequod are rapacious and stingy religious hypocrites. The ship's business is to butcher whales

and turn them into an industrial energy product... Elijah the prophet—from the American artist caste—foretells the Pequod's doom, which comes about because the chief executive, Ahab, is a megalomaniac who wants to annihilate nature. Nature is symbolized by a big white whale, which has interfered with Ahab's personal freedom by biting off his leg and refusing to be slaughtered and boiled. The narrator, Ishmael, represents journalists; his job is to warn America that it's controlled by psychotics who will destroy it, because they hate the natural world and don't grasp the fact that without it they will die." Similar, if less entertaining, readings have been advanced by numerous scholars, from Laurie Robertson-Lorant ("Moby Dick's survival affirms the existence of spiritual forces in Nature that man should treat with reverence, not contempt") to Edward F. Mooney ("Schopenhauer found at the inner core of things the wonder of music; Ahab finds a repulsive stench"). See Laurie Robertson-Lorant, *Melville: A Biography* (Amherst, MA: University of Massachusetts Press, 1996), 280; and Edward F. Mooney, "Passion, Reverie, Disaster, Joy," in *Melville among the Philosophers*, 47. My reading is slightly different, since, in my view, Melville is attending not to nature as such but to the natural forms, forces, and relationships that are constitutive of beauty.

9. This is not to say that Melville was uninterested in the science and philosophy of atoms. On the contrary, Melville belonged to a tradition of writers who sought to integrate atomic theory into literature. See Mark Noble, *American Poetic Materialism from Whitman to Stevens* (New York: Cambridge University Press, 2014).
10. Melville, *Moby-Dick*, 320, 440, 7, 195.
11. *Oxford English Dictionary*, ed. John Simpson and Edmund Weiner (Oxford: Oxford University Press, 1989).
12. Simone Weil, *Waiting on God* (New York: Routledge Revivals, 2010), 67.
13. See, respectively, Cameron, *Impersonality*, 180–205; Sanborn, "Melville and the Nonhuman World"; and Jonik, *Herman Melville and the Politics of the Inhuman*.
14. Melville, *Billy Budd, Sailor*, 102; Melville, *Moby-Dick*, 312.
15. Sharon Cameron, *The Corporeal Self: Allegories of the Body in Melville and Hawthorne* (New York: Columbia University Press, 1991), 41–2.
16. Jonik, *Herman Melville and the Politics of the Inhuman*, 14, 16.
17. Melville, *Moby-Dick*, 263, 333, 374, 199, 263, 362.
18. Melville, *Moby-Dick*, 364.
19. For more in-depth analyses of the limits of language and representation in *Moby-Dick*, see Katie McGettigan, *Herman Melville: Modernity and the Material Text* (Durham, NH: University of New Hampshire Press, 2017), especially 84–116, and Gayle L. Smith, "The Word and the Thing: *Moby-Dick* and the Limits of Language," *ESQ* 31 (1985): 260–71.
20. Melville, *Moby-Dick*, 456; McGettigan, *Herman Melville*, 1.
21. D.H. Lawrence, *Studies in Classic American Literature*, ed. Ezra Greenspan, Lindeth Vasey, and John Worthen (Cambridge: Cambridge University Press, 2003), 134.
22. Melville, *Moby-Dick*, 307.
23. Otter, "Melville, Poetry, and Prints."
24. For Hegel, aesthetic experience consists in a spiritual and intellectual elevation above nature: "the beauty of art is *higher* than nature. The beauty of art is *born of the spirit and*

born again, and the higher the spirit and its productions stand above nature and its phenomena, the higher too is the beauty of art above that of nature." Schiller not only addresses his aesthetic letters to an aristocrat; he pitches aesthetic education as a kind of preparatory training for the political elite. The "natural character of man," Schiller posits, is too "selfish and violent" to preserve "the living clock-work of the state," so society requires a small class of rulers, educated in art and aesthetics, who can balance reason with feeling and exercise the power of the law "without retarding the development of [their] moral character." And Kant's universalism meets its limit as soon as he considers race: "a negro must have a different normal Idea of the beauty of the [human figure] from a white man, a Chinaman a different normal Idea from a European, etc. And the same is the case with the model of a beautiful horse or dog (of a certain breed)." Melville encountered some of these aesthetic ideas through his books, and through his momentous conversations with George Adler during his trip to Europe in the late 1840s. As Melville noted in the October 22, 1849, entry in his *Journals*, he spent most of the previous night with Adler (a professor at New York University who was apparently quite fond of alcohol) drinking whiskey and talking philosophy: "We had an extraordinary time & did not break up till after two in the morning. We talked metaphysics continually, & Hegel, Schlegel, Kant &c were discussed under the influence of the whiskey." Georg Wilhelm Friedrich Hegel, *Aesthetics: Lectures on Fine Art*, Vol. 1, trans T.M. Knox (Oxford: Oxford University Press, 1975), 2; Friedrich Schiller, *The Aesthetic Letters*, trans. J. Weiss (Boston, MA: Charles C. Little and James Brown, 1845), 9–10; Kant, *Critique of Judgment*, 40; Melville, *Journals*, 8.

25. To put this another way, the novel's philosophy of disability is intimately bound up with its philosophy of beauty. For Melville, beauty consists neither in wholeness nor in perfection but in a variety of shapes, forms, and relations. On Melville and disability, see the March 2006 special issue of *Leviathan: A Journal of Melville Studies* and Ellen Samuels's *Fantasies of Identification: Disability, Gender, Race* (New York: NYU Press, 2014).

26. Nehamas, *Only a Promise of Happiness*, 77.

27. Melville, *Moby-Dick*, 307.

28. Barnard provides a cogent account of Melville's biocentrism in "The Cod and the Whale," 851–79.

29. "Melville cannily cycles through all of analogy's functions," Duquette writes, and those functions are wide ranging: "analogy...helps to establish and maintain particular perspectives on the world which we might call philosophies; it can be justificatory or descriptive (examples and parables and similes), in which capacity it helps to clarify perception; and it can be heuristic, leading to startling discoveries and surprising insights." Elizabeth Duquette, *"The Confidence-Man between Genres,"* in *The New Melville Studies*, 100.

30. Ralph Waldo Emerson, "The Problem," in *The Complete Works of Ralph Waldo Emerson*, Vol. 9: Poems (Boston, MA: Houghton Mifflin, 1904), 7. Michelangelo's artistic redesign is described in John Murray, *Handbook for Travellers in Central Italy* (London: Murray, 1843), which Melville borrowed from the Astor Library. Michelangelo, the *Handbook* notes, "immediately returned to the design of a Greek

cross, enlarged the tribune... strengthened the piers... and declar[ed] that he would raise the Pantheon in the air" (335).
31. Murray, *Handbook for Travellers in Central Italy*, 338.
32. Madame de Staël, *Corinne; or, Italy*, trans. Isabel Hill (London: Bentley, 1833).
33. Giorgio Vasari, *Lives of the Most Eminent Painters, Sculptors, and Architects*, trans. Mrs. Jonathan Foster, 5 vols. (London: H.G. Bohn, 1850–2). Vasari discusses Michelangelo's life and art in Vol. 4.
34. Melville, "Statues in Rome," 314.
35. In that regard, the beauty of the whale is at once aesthetic and theological. The skin, or "blanket," is not simply "crossed and re-crossed with numberless straight marks in thick array"; it is also a visual manifestation of *mana*. Melville was deeply influenced by the culture and history of the Maori, and, as Geoffrey Sanborn has documented, Melville was particularly intrigued with "mana" and its associations of sacred power and esoteric inscription. This is why tattoos in *Moby-Dick* become, as Sanborn puts it, the symbolic "antithesis of whipscars": "If whipping signifies the massive mana of the Law—just as, say, a lightning-bolt signifies the massive mana of God or Nature—then, if this is a world to which there is any kind of prospect for the human dignity to which Melville is so fiercely attached, we have to have some way of expressing our own mana in turn. Since we cannot strike God, Nature, or the Law, we can only resignify the thing that they strike: the surface of the body." This resignification, I would suggest, extends to whales (and beyond) and plays an integral role in the novel's aesthetics. Geoffrey Sanborn, *Whipscars and Tattoos: The Last of the Mohicans, Moby-Dick, and the Maori* (Oxford: Oxford University Press, 2011), 123.
36. Melville, *Moby-Dick*, 340, 306, 340.
37. Barnard, "The Cod and the Whale," 867; Colin Dayan, "Melville's Creatures, or Seeing Otherwise," in *American Impersonal: Essays with Sharon Cameron*, ed. Branka Arsić (London: Bloomsbury Publishing, 2014).
38. As Dayan posits, "Reading Melville depends on a devotion to the possibilities of revelation, even if the revelation turns out to be seeped in a terrain of rot, waste, and stink" ("Melville's Creatures," 53).
39. Melville, *Moby-Dick*, 143, 334.
40. For an alternative account of beauty's role in the novel, see Davis's perceptive and compelling essay, "Melville's Ornamentation." Focusing on the narrator's treatment of Pip and "The Grand Armada" chapter, Davis contends that *Moby-Dick* is at once a book seeped in beauty and a narrative that tends to evacuate beauty of any stable ethical force. As Davis puts it, "The ornamental aesthetics in *Moby-Dick* flout any demand that beauty be ethically meaningful, as beauty remains and even flourishes in the midst of cruelty and desolation. *Moby-Dick* is a text in which absolute disappointment is garlanded by inordinate, ornamental beauty" (45). I read the novel along slightly different lines, approaching beauty as co-extensive with the organic forms and relations from which Ahab has tragically alienated himself.
41. Melville, *Moby-Dick*, 195, 168. As Christopher Freeburg posits, Pip is "a symbol of blackness itself, a living emblem of joy, music, and festive camaraderie—so full of life that he is removed from the drudgery of whaling." So when the crew members abandon him in "The Castaway," Pip comes to embody "the tragic destruction of social bonds."

Christopher Freeburg, "Pip and the Sounds of Blackness in *Moby-Dick*," in *The New Melville Studies*, 42, 47.

42. Freeburg, "Pip and the Sounds of Blackness in *Moby-Dick*," 108–9; *Moby-Dick*, 143, 121, 212, 266, 333. Whenever Melville discusses war, he tends to depict it as a violation of nature. *Battle-Pieces* depicts the Civil War through a range of such violations, from the brutal emergence of "plain mechanic power" to the scorched earth that is left behind by the invading armies leaving naught but "burning woods," churches transformed into sites of pain, and landscapes strewn with "iron cones and spheres of death" (Melville, *Published Poems*, 97, 44, 130). *Billy Budd* similarly distinguishes between war (and its forms of law) and natural states, a tension embodied in the conflict between the martial officers (Vere and Claggart) and Billy (the "Barbarian" who acts and speaks as though he comes from a state of primal nature, "like Caspar Hauser"). Melville, *Billy Budd, Sailor*, 52, 53. On Melville and warfare, see also Robert S. Levine's compelling reading of *Israel Potter* in "Beautiful Warships: The Transnational Aesthetics of Melville's *Israel Potter*," in *Race, Transnationalism, and Nineteenth-Century American Literary Studies* (New York: Cambridge University Press, 2018), 98–115. As Levine contends, Melville tends to use aesthetics to demonumentalize, to refocus our attention on beauty that is common—like the beguiling beauty of warships. Other incisive accounts of Melville's pacifism can be found in Cynthia Wachtell, *War No More: The Antiwar Impulse in American Literature, 1861–1914* (Amherst, MA: University of Massachusetts Press, 2010), 41–60; Yothers, *Sacred Uncertainty*, 131–62; and Michael Warner, "What Like a Bullet Can Undeceive?" *Public Culture* 15.1 (Winter 2003): 41–54.
43. Melville, *Correspondence*, 190; Melville, *Moby-Dick*, 281, 285–6.
44. By "profane," I mean the refusal or violation of the "sacred," as Brian Yothers defines that term. Melville sustained a lifelong interest and investment in what he called "that sacred uncertainty which forever impends over men and nations" (Melville, *Published Poems*, 185). Melville's phrasing, Yothers argues, pulls in two directions: "On the one hand, the use of the term 'sacred' points broadly toward moral earnestness and a numinous sense of awe. On the other, 'uncertainty' undermines the prospect that earnestness and awe can lead to either arrogance or a conclusive faith" (*Sacred Uncertainty*, 5). Stubb's murder—and it is, indeed, treated as a homicidal act—violates the sacred in both of these ways, by acting out of certainty and by substituting violence for a sense of divine wonder.
45. *Oxford English Dictionary*, ed. Simpson and Weiner.
46. Melville, *Moby-Dick*, 286, 117, 119, 279.
47. Melville, *Moby-Dick*, 293. On the novel's antiracist aesthetics, see also Sterling Stuckey, *African Culture and Melville's Art: The Creative Process in Benito Cereno and Moby-Dick* (Oxford: Oxford University Press, 2009); Freeburg, "Pip and the Sounds of Blackness in *Moby-Dick*," 42–52; Christopher Charles Freeburg, *Melville and the Idea of Blackness: Race and Imperialism in Nineteenth-Century America* (New York: Cambridge University Press, 2012), 20–60; and Samuel Otter, *Melville's Anatomies* (Berkeley and Los Angeles, CA: University of California Press, 1999), 101–71.
48. Melville, *Moby-Dick*, 302, 299, 300.
49. For a fuller interpretation of the novel's treatment of "animal capitalism," see Barnard, "The Cod and the Whale."

50. Melville, "Hawthorne and His Mosses," in *The Piazza Tales*, 243; Melville, *Timoleon*, 280.
51. In this respect, my reading of beauty in the novel converges with Branka Arsić's account of "ambient personhood" in Melville, wherein personhood is dispersed and distributed across both organic and inorganic matter. See Branka Arsić, *Ambient Life: Melville, Materialism, and the Ethereal Enlightenment* (forthcoming).
52. Melville, *Moby-Dick*, 557.
53. Melville, *Moby-Dick*, 571.
54. As James remarks, "This is Melville's vision": "[the] world is heading for a crisis which will be a world crisis,... in every sense of that word" (*Mariners, Renegades, and Castaways*, 34). Cesare Casarino similarly finds in the novel an eerie warning about impending catastrophe and transformation: "Prescience of crisis so thoroughly infuses each and every page of *Moby-Dick* right from the very opening lines—the first chapter is appropriately titled 'Loomings,' and the first paragraph is imbued with intimations of melancholia and suicide—that, when the long-expected catastrophe does arrive, one is left with a sensation of excess of crisis" (*Modernity at Sea*, 68).
55. Melville, *Moby-Dick*, 122, 153.
56. C.B. MacPherson, *The Political Theory of Possessive Individualism: Hobbes to Locke* (London: Oxford University Press, 1962), 3.
57. Melville, *Moby-Dick*, 129, 560, 125.
58. Melville, *Moby-Dick*, 545.
59. Elizabeth Schultz, "Melville's Environmental Vision in *Moby-Dick*," *Interdisciplinary Studies in Literature and the Environment* 7 (2000): 97–113 (100); Jonik, *Herman Melville and the Politics of the Inhuman*, 23. On Melville's relationship to the environment, and to matter itself, see also the intriguing essays in Meredith Farmer and Jonathan Schroeder, ed., *Ahab Unbound: Melville & the Materialist Turn* (Chicago and Evanston: Northwestern University Press, 2022).
60. Melville, *Moby-Dick*, 120. In this regard, Ahab resembles the mad inventor, Bannadonna, who sees art only in terms of exceptionalism. There "is a law in art," Bannadonna proclaims, "which bars the possibility of duplicates" (Herman Melville, "The Bell-Tower," in *The Piazza Tales*, 179). The aesthetic philosophy woven throughout *Moby-Dick* differs radically from Bannadonna's vision, prioritizing life, community, and relationality.
61. Eliza Richards, "Weathering the News in US Civil War Poetry," in *The Cambridge Companion to Nineteenth-Century American Poetry*, ed. Kerry Larson (New York: Cambridge University Press, 2012), 116; Melville, *Moby-Dick*, 123, 124, 436.
62. Melville, *Moby-Dick*, 482–3.
63. The reading method best suited for *Moby-Dick* thus resembles the reading method that Justine S. Murison adopts for *The Confidence-Man*, approaching the novel as a multilinear—or "temporally vertiginous" (20)—narrative marked by an intricate series of loops, leaps, and returns. See Murison, "Paranoid Reading," 13–26.
64. Melville, *Moby-Dick*, 184–5.
65. Melville, *Moby-Dick*, 542.
66. Melville, *Moby-Dick*, 543.

67. On the development of "enchantment" as a word, idea, and practice, see Jane Bennett, *The Enchantment of Modern Life: Attachments, Crossings, and Ethics* (Princeton, NJ: Princeton University Press, 2001) and Emily Ogden, *Credulity: A Cultural History of US Mesmerism* (Chicago, IL: University of Chicago Press, 2018). As Bennett posits, "enchantment entails a state of wonder" as well as "an energizing feeling of fullness or plenitude" (5).
68. Leslie E. Sheldon, "Messianic Power and Satanic Decay in *Moby-Dick*," in *Melville & Milton*, 25–46.
69. Melville, *Moby-Dick*, 543.
70. Melville, *Moby-Dick*, 330, 550, 543.
71. Melville, *Moby-Dick*, 30.
72. Melville, *Moby-Dick*, 50.
73. Melville, *Moby-Dick*, 25; Looby, "Strange Sensations."
74. Melville, *Moby-Dick*, 478.
75. Peter Coviello, *Intimacy in America: Dreams of Affiliation in Antebellum American Literature* (Minneapolis, MN: University of Minnesota Press, 2005), 124.
76. Coviello, *Intimacy in America*, 3, 51; Melville, "Hawthorne and His Mosses," 250. On the affective and erotic undercurrents of Melville's relationship with Hawthorne, see Jordan Alexander Stein, "Herman Melville's Love Letters," *ELH* 85.1 (Spring 2018): 119–40.
77. Melville, Letter to Hawthorne (November 1851), in *Correspondence*, 212.
78. Melville, *Moby-Dick*, 416.
79. Melville, *Moby-Dick*, 492, 153.
80. Richard Hardack, *Not Altogether Human: Pantheism and the Dark Nature of the American Renaissance* (Amherst, MA: University of Massachusetts Press, 2012), 3.
81. Edward Slowik, "Descartes's Physics," in *The Stanford Encyclopedia of Philosophy* (Stanford, CA: Stanford University Press, n.d.): https://plato.stanford.edu/entries/descartes-physics/. As Maurice Lee points out, "It is no coincidence that Melville refers to Descartes in *Moby-Dick* at a moment when Ishmael nearly 'loses his identity.' A curious dynamic in Melville's career is that the more committed he becomes to philosophical explorations of identity, motive, and agency, the more he suspects that human psychology and character lie beyond the reach of philosophical explanation." Maurice Lee, "Skepticism in *The Confidence-Man*," in *The New Cambridge Companion to Herman Melville*, 178.
82. Lee, *Uncertain Chances*, 48–9.
83. Melville, *Moby-Dick*, 320; Lee, *Uncertain Chances*, 56.
84. Melville, *Moby-Dick*, 214–15.
85. Michael Jonik, for example, notes the referential depth of Melville's "Loom of Time" (a figure that reaches back to ancient Greece) while John Wenke emphasizes the role of "cooperative labor" in the chapter, linking cooperation writ large to the metaphysics of "The Mat-Maker." Maurice Lee reveals two related dimensions of the chapter: the way it engages with Davenant's *A Discourse upon Gondibert* (1650), from which Melville lifts the metaphor of "the indifferent sword of chance"; and its structural placement— i.e. the Loom of Time is unfinished and their weaving is interrupted by the sighting of a

whale. Jonik, *Herman Melville and the Politics of the Inhuman*, 25–32; Wenke, *Melville's Muse*, 108; Lee, *Uncertain Chances*, 61–2.
86. Melville, *Moby-Dick*, 375, 570, 164, 117.
87. Melville, *Moby-Dick*, 278.
88. Melville, *Moby-Dick*, 375–6.
89. Melville, *Moby-Dick*, 449–50.
90. Illana Pardes, *Melville's Bibles* (Berkeley and Los Angeles, CA: University of California Press, 2008), 63.
91. Pardes, *Melville's Bibles*, 491–2.
92. *Oxford English Dictionary* online: https://www.oed.com. I am also drawing on Caroline Levine's definition of "network" as a distributed form in which "patterns of interconnection and exchange" at once shape and "organize...experience." Levine, *Forms*, 113.
93. George Santayana, *The Sense of Beauty: Being the Outlines of Aesthetic Theory* (New York: Scribner's, 1896), 53. One of the reasons I draw on Santayana here is that he articulates a view of beauty that exceeds the bounds of the human: "The fine arts...are by no means the only sphere in which [people] show their susceptibility to beauty. In all products of human industry we notice the keenness with which the eye is attracted to the mere appearance of things: great sacrifices of time and labour are made to it in the most vulgar manufactures; nor does man select his dwelling, his clothes, or his companions without reference to their effect on his aesthetic senses. Of late we have even learned that the forms of many animals are due to the survival by sexual selection of the colours and forms most attractive to the eye. There must therefore be in our nature a very radical and wide-spread tendency to observe beauty, and to value it. No account of the principles of the mind can be at all adequate that passes over so conspicuous a faculty" (1–2).
94. Melville, *Moby-Dick*, 371.

Postscript

1. William James, *Pragmatism: A New Name for Some Old Ways of Thinking* (New York, Bombay, and Calcutta: Longmans, Green, & Co., 1907), 45.
2. W.H. Auden, "In Memory of W.B. Yeats," in *Collected Poems* (New York: Random House, 1976), 248.
3. Hester Blum, "Introduction: Academic Positioning Systems," in *Turns of Event: Nineteenth-Century American Literary Studies in Motion* (Philadelphia, PA: University of Pennsylvania Press, 2016), 2.
4. Joseph North, *Literary Criticism: A Concise Political History* (Cambridge, MA: Harvard University Press, 2017), 1.
5. Laura R. Fisher, *Reading for Reform: The Social Work of Literature in the Progressive Era* (Minneapolis, MN: University of Minnesota Press, 2019); Eden Wales Freeman, *Reading Testimony, Witnessing Trauma: Confronting Race, Gender, and Violence in American Literature* (Oxford: University Press of Mississippi, 2020); Jessica Hurley, *Infrastructures of Apocalypse: American Literature and the Nuclear Complex*

(Minneapolis, MN: University of Minnesota Press, 2020); Alvin J. Henry, *Black Queer Flesh: Rejecting Subjectivity in the African American Novel* (Minneapolis, MN: University of Minnesota Press, 2020); Lori Merish, *Archives of Labor: Working-Class Women and Literary Culture in the Antebellum United States* (Durham, NC: Duke University Press, 2017).

6. Stephen Best and Sharon Marcus, "Surface Reading: An Introduction," *Representations* 108.1 (Fall 2009): 1–21 (1).
7. Bruno Latour, "Why Has Critique Run Out of Steam? From Matters of Fact to Matters of Concern," *Critical Inquiry* 30.2 (Winter 2004): 225–48 (238–9).
8. Rita Felski, *The Limits of Critique* (Chicago, IL: University of Chicago Press), 17. The term "hermeneutics of suspicion" was coined by Paul Ricoeur, who identifies it with the interpretive traditions that have evolved out of the writings of Friedrich Nietzsche, Sigmund Freud, and Karl Marx. Paul Ricoeur, *Freud and Philosophy: An Essay on Interpretation* (New Haven: Yale University Press, 1970).
9. Felski, *The Limits of Critique*, 2, 10.
10. North, *Literary Criticism*, 3.
11. Richard Rorty, *Philosophy and the Mirror of Nature* (Princeton, NJ: Princeton University Press, 2009), 8.
12. Fredric Jameson, *The Political Unconscious: Narrative as a Socially Symbolic Act* (Ithaca, NY: Cornell University Press, 1982), 1.
13. See Kellen Bolt, "Squeezing Sperm: Nativism, Queer Contact, and the Futures of Democratic Intimacy in *Moby-Dick*," *ESQ: A Journal of Nineteenth-Century American Literature and Culture* 65 (2019): 293–329.
14. Bolt, "Squeezing Sperm," 299.
15. Maurice Lee, "Falsifiability, Confirmation Bias, and Textual Promiscuity," *J19* 2.1 (Spring 2014): 162–71 (165). Lee also provides a fascinating account of the nineteenth-century origins of the information revolution in Lee, *Overwhelmed*.
16. See Marrs, *Nineteenth-Century American Literature and the Long Civil War*; and Cody Marrs, *Not Even Past: The Stories We Keep Telling About the Civil War* (Baltimore, MD: Johns Hopkins University Press, 2020).
17. Tim Dean calls this criticism the "New Descriptivism," a method that follows in the footsteps of Stanley Cavell to view "description as a method superior to interpretation rather than preparatory to it." Tim Dean, "Genre Blindness in the New Descriptivism," *MLQ* 81.4 (2020): 527–52 (527). Some of the best work in this vein includes Branka Arsić, *Bird Relics: Grief and Vitalism in Thoreau* (Cambridge, MA: Harvard University Press, 2016); Christopher Hanlon, *Emerson's Memory Loss: Originality, Communality, and the Late Style* (New York: Oxford University Press, 2018); Toril Moi, *Revolution of the Ordinary: Literary Studies after Wittgenstein, Austin, and Cavell* (Chicago, IL: University of Chicago Press, 2017); Jed Deppman, *Trying to Think with Emily Dickinson* (Amherst, MA: University of Massachusetts Press, 2008); Michael Jonik, "'Wild Thinking' and Vegetal Intelligence in Thoreau's Later Writings," in *Dispersion: Thoreau and Vegetal Thought*, ed. Branka Arsić (New York: Bloomsbury, 2021); and Mastroianni, "Perfectionist *Pierre*"; and Mastroianni, *Politics and Skepticism in Antebellum American Literature*.

18. See Levine, *Forms*; Morgan, *The Outward Mind*; Cristanne Miller, ed., *Emily Dickinson's Poems: As She Preserved Them* (Cambridge, MA: Harvard University Press, 2016); Otter, "Melville's Style," 114–38; as well as Amanda Anderson, Rita Felski, and Toril Moi, *Character: Three Inquiries in Literary Studies* (Chicago, IL: University of Chicago Press, 2019). The quote comes from Levine's *Forms* (3).
19. Examples include Cindy Weinstein, *Time, Tense, and American Literature* (New York: Cambridge University Press, 2015) and *Writing about Time: Essays on American Literature*, ed. Weinstein (New York: Cambridge University Press, 2018); Jeffrey Insko, *History, Abolition, and the Ever-Present Now in Antebellum American Literature* (New York: Oxford University Press, 2018); Sandra M. Gustafson, "The Varieties of Religious Expression in Early American Literature," in *A Companion to American Literature*, ed. Susan Belasco, et al. (London: Wiley, 2020); and LaFleur, *The Natural History of Sexuality in Early America*.
20. Steven Knapp and Walter Benn Michaels, "Against Theory," *Critical Inquiry* 8.4 (Summer 1982): 723–42.
21. This co-evolution is documented by Lee in *Uncertain Chances* and Richard Poirer in *Poetry and Pragmatism* (Cambridge, MA: Harvard University Press, 1992).
22. Looby and Weinstein, "Introduction" to *American Literature's Aesthetic Dimensions*, 31.
23. John Dewey, *Art as Experience* (New York: Penguin, 2005), 3.
24. Dewey, *Art as Experience*, 2.
25. Dewey, *Art as Experience*, 13.
26. John Tooby and Leda Cosmides, *The Adapted Mind: Evolutionary Psychology and the Generation of Culture* (Oxford: Oxford University Press, 1995), as quoted by Dennis Dutton in *The Art Instinct: Beauty, Pleasure, and Human Evolution* (New York: Bloomsbury, 2009), 105.
27. Dutton, *The Art Instinct*, 2–3.
28. Dewey, *Art as Experience*, 112, 200.
29. Dewey, *Art as Experience*, 329, 338.
30. Melville, *Published Poems*, 280.

Index

For the benefit of digital users, indexed terms that span two pages (e.g., 52–53) may, on occasion, appear on only one of those pages.

Aesthetics v–x, 17, 21, 54, 72–3, 82–3, 101, 111–13
  and consciousness 1, 13–14, 22–3, 78–9, and philosophy 12–15, 24, 33–6, 56, and sensation 6–7, 9, 42, and suffering v, xi, and Marxism 21, and racism 22–3
American literary studies 27, 107–8, 111
  history of 17, 22
Arnold, Matthew 28
Arsić, Branka 4, 49, 111

"Bartleby, the Scrivener," 9
Barnard, John Levi 85–6
Battle-Pieces vi–viii, xi
Bayle, Pierre 33–6
Beauty viii–xi, 1–3, 5–6, 13–14, 25–30, 32–3, 43–51, 61, 65, 70, 73, 77–8, 96–7, 99–102
  and consciousness 1, 3, 9, 29–30, and hope 23, and identity 3, 64–5, and materialism 38, and multiplicity 9, 12, 22–3, 25–6, 29–30, 57, and natural forms 30–1, and non-possession 3, 57–9, 82–3, and non-sovereignty 1–3, 14–15, 38, 42–4, 48–9, 52, 54, 58–9, 64–5, 67–8, 70, 75–6, 79, 91–2, 96, and play 8–9, 100–1, in twentieth-century art 20, of flowers 52–4, 58, 73, of whales 7–9, 13–14, 77–8, 80–2, 91, of worms 25–6, versus the sublime 5, 7, woven 101–2, 105–6
Benjamin, Walter viii
Best, Stephen and Sharon Marcus 108
Billy Budd 7, 62–3
Blum, Hester 107–8
Bolt, Kellen 109–10
Bourdieu, Pierre 21
Bryant, John 54
Burke, Edmund, *see* Melville, Herman and Edmund Burke

Cameron, Sharon 14, 62, 79–80
Castiglia, Christopher 23
Channing, William Ellery 12
Chuh, Kandice x
Coleman, Dawn 12

Coviello, Peter 98
Civil War vi–viii, x–xi, 110–11

Davis, Theo 3–5, 48–9, 140n.40
Dayan, Colin 85–6
Deleuze, Gilles 17
Dewey, John 111–13
Dillingham, William B. 30, 62–3
Duquette, Elizabeth 84
Dryden, Edgar 30

Epicurus 31–2, 42–3

Felski, Rita 109
Flowers, *see* "Beauty, of flowers"
Fredricks, Nancy 43–4
Freeburg, Christopher 141n.42
Fretwell, Erica 4–5

Goethe, Johann Wolfgang von 14–15
Greiman, Jennifer 123n.57

Hanlon, Christopher 111
Hardack, Richard 99
Hawthorne, Nathaniel 14–15, 31–2, 61, 71–3, 98
Hazlitt, William 10–12, 39–41
Hurh, Paul 9, 14, 62
Hsu, Hsuan viii

James, C.L.R. 78
James, William 107
Jameson, Fredric 109–10
Jonik, Michael 14, 62, 79–80, 92, 111

Kant, Immanuel 32
Kevorkian, Martin 54

Latour, Bruno 108
Lawrence, D.H. 81
Lee, Maurice 99, 110
Levine, Caroline 111
Levine, Robert S. 141n.42
Lloyd, David 22
Looby, Christopher 4–5, 72–3, 97, 111

INDEX

Lorrain, Claude 39, 41
Ludot-Vlasak, Ronan 31–2

Marr, Timothy 51
Marsoin, Édouard 4–5
Mastroianni, Dominic 111
Mayo, Sarah 60
McGettigan, Katie 81
Melville, Elizabeth 52, 54, 68
Melville, Herman, and architecture 47–51, 84–5 and classical antiquity 25–6, 37, 51, and collectivity 1–3, and Edmund Burke 6–9, 32, and ekphrasis vii, and luminism vii, and pacificism ix, 86–7, and philosophy 3–4, 12–13, 24, 31–2, 34–6, 56, 61–3, 67–8, 98–9, and perspective viii, and politics v, xi, and reading 6–7, and Rome 2–3, and style 3–4, and the sublime 5, 9, and travel 28–9, career of 16–17, 54, 62–3, 65, reception of 19–20
Miller, Cristanne 111
Moby-Dick vii–ix, 7–9, 13–14, 16, 77–83, 86–7, 93, 105–6
Mode (theory) 15–17, 27–8, 56
Moi, Toril 111
Morgan, Benjamin 38, 111
Mumford, Lewis 29
Murdoch, Iris viii

Nehamas, Alexander 82–3
New Americanists 22
New Criticism 18
Ngai, Sianne 3–4
Nonhuman 14, 25–6, 30–8, 45–8, 52–3, 56–7, 60, 69–70, 78–80, 84–91
North, Joseph 108–9
Nurmi, Tom 12–14, 32

Osborne, Gillian 54, 61, 71–2
Otter, Samuel 4–5, 14, 33–4, 82, 111

Pardes, Ilana 103–4
Parthenon 33–4, 38
Pfister, Joel v
Piombo, Sebastiano del 10–11

Piranesi, Giovanni 82
Picturesque 10
Plato 24, 98–9
Possessive individualism 91–2
Pragmatism 107–10, 113–14
Prum, Richard 23
Pyrrhonism x, 62, 99

Racism 22–3, 88
Radway, Janice 22
Renker, Elizabeth 17–18
Richards, Eliza 92–3
Riley, Peter 30
Robillard, Douglas 30
Rorty, Richard 109
Rowe, John Carlos 22
Ruskin, John 10–11, 33

Said, Edward 75
Saint Peter's Cathedral 83–5
Sanborn, Geoffrey 1, 4–5, 33–4
Scarry, Elaine 43–4, 78
Schopenhauer, Arthur 28, 59, 61–4, 67–8
Schultz, Elizabeth 92
Shelley, Percy Bysshe 3
Short, Bryan 34
Spinoza, Baruch 34–6
Staël, Madame de 10–11, 84
Sugden, Edward 115n.4, 118n.11
Sweet, Timothy viii

Tamarkin, Elisa 30, 32–3
Timoleon 1, 16, 25, 51

Ugliness 5, 10

Vedder, Elihu 30, 32, 34

Wallace, Robert K. v, 41
Weeds and Wildings 16, 52–4, 56–9, 64, 67–8, 73
Weinstein, Cindy 4–5, 111
Williams, Raymond 21

Yothers, Brian 116n.17, 141n.44